The Native World-System

ISSUES OF GLOBALIZATION
Case Studies in Contemporary Anthropology
Series Editors: Carla Freeman and Li Zhang

The Native World-System

An Ethnography of Bolivian Aymara
Traders in the Global Economy

NICO TASSI

New York   Oxford
OXFORD UNIVERSITY PRESS

Oxford University Press is a department of the University of Oxford.
It furthers the University's objective of excellence in research,
scholarship, and education by publishing worldwide.

Oxford   New York
Auckland   Cape Town   Dar es Salaam   Hong Kong   Karachi
Kuala Lumpur   Madrid   Melbourne   Mexico City   Nairobi
New Delhi   Shanghai   Taipei   Toronto

With offices in
Argentina   Austria   Brazil   Chile   Czech Republic   France   Greece
Guatemala   Hungary   Italy   Japan   Poland   Portugal   Singapore
South Korea   Switzerland   Thailand   Turkey   Ukraine   Vietnam

Published by Oxford University Press
198 Madison Avenue, New York, New York 10016
http://www.oup.com

Oxford is a registered trademark of Oxford University Press

Library of Congress Cataloging-in-Publication Data
Names: Tassi, Nico, author.
Title: The native world-system : an ethnography of Bolivian Aymara traders in
    the global economy / Nico Tassi.
Description: New York : Oxford University Press, 2017. | Series: Issues of
    globalization : case studies in contemporary anthropology | Includes
    bibliographical references and index.
Identifiers: LCCN 2015046544 | ISBN 9780190255220 (pbk. : alk. paper)
Subjects: LCSH: Aymara Indians--Commerce. | Aymara Indians--Economic
    conditions. | Informal sector (Economics)--Bolivia. | Bolivia--Commerce. |
    Bolivia--Economic conditions--1982-
Classification: LCC F2230.2.A9 T374 2016 | DDC 382.089/98324084--dc23 LC
record available at http://lccn.loc.gov/2015046544

Printing number: 9 8 7 6 5 4 3 2 1

Printed in the United States of America
on acid-free paper

In memory of
José María and Pier Paolo,
Elena and Momo.
And to Bolivia
that made me live again.

CONTENTS

ACKNOWLEDGMENTS

....

This book is the product of an ongoing process of collective reflection with Bolivian traders, truck drivers, butchers, artisans, cooks, guilds, and brotherhoods, as well as the research collective *Vas a disculpar* with whom I have been sharing ideas and uncertainties for years. Those thoughts and reflections have infected my spirit and body but also materialized "another country" and other possibilities that sometimes elude the erudite and considered gaze of hardened analysts.

In Bolivia, behind the walls of discrimination and indifference, in the cracks of social exclusion, another unofficial world has been sprouting, kicking, and pushing. I was invited to climb those walls, to live in those cracks where tenderness and fury were the propelling forces outlining a spectrum of unexpected possibilities. In Bolivia, one often forgets how accustomed we are to thinking and acting from other angles, to scouting new potentials tangential to the inescapable destinies of history and global politics. This book is a humble tribute to Bolivia's overflow of possibilities and to the people who have produced it.

I am grateful to the International Institute of Environment and Development, the *Centro Mainumby Ñakurutu*, the *Centro de Investigaciónes Sociales* and the *Programa de Investigación Estratégica en Bolivia* for supporting different phases of the research over the years. I felt incredibly privileged to be a recipient of the Hunt Fellowship of the Wenner–Gren Foundation and to have the opportunity to comfortably and exclusively work on the manuscript over months. PIEB, John Wiley and Sons, I.B. Tauris and Bonilla Artigas Editores were kind enough to let me reproduce parts of my previous publications. I thank the OUP editors for believing in this project and for helping me to give shape and direction to the book.

Great gratitude goes to my teachers, friends and colleagues of the anthropology department at the University College London. This has been not only a nurturing environment in which to grow professionally, but also a refuge to cultivate and pursue independent ideas and counterintuitive aspirations. To my narrow and extended families in Bolivia, Italy, and the United Kingdom I express my deepest appreciation for trying to understand and support me in myriad different ways.

Oxford University Press thanks the following people who formally reviewed the manuscript: William L. Alexander, University of North Carolina at Wilmington; Caroline S. Conzelman, University of Colorado at Boulder; Maria F. Curtis, University of Houston–Clear Lake; Teresa E. P. Delfín, Whitter College; Alan L. Kolata, University of Chicago; Manuel Lizarralde, Connecticut College; Deborah Poole, Johns Hopkins University; and Stacey Schwartzkopf, Hendrix College.

"On Our Own Terms": Indigenous Traders in the Global Economy

Born into a peasant family in the Aymara village of Taraco on the shores of Lake Titicaca at 13,000 feet above sea level, Silveria[1] is an unassuming widow in her seventies. She wears a large, traditional Andean skirt (*pollera*), borsalino bowler hat, dark shawl gathered with a pin over her chest, and long hair tidily plaited. The reassuring image of a traditional, aging Andean woman is spoiled by the fact that Silveria owns a five-story house and runs four electrical goods shops displaying the newest Chinese technology on the main commercial street in La Paz: the Eloy Salmón.

One of the early members of the Eloy Salmón's trade union and a pioneer rural trader, Silveria left the countryside when she was still a teenager, a few years after the agrarian reform of 1953. In her first years in La Paz, in the morning she sold lake fish that relatives would bring in from the countryside and in the afternoon she retailed secondhand sewing machines, smuggled from Peru to Taraco on a rowing boat by a *compadre*. Silveria soon moved on to batteries and portable radios, and her strip of coarse cotton cloth on the sidewalk was replaced by a sheltered wooden stall. Alerted by her swift economic success, relatives from Taraco poured into the city and—through a system of rotating loans and credits (*pasanako*)—established their stalls on the sidewalks of the Eloy Salmón, extending their commercial control over the neighborhood.

From transistor radios to black-and-white televisions, from stoves to refrigerators, little by little Silveria's and the Taraqueños's businesses evolved both in quality and in volume. They began renting garages and stores and displacing the workshops of *mestizo* shoemakers and tinsmiths. The Taraqueños thrived thanks to their Peruvian connections. However, they were quick to extend their commercial networks to include Lebanese wholesalers (*turcos*) and local employees of the railway and the national airline who would often come back from their trips to Chile and the United States with "tax-free" commodities.

Silveria attributes the steady commercial growth of the Eloy Salmón to the miraculous Lord of Gran Poder, who had made the neighborhood "fertile" for business. Associated with the Holy Trinity but highly reminiscent of indigenous deities, this three-faced image of Christ was hosted in the shops and homes of the Eloy Salmón neighborhood after its "expulsion" from a Catholic convent as a result of its unorthodox iconographic features. Like the Taraqueños, the Holy Trinity image was a newcomer (*forastero*) to the area that had been forced out of its home, stridently disagreeing with the modern canons of urban propriety and remaining associated with a rural and indigenous past supposedly on the verge of disappearance (Guss 2006).

The Lord of Gran Poder.

The formation of the Eloy Salmón's trade union was paralleled by that of a religious fraternity of Taraqueños that, together with other traders' guilds, participated in the annual fiesta and dance parade in honor of the Lord of Gran Poder. Despite the peripherality of both Aymara traders and the Gran Poder neighborhood in the urban geography, the fiesta has lately transformed into one of the region's largest religious celebrations (Albó and Preiswerk 1986; Guss 2006; Himpele 2003; Tassi 2010). Together with her late husband Pedro, Silveria was fiesta steward (*pasante*) of the Eloy Salmón fraternity in 1984—an event that sanctioned her definitive social recognition among "popular" traders in the city. The Gran Poder festival had become an ideal platform for expressing the success of newly rich rural settlers of indigenous origin in an urban context that tended to exclude them and overlook their social and economic achievements.

In the 1970s, Silveria began traveling with her *comadre* Delia to the Colón duty-free zone in Panama. She would place large orders for commodities that she would then redistribute to her numerous relatives in the Eloy Salmón. A few years later, Silveria became a habitué of the newly

MAP 1 Map of the main locations of regional trade mentioned in the text.

established duty-free zone in Iquique in the north of Chile. She would travel to Chile on her godson's father's truck, with thousands of dollars in cash strapped around her belly. In the duty-free zone she became the customer (*casero*) of "Mauricio," an Arab importer who provided her with appliances and electronics of mainstream brands not officially represented in Bolivia. She would often buy on credit from her Arab *casero*, and with a simple verbal agreement, her godson's father would transport thousands of dollars' worth of her goods to La Paz along unpaved mountain roads, avoiding—or negotiating with—customs officials or depositing goods in hidden store-houses in the Aymara villages along the route with the help of the locals.

China was Silveria's next challenge. She first traveled to China in the early 1990s, "mute and deaf," as she put it, without speaking a word of Mandarin or English. Only later did she pick up some English words from

MAP 2 Map of the main Chinese locations linked with Aymara trade.

her daughter's exercise book. Today she travels regularly, two or three times a year, to Guangzhou (Canton) and Shenzhen. She goes with relatives and members of the guild. They place joint orders with Chinese family-run consortia and they share the costs of the container, although in some cases they might negotiate individually with the producers. Although electronics is Silveria's main business line, she has begun importing water tanks, mobile phone accessories, and particularly motorbike parts that her grandson assembles in his workshop. By importing parts, they save on customs taxes and transport costs and they are able to place the family brand label on the bikes, claiming to be the first brand of "Bolivian motorbikes." Before each trip to China, Silveria visits *tío* Evaristo, a ritual specialist who "reads" in cards and coca leaves whether the investment is going to turn out positively. Sometimes they prepare offerings for deities with condor wings, so that their requests (*pedidos*) will be heard as far away as China.

Indigenous Peoples and Global Capitalism

In Bolivia, the emergence of Aymara traders such as Silveria has been going on for some decades under the unconcerned gaze of the white-*mestizo* sectors. Similar to other Latin American countries, the recent economic bonanza is not uniquely enjoyed by the elites and the ruling classes because an increasing portion of the "popular sectors"[2] have managed to participate successfully in new circuits of trade and consumption (Arellano and Burgos 2010). Overlooked by economic policies and considered incapable of properly progressing by conventional economic theory and development experts (UNDP 2005), popular sectors have often been of scant interest to both public servants and ruling classes. Destined to decline in the contact with the global economy and incapable of adopting behavioral and economic practices suited to a middle-class lifestyle (they would not go to Miami for holidays and they would not start a franchise of a foreign brand), Aymara traders were now displacing the traditional middle class and presenting themselves as a key economic force in the transformation of the country. When it became apparent that they were challenging the established social, economic and colonial hierarchies and boundaries separating middle-class urban families from "indigenous" newcomers, their emergence came to be labeled a "problem."

This book addresses some of these transformations and delves into the modalities of social and economic affirmation of Aymara traders. It seeks to understand how a marginal socioeconomic form that developed in the cracks of the state has been able to transform a space of social and economic exclusion into one of affirmation, setting up economic networks ranging from Brazil to China and consolidating national and regional chains of supply and distribution. Popular and indigenous economies are often characterized as being local, marginal, and subsidiary to the official one (Applbaum 2005) and as having limitations in access to capital, technology, and information (Long and Roberts 1984; Quijano 1998). Expressions such as "jungle of prices," "inhomogeneity of goods," and "cacophony and contradictions" of popular markets (Geertz 1979: 217) tend to be used to describe the precarious institutional modalities and economic strategies of popular economic actors. However, Aymara traders' capacity for social organization and mobilization and their strategies of economic protection and expansion appear to have become consolidated into an economic system structuring national and, partially, regional flows.

Today, the Aymara[3] are renowned in the Andean countries—and even among some traders in the United States and China—for controlling the trade, routes, and markets of a wide range of commodities in some of the major cities of Bolivia and Peru. Despite being a landlocked country, Bolivia has in the past few decades become the fulcrum of an intense traffic of commodities. After entering the harbors of northern Chile and being either smuggled or imported into Bolivia, commodities are then redistributed to most countries on the continent, including Chile itself. Such trade is almost entirely controlled by the Aymara through extensive and sophisticated kinship networks and informal but solid economic agreements rarely put on paper or legalized.

The Aymara traders at the center of this process of economic expansion have had limited access to formal education and a long trajectory of exclusion from official institutions such as state bureaucracy, universities, and professional associations. As in the case of Silveria, we are not talking about civil servants or local elite families who profited from substantial state benefits and *ad personam* policies, as often happens to the region's ruling elites. Nor has this group been benefiting from recent involvement in an international export economy, the influx of foreign capital, or the emergence of richer peasant farmers connected to a plantation economy. On the contrary, they are former members of farming communities involved in small-scale agriculture in one of the continent's toughest, most isolated regions with the most adverse climate conditions. Interestingly, the unlikely global success of these traders has been paralleled by the strengthening of their local organizations and institutions as well as by the intensification of their ritual and religious activities, some of which are crucial in the reproduction and extension of the local power structure.

In the Andes, indigenous cultural and socioeconomic forms have often been associated either with poverty (Perry et al. 2006; Poole 1992) or with an impediment to the modernization and progress of the nation, if not being considered a reason for its backwardness (Ávila Molero 2000; Holmberg 1952). This deep-rooted history depicting indigenous actors as incomplete or deficient subjects has fostered a tendency, still very much alive today, to envision these actors as requiring intervention, redefinition, and integration. Their economic practice was therefore framed in normative terms: their local institutions had to be restructured to become economically more efficient and to incentivize an effective capital formation; "technical assistance" was required because their lack of formal education hindered stable trends of development; and partnerships with mainstream entrepreneurs were encouraged to promote integration into the market and enable them to learn the tricks of a global economy. Unexpectedly, these narratives and forms of intervention came to be challenged by intrepid indigenous entrepreneurs positioning themselves as the engine of dramatic economic transformations.

Politicoeconomic analyses of indigenous peoples' involvement with global capitalism have often tended to focus on a loss of culture following the incursion of the monetary economy and of conventional technologies (cf. Bohannan 1959; Turner 1995) and unequal forms of integration into an unbalanced and exploitative world economy that tended to treat them as either cheap labor or mere purveyors of raw materials (Wolf 1982). Culture-based studies would emphasize the emergence of new meanings, the resignification of capitalism (Appadurai 1986, 1996) produced by the incursion of indigenous concepts, forms, and aspirations in the economic field, and the extension of local categories and imaginaries to potentially converge into indigenous world-systems (Sahlins 2000), namely, interpretations of the world from local and indigenous perspectives.

In more recent years, scholars (Andolina et al. 2009; Comaroff and Comaroff 2009; DeHart 2010) have begun to address how the increasing transnationalization of indigenous movements and identities and their links with international development agencies has brought about a reconceptualization of ethnicity as an asset to development rather than an obstacle (Andolina et al. 2009: 11). What was often implied was the cooption of ethnicity by neoliberal institutions and policies (DeHart 2010: 1–3) and the reproduction of a pattern whereby indigenous peoples could be recognized as subjects or "agents" as long as they were integrated into predefined ideas of economic change/development formulated elsewhere. From a different perspective, theorists (see Escobar 1995, 2005) have suggested forms of mobilization of ethnicity directed toward practices of "counterwork," namely, alternative economic projects tied to often-marginal indigenous and subaltern strategies of localization aimed at counteracting violent forms of economic exclusion, deterritorialization, and globalization.

In this book, I argue that Aymara forms of organization and control of local commercial spaces have been strategic tools allowing them to expand their sociopolitical structure and economy by means of flexible translocal networks (Ribeiro 2006), reaching out to regions where neither the state nor the mainstream enterprises were able to operate or interested in doing so. This concomitant expansion of economic scope and sociopolitical institutionality, rooted in a series of traditional cultural forms and practices, conforms neither to a mere resignification or generation of cultural meanings nor to a simple political resistance to capitalist powers. Keeping international agencies and state institutions at bay through the capillary control of locality, the forms of appropriation of capitalism and globalization by Aymara traders have become proactive tools engendering specific microeconomic practices and strategies of business administration, consolidating the local power structure and outlining tactics to access the market on their own terms (Tassi et al. 2013). Aymara traders have been able to configure a rhythm of operation and a level of autonomy in their economic management that places them as "economy makers" (Escobar 2008: 100) in the sense that the economy is something they act on rather than something that is imposed on them. Interlocked with cosmological reproduction and political self-determination (Colloredo-Mansfeld 1999; Guyer 2004; Maurer 2005), this emergent economic know-how is posing a challenge to conventional economic narratives and principles forecasting the dissolution of indigenous economic forms and their absorption by larger and more modern conglomerates (cf. Yang 2000) while outlining a mode of affirming indigenous logics and practices from the interstices.[4]

Cosmoeconomics and Globalization from Below

The "cultural turn" movement of the 1970s/1980s produced a tendency to downplay overarching economic and political dynamics to promote a cultural mode privileging difference, specificity, and identities (cf. Jameson 1998; Santos 2008) and placing emphasis on meaning and culture as the focus of contemporary debates. In reaction to the cultural turn and on the wave of the recent economic crisis, scholars have begun to critically reemphasize global dynamics and sound a caution about the capacity of capital to engulf local and culturally specific practices (Comaroff and Comaroff

2006, 2009; Žižec 1997). This tension has been feeding two opposed trends. On the one hand, the focus on "local identity" has tended to overshadow concerns about economic inequalities and uneven access to and distribution of resources among indigenous and marginal sectors of society (Kohl and Farthing 2006; Wolf 1982). Somehow this made it possible to reproduce and normalize a system of exploitation that subdued indigenous and local peoples, forcing them to provide raw materials and cheap labor (Ferguson 1999; Mitchell 2002). On the other hand, the depiction of local/indigenous economic actors as marginal or irremediably destined for a natural absorption by dominant forces reasserted the primacy of Western thought and practices by inserting the non-Westerns into the market and therefore overlooking their creative capacities and ability to engender their own politicoeconomic concepts and practices, often challenging taken-for-granted ideas and categories (Goody 2010; Sahlins 2000).

Some scholars (Escobar 2005, 2008; Gibson-Graham 1996; Santos and Rodríguez-Garavito 2005; Yang 2000) have suggested that capitalism's capacity to overpower subordinate local cultures is paralleled by the constant emergence of economic practices and interstitial strategies shaped by this same process of exclusion, which have the potential to articulate "other" economic projects and models. Excluded, deterritorialized, and displaced by forms of delocalization intrinsic to a new global division of labor, local and indigenous groups appeared to produce both new alliances and strategies of appropriation, revitalization, and reterritorialization of local spaces and concepts, outlining unexpected meanings and knowledges. This shapes a multiplicity of possible globalizations, political and economic configurations, and socioenvironmental designs (cf. Escobar 2008; cf. Mignolo 2000). Consequently, scholars have been encouraged to question the idea that capitalism and globalization are intra-European phenomena (Escobar 2005: 24; Goody 2010) as a strategy to highlight the dark side of these models and concepts and to foreground those subordinated practices and knowledges that are suppressed, disqualified, or overlooked by conventional powers.

Over the past few years, sociological and anthropological analyses of practices of globalization and international trade have recorded the emergence of unconventional economic actors encountering a degree of "agency" and success in the interstices of global economic processes. A number of symptomatic works (Harriss-White 2003; Harriss-White and Sinha 2007; Mathews et al. 2012; Neuwirth 2011; Simpfendorfer 2011) have suggested that there has been a rise of popular and informal sectors traditionally excluded or subordinated to the dominant interests of the mainstream economy, which has led to these sectors becoming key actors in third world flows. Although scholars have been cautious when addressing the possible durability of these processes and actors (cf. Ferguson 1999) or their propensity to counteract capitalism (Ribeiro 2012), a new debate on non-hegemonic global economies (Mathews 2011; Mathews and Yang 2012) has begun to spring up.

Not only did such non-hegemonic global economies show unexpected resilience, self-organization, and cunningness when confronted with global capitalism, but also they appeared—in some cases—to be scaling up (Neuwirth 2011). Although popular, indigenous, and informal economies have often been characterized in terms of their inability to develop consistent forms of capital accumulation and as a "handful of market women selling a handful of shriveled carrots to earn a handful of pennies" (Neuwirth 2011: 18), this "economy of desperation" suddenly appeared to be on the verge of change. As transportation and communication technologies expanded, third world popular economies expanded too, transforming into a sector not only capable of generating accumulation but also of providing access to forms of employment that traditional institutions and development agencies were unable to provide and eventually propelling many third world cities and countries into more or less sustainable forms of "modernity" (Neuwirth 2011; Scarborough 2013).

Neuwirth (2011) argues that this is partly the consequence of the inability of legal businesses and large conglomerates to obtain enough profit from bringing cutting-edge commodities and technology to the third world. In recent years, this has been counteracted by the willingness of small Chinese manufacturers not so concerned with "legal insecurity"[5] to engage directly with third world traders (Mathews and Alba Vega 2012). Together with Chinese manufacturers' capillary capacity to distribute goods to the most remote regions of the globe, the flexibility of their productive system has enabled them to produce in small batches according to the requirements of local traders and markets, thus activating interstitial global trade flows unmediated by large firms, while allowing third world popular sectors to access global commodities at affordable prices (Mathews et al. 2012).

The tendency of informal/popular economic practices to scale up and the emergence of a series of organizational structures and networks that attempt to replace the "formal" economic institutions (cf. Laville 2009) have been sparking a debate on "globalization from below" (Mathews et al. 2012; Ribeiro 2012), "low-end globalization," and "non-hegemonic world-systems" (Ribeiro 2006). This intellectual ferment on the subject also mirrors the emergence—or the recent awareness—of a global system of non-hegemonic actors, cemented by networking and brokerage, that is operating "under the radar of the law" (Mathews and Yang 2012: 97) and tangential to the logic of traditional power holders connected to state apparatuses and private firms.

Yemeni traders of the Hadrami tribe investing in Yiwu (Simpfendorfer 2011), Malian entrepreneurs in Guangzhou running shipping companies to sub-Saharan Africa (Li et al. 2007), the Igbos of Hong Kong (Rojas 2009), or the networks of Fujian villagers in New York (Chu 2010) appear to weave together different ideas and forms of economic globalization often invisible to conventional analyses (Mathews and Yang 2012). All these actors symbolize a new wave across the world, incessantly engendering sociocultural practices and strategies that are often sustained by local institutions and translocal alliances, to participate in the global economy and counteract the unequal balances and supposedly universal rules of global phenomena.

Deploying limited amounts of capital in semilegal transactions, this is a kind of "business without lawyers and copyrights, run through skeins of personal connections and wads of cash" (Mathews and Alba Vega 2012: 1; Mathews 2011). Although referred to by some as a problem or as criminals (Naím 2005) for circumventing the official rules of economic interaction often defined by the converging interests of states and transnational conglomerates, these emerging actors produce a variety of unorthodox strategies in negotiating with established legal structures, systems of production, global transport, and local demands. Not only does this end up blurring a reified distinction between formal and informal economies and between illicit and licit activities,[6] but also it has begun to create pressure on official institutions and international agencies to redefine policies and laws favorable to conventional firms and large investors (Gustavo Lins Ribeiro, personal communication; Santos and Rodríguez-Garavito 2005) to address the interests and the practices of these unconventional economic actors.

These non-hegemonic actors are often instrumental in generating employment locally, improving access to resources that global capitalism is not interested in guaranteeing (Karaganis 2011) and, in the inapplicability of or exclusion from formal regulations, consolidating locally based, nonofficial regulatory structures that allow the economy to function (cf. Grégoire and Labazée 1993; Benjamin and Aly Mbaye 2010). Additionally, the emergence of this variety of unorthodox global economic actors (Chu 2010; Xiang 2005; Yang 2000) dodging mainstream economic institutions and models has been stimulating a direct crossbreeding among "local" groups, sociocultural institutions, and economic forms that are unmediated by dominant conglomerates, contributing to the creation of an interstitial global economic space (see Chapter 3).

The dynamics of globalization from below and the new emphasis on local/indigenous economic institutions and practices as the sites onto which these global transformations are mapped encourage us to downplay the epistemological gap established between local cosmology and global economic forces and to reflect on the double-bind relation existing between economy and cosmology (da Col and Rio 2013). For indigenous groups such as the Aymara, scholars have tended either to differentiate between two separate spatiotemporal dimensions, namely, the community-like dynamics versus the market economy (Temple 1997), or to forecast a linear transition from rural backwardness to global capitalism (cf. Bohannan 1955; Turner 1995). Non-hegemonic global actors often dwell in a liminal terrain at the confluence of global flows, ethnic networks, and culturally specific economic concepts.

Although we tend to identify the rationale of indigenous economies as either "successive" or "concurrent" to the logic of global market systems (cf. Applbaum 2005; Mandel 1972), I ponder here how the two might interact with each other. We are living in a time when a series of ideological, economic, and military interests appear to shape a constellation of powers in which violent and coercive types of enforcement have increasingly become tools to regulate peoples and economies (Asad 2010; Boot 2002; Joxe 2002). However, this should not lock us into reading the incursion of the market and globalization into local spaces as a stoppage in the ability of local cultures to produce techniques, ideas, and myths to act pragmatically according to the rules of the market and using the instruments of the market. In contrast to local elites' historical dependence on and subordination to modernist developmental models (Arguedas 1975: 170), the Aymaras's contact with modernity and the market economy has enhanced both their ritual production and their capacity to engender economic concepts and narratives of their own (Arbona et al. 2015; cf. Bird-David 1992; Codere 1950; Colloredo-Mansfeld 1999; Grotti 2013), often through practices of appropriation.

Anthropological concepts such as "economies of fortune and luck," "spiritual economy," and more recently "cosmoeconomics" (da Col and Rio 2013) have often referred to the symbolic and theological roots of economic phenomena and orders but also emphasized the role of economic cosmologies as heuristic tools for rethinking conceptions of economy, well-being, and prosperity. The emphasis on economic cosmologies is often read as a focus on locally circumscribed and economically marginal practices and concepts that may outline principles or logics of functioning challenging conventional economic forms and ideas. What I am suggesting here is an expansion of the idea of cosmoeconomics (da Col and Rio 2013), envisioning it not only as a set of principles but also as a tool to respond to and counteract the demands of global capitalism (Ong and Nonini 1997) as well as a structure mitigating its inequalities and hierarchies, outlining possibilities, rhythms, and patterns of participation in the global economy defined translocally. This may induce us not to simply trace the integration of Aymara traders into a global imaginary with local coloring, but to outline an economic venture that attempts to appropriate and resignify trade and to practice global flows by building on local strategies and concepts (Escobar 2001).

The modern science of economics has been created and reproduced through narratives that have tended to draw a distinction between market and community (Gudeman 2008, 2009), material and spiritual aspects (Espirito Santo and Tassi 2013; Keane 2007; Maurer 2005), kinship and capitalism (De Boeck 1999). The separation of these domains and dimensions constituted the basis on which a boundary was devised between proper and improper economic behavior and between modern market economies and local/indigenous unfulfilled stages of capitalism. The modalities and concepts of Aymara trade not only lead us to reconsider such dichotomies but also prove particularly valuable in forcing us to question and analyze how we create a distinction between these domains (market and religion, gifts and commodities, kinship and capitalism). Potentially, this may open the way to a review of taken-for-granted conceptual categories such as "the market" (cf. Dilley 1992) and "globalization" (Inda and Rosaldo 2007; Meyer and Geschiere 1999).

The modalities of operation of this interstitial trade encourage us both to recognize and to scrutinize new politicoeconomic dynamics at the heart of global capitalism and to dwell on a series of local concepts, cosmological forms, and practices creatively and proactively outlined as a response to global economic dynamics. They also force us not to lose sight of the power discrepancies and differences of scale between global flows and local actors. In fact, it leads us to simultaneously explore the possibilities and limitations of a globalization from below (Mathews et al. 2012; Ribeiro 2012) and the cosmological concepts, practices, and logics (cf. da Col and Rio 2013) that frame their participation in the global economy on their own terms.

In the Cracks of the State: Indigenous Counter-Hegemonic Strategies and Institutions

The processes of sociopolitical exclusion of indigenous minorities often produce an overlap of denial of basic rights and services with the implosion of local socioeconomic structures recursively weakening their capacity for negotiation with external forces. In Bolivia, the marginality and destruc-turation of indigenous groups was counteracted by their absolute majority in terms of population (Arnold 2008; Rivera 2010c) and by the persistence and reconfiguration (cf. Dover 1993) of a series of sociopolitical structures that were able to repeatedly challenge the official institutions (Hylton and Thomson 2007). Today it would be impossible to grasp the recent political transformations or make sense of the emergence of Aymara traders with-out understanding the weight of indigenous and popular institutionality (Medeiros et al. 2013).

The interstitial institutionality of highland indigenous groups and their tendency to operate in the fissures of the official economic and ad-ministrative system dates back a long way in history. The constitution of the Republic of Indians during the colonial times originated a semiau-tonomous governmental structure based on "indigenous law" that sepa-rated indigenous politics and jurisdiction from the sphere of colonial power (Fernandez 2000: 15). Although aimed at the political exclusion of indigenous people, the indigenous legislation with its authorities and norms managed to preserve and reproduce some of the local juridical and institutional practices. Similar contradictions operated in the economic field. On the one hand, the Spanish Crown was exerting a monopoly over the exploitation and commercialization of precious metals in the region in an attempt to hinder local people's control of strategic economic resources (Escobari 1985). On the other hand, its capacity to control the territory was limited to some of the main urban centers (Klein 1995), making the colonial authorities economically highly dependent on the indigenous populations in terms of both labor and food supply and socioeconomic structures of distribution. This created a paradoxical situation whereby the socioeconomic articulation of the colonial territory was in the hands of indigenous lineages that were excluded *de facto* from forms of political and economic participation (Glave 1989; Rivera 2010a).[7]

Based on the provision/exploitation of indigenous labor and the pay-ment of tribute, this political and economic system granted local popula-tions the possibility to administrate local parishes according to indigenous forms and practices of authority (cf. Choque 1987; Platt 1982a; Thompson 2002). Although founded on forms of forced labor in the mines and un-equal taxation of the indigenous population, such economic measures consolidated "indigenous economic spaces" (cf. Glave 1989) in political and economic interstices and marginal areas. In economic terms, this made it impossible for official institutions to establish conventional forms of agrarian capitalism in highland rural areas (Platt 1982a). It also led to the springing up of a local system of rural weekly markets (*ferias*)[8] whose commercial rhythms remained defined by indigenous communities and logics (Langer 2004).

As explained by Brooke Larson (2004), the creation of the Bolivian state was characterized by two opposed movements. On the one hand, the white-*mestizo* elites were attempting to recreate the forms and practices of European liberal democracies and to consolidate an integral and homogeneous nation. On the other, they strove to limit the principles of liberalism by instituting "innate" ethnic differences in the attempt to build an apparatus of nation-making that simultaneously integrated and marginalized the indigenous populations (cf. Irurozqui 1994; Gruzinski and Wachtel 1997; Goodale and Postero 2013). These dynamics generated a contradictory situation where the exclusion of the indigenous peoples from the official economy and their repeated characterization as obstacles to progress, incapable of participating in the "history of the country,"[9] was counteracted by the consolidation of relatively autonomous indigenous spaces and even institutions relegated to marginal areas and spaces (Platt 1982a).

In fact, the creation of the Bolivian state (in 1825) reproduced the tension between an inconstant and exclusive officialdom and the indigenous sectors and organizations—particularly Aymara—with a defined idea of "nation" (Zavaleta 1986) and also a two-level layering of the economy. Based on the alliance or identification between the bureaucratic apparatus and the enlightened ruling classes of Spanish descent, the Bolivian state has traditionally constituted a tool to further the economic interests of a small sector of the population and maintain a regime of exploitation of the indigenous majority (Zavaleta 1986; cf. MacGaffey and Bazenguissa-Ganga 2000). In other words, the state was the instrument that granted participation in the formal economy to a small group of enlightened citizens (cf. de Soto 1986), while subjecting the rest of the population to the absence of a regulatory framework for their economic activities.

These modalities of operation of the state activated a kind of vicious circle. As state bureaucrats use the state to further their own interests, national resources and revenues begin to decline and the state apparatus becomes increasingly unable to provide services and perform its role (Gill 2000). As the official system collapses, on the one hand, more and more people turn to unofficial activities that sometimes manage to work in extraordinarily ingenious ways, whereas on the other hand, unofficial institutions and organizations tend to fill the gaps and replace the role of the state both in the regulation of economic activities and in the provision of basic services.

The decline of national revenues became apparent with the neoliberal policies of the 1980s and 1990s that are often associated with the withdrawal of the state from the economic field, the weakening of trade unions, and a general process of social and moral deterioration (García Linera 2008). In Bolivia, the affirmation of Aymara traders and the popular economy has been often connected to the fragmentation of trade unions, the incursion of capitalism, and a general recomposition or flexibilization of forms and practices of sociopolitical organization (García Linera 2008; UNDP 2005). On the one hand, neoliberal policies weakened the prebendal relation between state and trade unions (Rodríguez Ostria 2014) based on the provision of public employment and welfare relief[10] and, in some cases, managed to reduce the corporatist control of strategic resources by privileged social sectors (see Spedding 2009 in the case of transport). On the other hand, neoliberal policies visualized the organizational and political substrata of popular and indigenous sectors (Saravia and Sandóval 1991) which had been consolidating on the margins, maintaining a degree of autonomy from the state (cf. Platt 1982a; Rivera 1983; cf. Rivera 2010c) and which had been complementing mainstream trade unionism. This not only did away with an old system of union leaders and sectorial political demands but also brought about forms of popular and indigenous organization and institutionality that neoliberal policies were unable to dismantle or absorb.

The Aymaras's sociocultural organization, their kinship networks, and their capacity to provide basic services, far from being the archaic traits of a people left behind, are now reframed as the attributes of a semi-autonomous "ungoverned" sector capable of defining the forms of the economy and the country itself. As we are witnessing in several parts of the Global South (Forment 2014), this institutional emergence of popular sectors not merely defined by the official institutions and disassociated from the prebendal relation with the state, instead of an impediment to the development of democracy (Lazarte 1991; Archondo 1991; Chatterjee 2004) or an emblem of social and moral deterioration, seems to provide an alternative set of institutions and possibilities with which to think about citizenship, the public sphere, and political parties (Forment 2014).

Appropriating the Other: Aymara Counter-Hegemonic Strategies

The Aymara built on the failure of the official institutions and economy— and their exclusion from them—to solidify the legitimacy and scope of their own organizations while simultaneously keeping opportunist conventional institutions at bay. Using both the weapons of their historical discrimination and exclusion and the mobilization of a purposely heightened ethnic difference,[11] the Aymara reasserted their indocile response to forms of control or assimilation and even managed to make the white-*mestizos* feel like foreigners in their own country (Himpele 2003). Their anchoring in the local territory and resources and their reliance on their own organizations and cultural codes operated as strategies to reiterate their role as legitimate owners of the space, openly defying the ruling classes whose sociocultural referents remained foreign (Toranzo 2007; Rojas Ortuste 2009).

This is not to say that the Aymara were radically locked into forms of closed corporatism (Schulte 1999). Their heightened sense of autonomy and reliance on their structures and organizations in the face of the inconstancy of official institutions was based not only on radical forms of resistance (Stern 1987a) but also on strategic practices of appropriation and resignification of external elements in the constant interaction with foreign institutions and forces (Abercrombie 1998). In fact, the interplay of forms of exclusion and assimilation of the indigenous sectors on unequal terms (cf. Gruzinski and Wachtel 1997) incentivized among the Aymara both withdrawals to their own world and space and forward movements of appropriation of officialdom.

The history of the Aymara is interspersed by a repeated and enhanced capacity to appropriate the ideas, spaces, and technologies of the dominant sectors to consolidate their own power structures, belief systems, and economies (Abercrombie 1998; Harris et al. 1987; Rivera 1983; Stern 1987b). These forms of appropriation are sometimes deemed either a cosmetic use of dominant symbols and forms to camouflage practices and ideas that remain indigenous at heart (Montenegro 1982; Montes Ruiz 1982) or to emphasize the ideological subordination of the indigenous groups to a more powerful and technologically advanced world. However, from Catholic rituals and images (Abercrombie 1998; Gose 2008; MacCormack 1991) to mercantile practices and money (Harris 1989; Platt 1992), foreign elements and technologies have become structuring components of the indigenous identity by being incorporated into and expanding local sociocultural and economic practices.

In economic terms, these forms of appropriation and resignification of dominant practices and systems have been striking. Steve Stern (1987b) suggests how the commercial initiatives of indigenous highlanders participating in a global mining economy could be read as strategies to strengthen indigenous economic forms and power structures. When international development agencies began advocating economic cooperatives and trade unions as tools to modernize the countryside and promote development (Ávila Molero 2000), the response of the Aymara was counterintuitive.

Aymara communities accepted the support of both development agencies and leftist intellectuals, but they often managed to maintain them at a distance from politicoeconomic decisions, repeatedly reasserting their autonomy (Rivera 1983). In other words, cooperatives and trade unions were often perceived as tools of local self-determination (Albó 1981) rather than foreign forms of organization, enabling a natural "adjustment" to the irreversible process of modern development.

This leads us to view the Aymara institutions and organizations not merely as subaltern structures and victims resisting the market and the state (Stern 1987a). Aymara people have been active *bricoleurs* in a process of assembling and linking new technologies with established and traditional practices. In so doing, they have appropriated these new materials, knowledges, and ideas, transforming them into indigenous ones and refashioning a sense of modernity and identity according to a pattern that is distinctively their own (cf. Bebbington 2000; Salomon 1986).

Compelling studies of popular economic institutions such as the bazaar (Geertz 1963, 1979) have concluded that such economic forms, although regulated by "ancient" and "fixed customs [sic]" of trade, often lacked proper trade unions or guilds, denoting a weak organizational capacity when faced with the power relationships of modern capitalism (cf. Meagher 2010). This leads the state to protect larger and better-structured firms from competition, enabling them to develop levels of accumulation of capital that the bazaar-like enterprises were unable to generate (Geertz 1963). Consequently, the fragmentation of popular and informal initiatives and their lack of institutionality are critical factors curtailing the lobbying capacity of these sectors (Meagher 2010). Particularly in third world countries, "legally" constituted foreign business conglomerates with an ample availability of resources are often much more likely to influence decision making and the adoption of favorable regulations by nation-states, again forcing popular economic actors into a semilegal existence.

In the case of Aymara traders, their local institutions achieved an organizational capacity and legitimacy that often overrode officialdom. They guaranteed popular and indigenous sectors not only the functioning of trade and the circulation of products but also forms of social control, sophisticated strategies for dealing with crimes, the provision of a local health-care system, and basic economic services (see Chapter 1). Often based on the appropriation of official procedures and regulations (Barragán and Cárdenas 2009), such unofficial organizations made it possible to limit the direct intervention of a dysfunctional bureaucratic apparatus—often uniquely preoccupied with furthering its own interests—and of foreign economic powers in the Aymara traders' political and economic arrangements and ecologies of patronage, re-distribution, and survival (see Chapter 2). This engendered a system of regu-lation from below based on local and existing resources and knowledges, which had not only acquired widespread legitimacy, but also constituted a system on which the state and official institutions themselves depended for their basic functioning (see Chapter 7).

The Overflow of the Cracks: Indigenous Modalities of Development

Generally, the regional imaginaries of traditionalism, poverty, and lack of a propensity to change that are associated with indigenous peoples were the motifs fostering measures of intervention, improvement, and development through a series of programs from external agencies and externally defined policies (Escobar 1995). Public policies and development projects were the tools used to imbricate indigenous groups into the conventional modes of economic modernization characterized by "expanding market relations and technical forms of expertise" (DeHart 2010: 141). However, the peculiar relational dynamics existing between official and Aymara institutions and economies encourage us to revise the representation of indigenous peoples as mere "beneficiaries" of external interventions. Rather than viewing them as eternally lacking possibilities, know-how, and organization or merely re-acting to the forms of exclusion of global capitalism, they urge us to enter-tain the possibility of thinking of them as bearers of specific strategies, institutions, and economic knowledge (see Chapters 4, 5, and 6).

In the region, indigenous peoples' conventional forms of development have been divided into three broad paradigms. The first has been associated with following in the footsteps of large entrepreneurs (Long and Roberts 1984; UNDP 2005). Considered unable to generate a surplus and capital re-production, local popular economies are said to require forms of association with large entrepreneurs and export chains to gain access to credit, technol-ogy, and know-how in a context where local actors' access to education and knowledge is as limited as their economic possibilities. As we shall see, the emergence of Aymara entrepreneurs and interconnected popular enter-prises has been challenging the conventional narrative of large firms paving the road to the development and legalization of "informal" actors.

A second option for development is that provided through investment by the state, both as a way to incentivize consumption and in terms of edu-cation, community development, and restructuring of local organizational forms (Holmberg 1952; Trebat 1983; cf. Ávila Molero 2000). State funds in the form of pensions, social security payments, and salaries for state officials may lead to the flourishing of commercial revenues, drawing local indigenous communities into the wider economy. In Bolivia in the past few years, the state has attempted to take on the role of lead entrepreneur, both as a strategy to speed up local development (local entrepreneurs joining state economic projects) and to prevent foreign multinationals from controlling the Bolivian economy (Postero 2013).

The third option is through the development projects of nongovernmental organizations (NGOs), especially those that support rural productive activities, facilitate local actors' entry into urban markets, produce forms of access to credit, and make local economic institutions more efficient. In Bolivia, the high percentage of failures of development projects over the past two decades has led scholars to question the NGOs' ability to understand local realities and aspirations (Rodríguez-Carmona 2009). A series of studies has begun observing development projects' dismantling of local social networks and survival strategies in the name of the market (see Elyachar 2005 in the case of Egypt) as well as the instrumental use of participatory strategies and methodologies as vehicles for consolidating the inflow of external ideas and interests into local areas (Walley 2004; Medeiros 1995; Rodríguez-Carmona et al. 2013). This has often resulted in a heightened capacity on the part of development agencies to coopt ethnicity and indigenous movements into their development concepts and ideas (Andolina et al. 2009; DeHart 2010), channeling them into predefined forms of development.

Escobar's (1995) "postdevelopment" project urges us to radically give up on an idea of development that imposed external political, economic, and technological innovations and redefined local actors and communities. He argues that the deterritorialization and dispersion of social forms imposed both by global flows and by conventional ideas of development may lead local and marginal groups to devise innovative visions and practices, which may become counter-hegemonic forces counteracting the domesticating efforts of conventional institutions, projects, and policies (cf. da Col and Rio 2013). Local and indigenous movements struggling with development imperatives may generate ways of reappropriating concepts and practices that were previously discarded (i.e., religious fundamentalism), but may also engender "hybrid" cultural productions and new rules, defying the official development logic.

Andean ethnographies have repeatedly signaled the proactive and creative capacities of indigenous groups when faced with projects of forced integration into the market economy or the destructuration of their cultural forms and institutions (Harris 1982; Platt 1982a, 1992). Local actors have been able to structure a series of strategies and market networks both to operate within and to protect themselves from mercantile flows that tended to subordinate them (Larson and León 1987). Such Andean strategies often operate in the margins allowed by global economic forces while simultaneously being able to limit and influence them (Harris et al. 1987).

Tristan Platt et al. (2006) observed how the availability of indigenous peasants to work in the mines was limited to short periods before the payment of their tributes to the state or before religious fiestas associated with remarkable expenditure. Harris (1982) describes the consolidation of a parallel economic circuit ("ethnic economy") recursively opening up to the market to make use of its benefits and closing off to avoid its threats. This was crucial to protect and expand the indigenous traders' power structure and reassert their control over the local means of production. Forced participation in the market reconfigured the rules and logics of operation and engendered new strategies. In recent decades, the Aymaras's participation in global flows and their connection with multiple markets have revamped ancient practices of mobility across the territory (Condarco Morales 1970; Murra 1975 [1972]), forms of double domicile, and an intercalated system of *ferias*, producing an investment in local assets and forms (Tassi 2012a).

Conventionally, modernization and development are seen as processes of "structural adjustment" and/or "rupture" with traditional ideas, practices, and organizations (cf. Holmberg 1952), signaling redemption from backwardness, tradition, and marginality. However, in recent decades Aymara religious festivals, kinship networks, and trade guilds have undergone a process of consolidation and expansion, coinciding with Aymara traders' firmer involvement in the global economy. Paceño religious fraternities have been venturing into new territories and creating "branches" in the tropical cities of the lowlands as well as among the Bolivian expat communities in Buenos Aires and São Paulo (Hinojosa and Guaygua 2015). Aymara socioeconomic networks have been able to establish their storage bays and workshops in the Iquique duty-free zone and also expanded their radius of operation toward the industrial hubs of São Paulo and Santos, from where they import building materials, shoes, and sewing thread. Through their networks, Peruvian cotton from central and northern regions could overcome the cold highland provinces and find new market niches in the tropical regions of Bolivia, and locally produced jeans could reach Peruvian and Argentinean cities on both the Pacific and the Atlantic coasts (Arbona et al. 2015).

These dynamics appear to be drawing a new and extended map of the Aymara economy in the region, ranging from metropolis to border towns, from harbors to rural provinces. Instead of rupture with tradition, abandonment of the interstices, and the sense of estrangement that characterizes processes of development and modernization (Keane 2007), Aymara traders' economic expansion takes the form of a simultaneous "widening" and "prolongation," both of the interstices they were forced to inhabit and of their socioeconomic networks and structures, thus outlining counterintuitive modalities of development.

The widening refers to the expansion of Aymara modalities of operation to domains from which they had been traditionally excluded, consequently defying conventional asymmetries between proper and improper economic actors and spaces and between expert urbanites considered bearers of economic knowledge and uneducated indigenous people of rural origin. This reconfigures both the local commercial landscape and the urban spatial divisions that had tended to segregate indigenous sectors. But it also reshuffles mainstream economic practices, from banking to consumption, investment to accountancy, which begin increasingly to revolve around Aymara sociocultural codes, logics, and institutions (see Chapters 4 and 5).

The second mode of affirmation of Aymara traders is the prolongation, namely, the geographical expansion of their radius of operation to include a variety of translocal spaces, leading to the creation of an interstitial global economy featuring an overlap of local networks and a capacity to move a variety of different products across vast territories. On the one hand, these spaces were often second-tier markets neglected by large conglomerates; on the other hand, the mode of prolongation of the interstices remained anchored to local practices of mobility and ramified, multiple, and flexible networks based on forms of kinship.

Widening the Interstices: The Appropriation of Exclusive Socioeconomic Spaces

This stretching of the interstices can first be observed in the conquest and appropriation of social spaces and domains traditionally reserved for white-*mestizo* sectors and institutions. The expansion of the commercial volume of the Eloy Salmón is paralleled by the extension and growth of religious fiestas, dance parades, and religious fraternities, which had become an indication of the gradual conquest of urban spaces by popular sectors. In the Eloy Salmón, increasing divergences are developing between the official Catholic groups linked to the clergy and the commercial guilds and fraternities involved in the organization of the religious festival of Gran Poder. The dispute developed as a consequence of the unorthodox religious practices adopted by traders during the festival and their limited participation in the official Catholic ceremonies. The traders' community was sidelining the church in the control of religious activities. In fact, they were able to insert into the Catholic ritual cycle practices that religious authorities were reluctant to accept. These practices included the Mass for the *pasante* with surprising transformations in the wording of the traditional liturgy, the mass blessing of the traders' fraternities with buckets of holy water outside the Sanctuary, and the offerings of food to the Lord of Gran Poder during the service.[12] In 2008, and from then onward, despite the protests of the Archbishop, the official procession on Holy Trinity Sunday was postponed to the following week so as not to interfere with the *Diana*, a crucial social event and parade performed by the traders' fraternities.[13]

The power of the traders was not only in their overwhelming of established mainstream institutions, but also in the consolidation and expansion of their legitimacy and authority. The appropriation of local media was crucial to this objective. Begun by the musician Carlos Palenque at the end of the 1980s with the television show *The Open Tribunal of the People* (cf. Himpele 2002), where indigenous people were portrayed for the first time as protagonists of urban life instead of folkloric and apolitical subjects, guilds of traders and religious fraternities continued the project of conquering spaces in the media. A series of traders' radio stations and popular TV channels began mushrooming. Initially, they were used as spaces to exchange messages, spread ideas, and call meetings. However, they were soon transformed into channels broadcasting the emergence of urban popular sectors, experimenting with practices of self-representation, and channeling specific aesthetic forms and aspirations. They even allowed butchers to run talk shows on national television and female indigenous traders to lead cooking programs. Instead of subaltern invisibility, the media granted even-handed forms of visual prominence to marginalized but emerging popular sectors, allowing them to experiment with their own forms and practices of upward mobility and to play with representation on their own terms. Above all, they made their presence unquestionable and undeniable; they were no longer associated with abnormal and backward clothing and beliefs or illicit economies, but had become an ascending social sector with a complex articulated social structure, which was appropriating spaces traditionally dominated by the elites.

The politicoeconomic field remains the crucial arena where the popular expansion and appropriation of spaces is played out. In a racially divided context with a tradition of weak formal institutions, Aymara traders have become strategic actors in providing basic socioeconomic services from health insurance to systems of neighborhood safety, from issuing trade licenses to implementing and organizing local transport (see Chapter 1).

Although deemed by modernist narratives as unprepared for global challenges, traders have been able to permeate and redefine according to their specific purposes and necessities the functioning of financial institutions, forms of banking, and marketing practices according to distinctively Aymara sociocultural patterns.

Prolongation: The Linkage with Translocal Spaces

If popular institutionality has been able to establish local forms of control of territory, markets, and chains of distribution and supply, the most astonishing feature of Aymara traders has been the prolonging of their radius of operation and networks, regionally and worldwide. In fact, they have been able to consolidate strategic commercial alliances and networks with Chinese family-run consortia in Guangzhou, Arab capitalists in Iquique, and even foreign entrepreneurs in La Paz. Despite their achievements, Aymara traders remain sharply differentiated from the conventional associations of entrepreneurs because of their indigenous provenance, socioeconomic modalities, and lack of formal education.

In general, among local conventional entrepreneurs, the idea of China's commercial potential has been obfuscated by the elitist imaginary that associated the Asian giant with cheap products, counterfeiting, and bad taste. For the urban middle classes, the United States remained the point of reference, the dispenser of modernity and of the most ingenious technological products brought about by globalization, despite—or because of—the restrictive measures obstructing local peoples' access to such products. Although local associations of formal entrepreneurs have only recently begun to discuss and address the "Chinese question," in the popular neighborhoods of La Paz, establishments with flashy neon signs, Oriental graphics, and ideograms, like the "Yiwu showroom" and the "Guangzhou commercial center," have begun to displace the ancient and decaying "Washington tailor shop" and "Miami travel agency" (Tassi et al. 2013: 116).

Conventional associations of entrepreneurs who envisage China as a commercial giant that produces everything—thus making export to that country impossible—are now advising Bolivian traders and entrepreneurs to form business partnerships with Chinese conglomerates and attract foreign capital to Bolivia.[14] Although these formal associations continue to promote unequal and often dependent economic partnerships with powerful overseas investors, Aymara traders have shaped strategic economic alliances with Chinese family-run consortia that are flexible enough to readjust their production to the requirements of local markets and supply goods in small quantities (Tassi et al. 2013).

Such alliances have enabled local traders to create their own brands of televisions and refrigerators produced in China, to find niches in the Chinese market for the sale of Bolivian products—as in the case of alpaca fiber—and to import Chinese technology to have it assembled locally. In La Paz, Aymara traders' capillary control of popular markets hindered Chinese investors from directly accessing local commercial spaces and forced them to use local kinship-based chains of supply and distribution reproduced through ritual events such as the fiesta of Gran Poder (Tassi et al. 2012).

The concept of prolongation refers both to the capacity of Aymara traders to devise practices of economic expansion, which remain anchored to traditional institutions and practices, and to a deep-rooted tendency to articulate different and multiple territories. Aymara history and cosmology are interspersed with a specific aptitude to weave relations among different territories, spaces, and groups (Platt 2009). Apart from their economic significance, such articulations are meant to actualize social and spiritual pathways, creative forms of communication, and exchange among different spaces and domains (see Chapter 4) associated with a multiplicative force and with forms of material and cosmic growth.

Development on Their Own Terms: An Aymara Cosmology of Socioeconomic Mobility

These dynamics suggest that the economic knowledge of these popular traders is becoming more complex and nuanced than expected, overturning the assumption that popular and indigenous sectors chronically need technical assistance and training in business management. In fact, these "different" entrepreneurial knowledges and economic strategies have begun displacing a whole professional sector from its leading role in economic decision making (see Chapter 7). Breaking with the ruling-class habit of transferring the economic surplus abroad, popular traders have reinvested their profits in the country, in their own structures and institutions. They have also outlined practices of commercial operation rooted in local necessities and possibilities rather than mimicking conventional economic models and recipes often unsuitable for and unconcerned with local potentials and limitations (Arbona et al. 2015).

The successful story of Aymara traders and their capacity to mold their own social and economic trajectory has undermined one of the main narratives on which the modern republican state had been constructed in Bolivia: the gradual and linear inclusion of urban indigenous sectors into the social and economic practices of the middle class by means of an acculturation process that would have rationalized and modernized indigenous thought and freed it from oppressive and traditional beliefs (Larson 2008; Rivera 1996; cf. Arguedas 1975; Quijano 1998). At an economic level, this meant the gradual absorption of popular indigenous economies, conceived as informal and generally characterized as localized and marginal because of their low levels of productivity and capital investment (Long and Roberts 1984; Quijano 1998), into a highly efficient, modern primary economy.

Rather than suggesting a pattern of gradual adoption of the practices, manners, and values of the urban middle classes, thus reproducing the dominant class system and its forms of exploitation (Rivera 1996), Aymara traders' economic emergence presents a series of divergences from mainstream patterns and even an explicit tendency to differentiate themselves from the middle classes. Father Marcelo, a priest at the Gran Poder sanctuary, defined the traders of the district as "a non-bourgeois upper-middle class" (Tassi 2010), implying that despite their striking economic success, they refused or were unable to fully adjust to the manners and behavioral canons of urban propriety. In fact, being "bourgeois" implied not only taking on conventional demeanors, but also "adjusting" to predefined and official practices, rules, and institutions and consequently recognizing the backwardness and/or inadequacy of local traditional forms and structures. Emerging Aymara traders determined to affirm and expand their own practices and institutions were therefore perceived as outlining a mode and a narrative of transformation that did not coincide with established patterns of bourgeoisization, modernization, or development.

Reactions to forms of social exclusion are also at the root of these peculiar dynamics. For decades, a series of social and professional barriers have been hindering Aymara traders, their sons, and their daughters from accessing jobs in banks and financial institutions, becoming high-ranking civil servants, or joining professional associations. Scholars have suggested that in the Andes, the upward mobility of indigenous sectors could only be achieved by renouncing their ethnic self-representation to be integrated into circles and institutions from which they had traditionally been excluded (Van den Berghe and Primov 1977). Instead of mimicking the white-*mestizos'* practices and demeanors, Aymara traders resorted to generating their own patterns and forms of upward mobility and expressions of status, as well as heightening their ethnic difference and affiliation by strengthening and expanding their bonds with a variety of popular guilds and rural and semirural relatives (cf. Harvey 2002).

Traders repeatedly reinvest in ritual practices and dance parades that reassert their indigenous provenance while threateningly invading the "public spaces" thought to be a prerogative of the white-*mestizos*. They constantly and creatively molded novel aesthetic forms and patterns embodying the specific taste and aspirations of popular sectors and reproduce their allegiance to rural kin both through ritualized forms of exchange and by reenacting their hardships and cultural marginalization (Himpele 2003). Instead of framing their socioeconomic mobility in terms of a rupture with the past and achievement of a new modern status thanks to individual capacities, they were careful to emphasize those specifically Aymara codes and features that connoted and distinguished their success. In other words, their project of socioeconomic expansion, stretching of the interstices, and challenging conventional rules and institutions was built on a social legitimacy granted to them by popular and indigenous sectors, thus outlining a specific pattern of social affirmation that prevented their integration into the circles of the local elites.

In an economy focused for centuries on the export of raw materials, elite families developed a tendency to look abroad for both economic and social referents, neglecting the consolidation of internal markets and socioeconomic models. This engendered a series of ideas, demeanors, and codes severed from local realities and difficult for the popular sectors to metabolize (Zavaleta 1986). Not only did the elites become alienated from the lower social strata, but also they were unable to put in place a socially hegemonic project (Zavaleta 1986). In the case of Aymara traders, their anchoring in the local economic possibilities and limitations, their acquaintance with the necessities and aspirations of popular sectors enable them to outline a socioeconomic project much more digestible to popular sectors because it also guarantees them access to employment and commodities. In a country that has historically been chronically dependent on socioeconomic models and standards defined abroad, this may not only sound tremendously refreshing, but also ultimately lead to the materialization of a series of local forms and practices of accumulation and internalization of surplus that have not preoccupied the local elites (Zavaleta 1986).

The emergence of Aymara traders has not produced a simple "replacement" of the elites (Salman and Soruco 2011) in the occupation of the bureaucratic apparatus or the official associations of entrepreneurs. In fact, in some cases Aymara entrepreneurs have rejected favoritism-based agreements with state institutions and displaced the role of the middle-class businessmen as local representatives of foreign capital and firms. Nor can we talk of new alliances between the new emerging sectors and the old oligarchy (Long and Roberts 1984) in the same way as occurred for European traders who migrated to Bolivia in the 20th century. Aymara traders have been forging modalities of social affirmation that differentiate them from other ascending sectors that have merged into the established ruling classes. These practices ultimately outline a counterintuitive social positioning that appears to define an understanding of "wealth" and social mobility that is not necessarily incompatible with being indigenous, "poor," and popular.

Another "Process of Change"? Aymara Traders and the Plurinational State

In the past decades, the worldwide (re)emergence of forms of local patronage tied to illicit economies has been often connected to a deterioration of the democratic conditions and the shrinking of the state apparatus and institutions during the neoliberal age (Comaroff and Comaroff 2006; Michelutti 2008). However, in Bolivia the emergence of Aymara traders and their complex institutionality coincided both with a progressive sociocultural revolution that attempted to consolidate the presence of the state and with state-run investments in infrastructures and social programs. On the one hand, state-run investments and social programs heightened the purchasing capacity of "intermediate cities" and rural provinces favoring the expansion of trade and the consolidation of local markets. On the other hand, Aymara traders' networks, institutions, and informality came to clash with the intention of Evo Morales's government to solidify the official presence in the territory and the economy.

In the context of Bolivia's "democratic cultural revolution" (*proceso de cambio*), Aymara traders' involvement with global capitalism, their marked sense of autonomy, and their defiant attitude toward conventional institutions have led to relations with the current government that are often tense and contradictory (García Linera 2011; Tassi et al. 2013). Most traders have been enlarging the voter base of the Aymara president, Evo Morales, although they have not been as visible and outspoken in their support for him as the miners and peasants have been. The predominantly Marxist position among state economic ideologists and the explicit attempt by the Morales government to strengthen the role of the state in the economy and beef up the collection of taxes have led on several occasions to clashes with independent guilds of semiformal traders. Such tensions have heightened a series of internal contradictions within the different currents of the ruling party, between politicoeconomic centralization and the idea of a plurinational state granting recognition and autonomy to multiple economic forms.[15]

Until the 2009 election, most of the traders' guilds were outspokenly supportive of the democratic cultural revolution.[16] In 2009, during the investiture of the fiesta steward of the butchers' fraternity for the Gran Poder celebration, the steward Víctor Carrillo refused to wear the traditional Western suit and tie and instead sported an outfit of raw wool with a coat bearing Andean patterns, which was reminiscent of the characteristic clothing of President Morales. While participating in the Gran Poder parade, Carrillo's nine brothers exhibited a peculiar dance step consisting of repeatedly lifting up and waving their left fists, a common gesture among *masista*[17] politicians. However, already during those years, a certain resentment of the government's lack of interest in or inability to capitalize on the skills of this politically and economically competent sector of the population could already be perceived among the guild leaders.

In the following years, the government's derogatory attitude toward traders translated into the issuing of a series of constitutionally shaky measures and laws explicitly directed to weakening popular economy and guilds as well as the execution of an increasing number of custom operatives against popular traders.[18] Campaigns in both progovernment and opposition media were waged against popular traders, reinforcing their association with illegality and emphasizing their allegedly unpatriotic sentiments as well as their challenge to the legitimacy and smooth running of official institutions.

Such tensions did not impede the existence of a number of complicities and overlaps between the politicoeconomic project of *proceso de cambio* and that of Aymara traders. In fact, the Aymara traders' institutionality and capacity to provide basic socioeconomic services in remote and marginal areas of the country turned out to be particularly useful to a state that aimed at strengthening its presence and control of the national territory. Both ministries and state enterprises had to rely on Aymara traders to consolidate their institutional presence along the sparsely inhabited eastern borders, to get to know the extension of the national road network, to develop partnerships with Chinese entrepreneurs, and for basic supply and distribution services.

Traders' business volume, together with their established connection with the harbors of northern Chile, have made these economic actors strategic in Morales's negotiations with the Chilean government to gain sovereign access to the Pacific for Bolivia. Fifty-four percent of sales in the Iquique duty-free zone (Díaz Brito 2007) and 73% of goods leaving the Chilean port of Arica[19] are destined for Bolivia, making the economy of the northern regions of Chile highly interconnected with, if not dependent on, Bolivian traders. Their forceful capacity for mobilization and their links both with truck drivers' guilds and with Chilean popular sectors (some of them of Aymara descent) have made it possible to mount massive protests and roadblocks in Chilean territory, paralyzing ports or entire cities.[20] On several occasions, leaders of both traders' and truck drivers' guilds, dissatisfied with the services provided and with the disparaging treatment by Chilean authorities, have threatened to transfer their commercial operations en masse to the harbors of southern Peru, such as Matarani and Ilo.[21]

These synergies and contradictions are key elements that hint at the complexity of the contemporary political conjuncture in Bolivia, the overlap of multiple politicoeconomic processes, and the double-bind relation between Aymara traders and the state. Indigenous economic actors, solidly organized in compact local guilds and extended commercial networks and daily circumventing the authority of the state, are in fact a crucial commercial sector that the revolutionary state must resort to for its basic functioning and to forge the new strategic geopolitical alliances required to challenge the established political and economic order.

Aymara traders and popular enterprises were key institutional and socioeconomic players well before Evo Morales came to power. However, their forcefulness and centrality became more visible with a *proceso de cambio* that, symbolically at least, placed popular sectors as the backbone of a country that had traditionally imitated social and economic models drawn up abroad. Despite political measures aimed at curtailing the politicoeconomic power of popular guilds, governmental actors were also forced to recognize the capacity of popular entrepreneurs to spin the current bonanza and increase in disposable income toward local markets and product categories exceeding the circumscribed primary economy of hydrocarbons at the root of the bonanza.

In contrast to the traditional elites who had historically sought personal advantage and protection of their interests and privileges from the state to reinvest abroad (Zavaleta 1990), Aymara traders tend to remain at a distance from the official institutions while "laying siege to" (*cercar*) the state through their control of the territory and the economy. Their knowledge, strategies, and investments trace a specific practice of nation-making (*hacer país*; Canessa 2005) that is often independent of state policies and initiatives and that aspires not to consolidate a "parallel state" but to achieve recognition as a constitutive element of the plurinational state.

Description of the Chapters That Follow

The idea of the Aymara trader, as well as the concept of the popular economy, has been informed by what it is not and what it should be. This has resulted in actors as diverse as Aymara importers traveling to China and peddlers selling their wares in marginal urban neighborhoods of major Bolivian cities being placed in the same category. This book does not fully

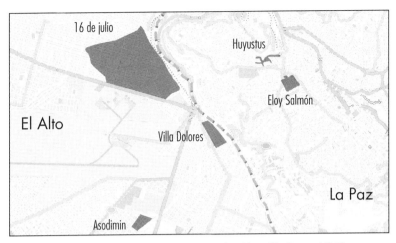

MAP 3 Map of the main commercial locations in the cities of La Paz and El Alto mentioned in the text.

address this heterogeneity, although it outlines a series of different economic practices and strategies informed by the features of different typologies of trading. The main lines of trade I have researched are electronics, food, garments, and vehicles, although the high levels of product diversification forced me to partly explore a variety of other categories. Generally, these typologies of trade imply different forms of linkage with suppliers and producers, markets, and places. My main informants were traders from five different markets[22] located in the cities of La Paz and El Alto. Through these traders, I have been able to identify a multiplicity of actors connected in network-like chains of supply and distribution.

Chapter 1 outlines the framework of interstitial and ethnic-based socioeconomic institutions that control and regulate local markets while simultaneously providing basic socioeconomic services in marginal neighborhoods and regions. In this chapter, I show how, rather than adapting to the requirements of global trade or adjusting to the conventional lessons of business administration, the global upswing of Aymara traders has become a tool for consolidating local power structures and institutions. Indigenous economies characterized by their improvisation and precariousness show a degree of organization often exceeding that of the official business establishment.

After describing the institutionality of local markets, Chapter 2 ventures into the flexible structures, forms of mobility, and extended kinship networks connected to and connecting Bolivia's popular markets. Such structures and networks bring together a variety of economic actors, from relatives in the countryside controlling the trade route to customs officials, from peripheral intermediaries to retailers in market towns. Often based on practices of clientelization, fictive kinship, and a series of shared cultural codes, these trade networks establish proper chains of supply and distribution across the region. These economic chains have been consolidating an extended and connected, although semiformal, economic structure that has gradually become the foundation of a national economy previously conceived as a sum of disarticulated enclaves.

In Chapter 3, I tackle the relationship of Aymara traders with Chinese family-run consortia and entrepreneurs operating in the region. Although mainstream entrepreneurs have been reluctant to bring cutting-edge commodities and technology to the third world because of the low profit margins and legal insecurity, the alliances among these popular businessmen and -women were founded on their recognition of the worth and aspirations of a peculiar type of developing world consumer. In addition, in contexts of rooted skepticism about official authorities, an unexpected overlap of Aymara and Chinese networks has generated inter-"ethnic" alliances and spaces of trust where commerce can occur. These dynamics not only suggest direct and counterintuitive commercial relations between local groups and ideas overstepping official institutions and enterprises, but also outline an interstitial global economic space.

Chapter 4 is based on an analysis of Aymara business management practices founded on a series of cosmological concepts and forms that often define the scope and rhythm of trade. The analyses of Aymara business management practices reveal a series of concepts and knowledges that challenge conventional microeconomic practices of investment and savings and outline indigenous ideas of wealth. In addition to highlighting Aymara concepts and ideas framing and regulating their economic activity in a global economy, I also outline indigenous modes of thinking of and dealing with global economies and of appropriating "foreign" artifacts, ideas, and forms. Last, I discuss the cosmoeconomic consequences of the extension of indigenous logics into a wider economic scenario.

In Chapter 5, I address another key tension in the Andean cosmology, namely, that between the individual and the collective. Specifically, I tackle the combination of forms of cooperation among Aymara traders that they use to access economies of scale with a heightened sense of autonomy, which has brought them to refuse unequal partnerships with large companies perceived as engulfing their independence and aspirations. The family/business is often a pool of different resources and a concatenation of different activities and strategies. Such relationships between the individual and the collective have stimulated the reframing of concepts such as "economies of scale," "accounting," and "competition." Furthermore, these peculiar structures and forms of organization may point to a fracture in the basic tenet of capitalism that relies on the principle of private property and private wealth.

In Chapter 6, I review some of the main commercial strategies adopted by Aymara traders to deal with the shifting trends in the global economy and the politicoeconomic instability of regional societies. Aymara traders have developed specific skills that allow them to move smoothly across a variety of markets and spaces, taking advantage of the price and legal discrepancies among countries of the region as well as among the urban boundaries between different social sectors. Such skills are combined with a high product diversification and a capacity to simultaneously handle product lines as diverse as electronics, mechanical parts, and garments.

In Chapter 7, I analyze the patterns of affirmation of Aymara traders, their capacity to convert economic activities considered marginal into emerging ones, and their ability to defy locally defined social and economic hierarchies. Reverting linear narratives of assimilation and integration of "marginal" and "informal" economic activities into formal and official ones, I outline a process of increasing "adaptation" of formal institutions and conventional entrepreneurs to the economic modalities of "informal" Aymara trade—a process that does not necessarily cancel out forms of discrimination and exclusion. Not only has this process appeared to displace the role of conventional institutions and economic experts in defining the rules of the economic game, but also it has led to an amplification of indigenous social and ritual practices and spaces as a means of expressing their success and transformation. In so doing, Aymara traders have been outlining a modality of being economically successful and indigenous, reconciling the possibility of being modern and traveling to China for business with belonging to the popular and indigenous sectors of society.

Some of the ideas about the institutionality of Aymara traders, their economic strategies and forms of business management have been previously addressed in a publication of the *Programa de Investigación Estratégica en Bolivia* (PIEB). Titled *Hacer plata sin plata: el desborde de los comerciantes populares en Bolivia*, the book collects the results of a research about the socioeconomic reconfiguration of Bolivia I conducted together with Carmen Medeiros, Juan Manuel Arbona, Antonio Rodríguez-Carmona and Giovana Ferrufino.

CHAPTER 1

Indigenous Institutions Regulating "Popular" Markets

La Paz stands on the vertiginous slopes that lead from the Andean plateau at an altitude of 13,000 feet to the bottom of a mountain canyon, and the view from both the top and the bottom is equally breathtaking. With a mixture of fear and affection, its inhabitants call La Paz *la hoyada*—the pit.

At the bottom of the canyon, the Choqueyapu River divides the city into two halves and the Spanish colony embraced and used this geographical division for administrative purposes. The Choqueyapu and the Mejawira rivers became the boundaries separating the social and political center of the colonial city, in the eastern part, from the three main indigenous *barrios* or "parishes"—San Sebastián, San Pedro, and Santa Bárbara—to which access was prohibited at night for nonindigenous settlers. The contemporary social and ethnic divisions in the urban structure of La Paz reflect that colonial partition (cf. Gill 2000). The western slope of La Paz, known in Spanish as *la ladera*, maintains a strong association with the urbanized indigenous world and practices and is clearly marked by their flair, markets, and religious celebrations (Tassi 2012b: 285).

Over the centuries this traditional zoning of the city has acquired different forms and features, breaking old and generating new urban frontiers. In the past century, the increasing immigration of Aymara settlers from the high plateau has pushed the white population of La Paz down the canyon (Gill 2000), resulting in new urbanizations in the so-called *Zona Sur*.

As a result of these processes, the initial segregation between the colonial administration on the eastern slope and the indigenous city on the western slope took on new forms. The epicenter of white-creole social life has been gradually sliding down the canyon. One can trace this process with a degree of precision by following the residential patterns of Paceño upper-class families. Whereas in the 1950s elite families still owned a house by the *Plaza de armas* close to the administrative heart of the city, it was not infrequent for the next generation to move to the residential neighborhood of *Sopocachi*, and their sons followed either by buying a house with a garden in the warmer and more comfortable *Zona Sur* or by directly moving to Santa Cruz, the booming settlement in the lowlands.

This should not mislead us into thinking that the participation of the indigenous population in the social and economic dynamics of the urban world was either a recent or a marginal process. The ethnohistorian Thierry Saignes (1992) has emphasized the degree of indigenous penetration in the activities of La Paz, where there was an unprecedented proximity between the indigenous *reducción*[1] and the Hispanic city, producing a curious and unique case of dual settlement in the colonial Andes. In the indigenous logic of organization of the territory, La Paz, or Chuquiago as it is known in Aymara, constituted the *taypi* (center or crossing) of multiple ecological, ethnic, and administrative jurisdictions, ranging from the high plateau to the tropical valleys (*yungas*). The Hispanic city came to constitute an extraterritorial settlement, at the confluence of multiethnic forces, whose fragility was deeply and repeatedly felt by its settlers (Saignes 1992: 64–65).

The Indigenous Economic Space

In some cases, the indigenous organization of the territory played a key role in structuring urban spaces. If we take, for instance, the urban guild of butchers, an economic organization with a long historical trajectory that included some of the indigenous pioneers in the urban market, it maintained the structure of an indigenous *ayllu*[2] in a central area of the city. In the parish of San Sebastián of the city of La Paz existed the so-called "*ayllu mañaso*" (Rivera 1996), where the ethnic structure was superimposed on membership of the guild of merchants traveling to the high plateau to fetch animals to be butchered. Through the guild and the religious brotherhood, the structure of the *ayllu* has been acquiring new forms and features while maintaining its economic and territorial relevance up to the present time.

Rossana Barragán (1997) identifies the consolidation of an indigenous urban sector anchored in indigenous structures and practices concomitant to the industrial growth of the 19th century. Among the female urban population, Barragán observes an unexpected event: an "intermediate" female social group, clearly economically differentiated from the elites and from the rural population, suddenly stops following the standard urban fashion modeled on the European style (Barragán 1997: 59–60). Particularly, what we observe in those years is that a specific item of clothing, the *pollera* layered skirt, gradually starts to disappear from the wardrobes of the elite and becomes an essential garment for this intermediate social group. Suddenly, this group stops imitating the ever-changing trends of the urban elites and chooses the *pollera* as the symbol of a new urban identity, associated with popular and indigenous sectors, which survives through today. The consequences of this change might have to do not only with economic factors but also with the conscious decision of this intermediate social group to seek a connection with the indigenous sectors rather than being the lowest and most disparaged tier of the Spanish *mestizo-criollo* world.

This intermediate indigenous urban sector became a referent for rural indigenous settlers during the waves of migration following the agrarian reform (1953), as well as for peasants from the high plateau seeking urban markets for their products. Aymara cattle producers from the high plateau settling in the city during the 1960s converged into the organizational structures—guilds and fraternities—and territories of the ancient *ayllu mañaso* (Tassi 2012a). Although it was not love at first sight between rural producers and urban butchers, it became apparent that in a racially stratified urban context Aymara rural producers needed the logistical support and knowledge of their urban relatives, whereas the latter would benefit from the organizational capacity of Aymara producers at a time of volatile political transformations.

In 1972, they created a fraternity of "meat workers," bringing together producers, butchers, and intermediaries. This enabled them to consolidate their control of the municipal abattoir and to build new commercial establishments. It is interesting to observe that the construction of some of the most central markets in La Paz was traditionally financed by the resources and initiatives of urban indigenous guilds rather than by the municipality. For instance, it was the butcher's guild that financed the construction of La Paz central market, Mercado Lanza (Aramayo 2014), by forcing all guild members to destine the profits from the sale of cattle skins for the building of the market. Although the municipality unloaded the costs of construction of basic urban infrastructure onto the shoulders of racially subordinate sectors, urban indigenous guilds used such initiatives as justification for expanding and imposing their forms of administration and decision making in public spaces and structures. In so doing, butchers also defiantly asserted the relevance and strength of their organizations and their capacity to dispense with official ones.

Already at the beginning of the 1920s Aymara rural traders and producers bringing their products into the city had established not only markets and stores for their products (*tambos*) but also urban shrines and ritual structures in the *ladera* of the city (Albó and Preiswerk 1986), thus beginning to appropriate for their own celebrations the public space that was being abandoned by the modernizing urban elites (Guss 2006). Besides consolidating forms of social and economic articulation with the city, such practices reproduced an indigenous ritual system and conceptualization of territory defined by scattered shrines linking the different social, economic, and ecological zones (cf. Platt 1996; Zuidema 1964). While both progressive and conservative local thinkers emphasized the incompatibility between indigenous traditionalism and a civilized or "industrialized" urban world (Larson 2004; Laserna 2005; Loza, cited in Wanderley 2003; Molina 2013), rural and urban indigenous settlers were remapping the country and weaving their participation in the market through a series of socioeconomic networks based on Aymara sociopolitical structures and cosmology.

It was through a system of guilds and religious brotherhoods, market spaces, and ritual celebrations that the variety of indigenous identities and spaces was often reconstituted and redefined in the city. Even today, the popular markets of the *ladera* are clearly differentiated according to the rural town or region of provenance of the traders, as well as according to the different waves of rural migration. These modalities of occupation of urban spaces are also visible in El Alto, a city whose population has grown tenfold in the past thirty years. Not only are the neighborhoods of the city named after the province or town of origin of its settlers, but also the main *feria*, 16 de Julio, is divided into spaces reflecting the boundaries between the regions of the high plateau.

These modalities of reproducing indigenous or rural provenance in the organization and occupation of urban spaces have been constantly challenged and incentivized by a long trajectory of institutional efforts to break up such indigenous structures (Mayer 2004) and to bar them from the official mercantile economy (Platt 1992). The interplay of forms of "assimilation," aimed at perpetuating practices of exploitation of the indigenous population, and "exclusion," connected to the inability or lack of interest of the state to deal with the increasing urban indigenous population (cf. Gruzinski and Wachtel 1997), contributed to generate both urban spaces with "indigenous jurisdictions" and strategies to conceal the modalities of operation of these sectors to official institutions. These indigenous economic spaces (cf. Assadourian 1982; Glave 1989) constantly reminded the elites that their project of modernizing the nation was tragically unaccomplished (Larson 2008). The emergence and increasing competition of indigenous entrepreneurs rooted in kinship networks, religious organizations, and local cultural practices was a constant reminder to official business practitioners that economic activity remained tied up with nonmodern practices (cf. Maurer 2005).

Interstitial Institutionality: The Consolidation of Popular Urban Markets

The anecdotal stories related to the construction of popular urban markets explicitly show the interweaving of forms of exclusion and concealment of popular indigenous sectors. As painful reminders of the enlightened middle class's failure to lead the nation onto the path of progress, popular areas and markets have been overlooked and neglected not only by official institutions but also by the official version of history. Nowadays, in a time of economic bonanza, the progressive leftist municipality of La Paz has suddenly taken on the role of a modernizing agent implementing a series of strategies that seek to "formalize," modernize, and/or suppress popular markets. In some cases, the construction of concentrated modern markets is adopted as a strategy to dismantle a resistant ethnic trade unionism (Molina 2013) supposedly incompatible with development and modernity. What the municipality is disregarding and underestimating is the century-long anchoring of those indigenous socioeconomic structures in the urban territory, their contribution to the infrastructural and social construction of the city, and ultimately their capacity to define the spatial dynamics and urban rhythms.

Social and Economic Transformations in the Markets of La Paz

In the case of the Eloy Salmón market, the formation of the trade union dates back to 1957. At the time, the actual area of Gran Poder was a sparsely populated space on the outskirts of the city. The neighborhood is still referred to today with the Aymara name of *Ch'ijini*—literally "pasture"—making reference to the rural area once bordering the expanding city. The transformation of this liminal part of the city into a commercial area clashed with the process of expansion of the local middle class, which sought to transform the neighborhood into a residential area and displace the surrounding peasant lands and settlements. With the agrarian reform of 1953 and the subsequent inflow of indigenous peasants from the high plateau into the city (Albó et al. 1981), the neighborhood began acquiring a new identity. The district was close both to the main bus terminals connecting the city to rural villages and to the storehouses (*tambos*) where vegetables and fruit from the surrounding countryside were stocked by Aymara wholesalers before being redistributed to retailers. As in the case of the butchers, urban Aymara wholesalers maintained good relationships with their suppliers in the countryside, offered them lodging in the *tambos* when they came to the city transporting their produce by mule, and developed forms of clientelization to guarantee continuous and secure flows of goods, although this ethnic complicity did not always imply social equality or the absence of forms of exploitation.

As explained in the case of Silveria, her town's long-lasting links with the city and the simultaneous connection with translocal economic actors on the other side of the Peruvian border enabled her to take part in a new flow of manufactured goods that were finding a new market niche among urban Paceño consumers. Already in the 19th century, a series of Aymara villages on the border with Chile, for instance, had been able to extend their forms of exchange and "ethnic economy" to mining enclaves on the northern coast of Chile. These famously intrepid traders came to act as a bridge between the Chilean coast and the Bolivian urban centers, particularly Oruro. This was often a consequence of both the central government's disregard of peripheral indigenous communities and the heightened mobility of such indigenous actors with connections to Aymara relatives on the other side of the border (Llanque and Villca 2011). In the case of Silveria and her fellow villagers from Taraco, the socioeconomic networks penetrating well into Peru were crucial for activating forms of bidirectional trade practiced on boats across Lake Titicaca, which enabled commodities such as sewing machines and their spare parts to appear in the urban markets of La Paz.

These highly mobile border traders were instrumental in the consolidation and development of Bolivia's urban markets. In the neighborhood of Gran Poder, migrants from Taraco began by renting rooms from the local middle class (*vecinos*) and occupying the sidewalk, from which they would sell sewing machines, needles, and machine oil on a strip of plastic sheeting. They would bring in goods from the lake and distribute them among fellow popular traders in the neighborhood. Within the trade union, they adopted forms of rotating loans (*pasanako*) that were allocated to relatives and kin, providing them with start-up capital to begin trading in the city. In this way, they consolidated forms of institutionality in a hostile urban space where they felt repulsed by the *vecinos* and disregarded by local and national institutions.

Rapid technological advancements and the parallel strengthening of an urban middle class aspiring to new consumer goods brought in a series of new commodities such as the transistor radio, the *tres-en-uno* (three-in-one: radio, cassette, and record player), and the television. The high profit margins on commodities that were often smuggled into the city would soon alter the urban equilibrium: Taraco's families started to rent garages from the *vecinos*, transforming them into shops and beginning to displace local corner shops, shoemakers, and smiths (Tassi et al. 2013). In the 1970s, Taraqueños had begun buying properties in the neighborhood, renovating and "modernizing" them according to their distinct taste and ingeniously integrating dwelling, storeroom, and shop. Now it was the traders renting out rooms to the *vecinos*.

Taraqueños also diversified their suppliers by turning to foreign traders running import houses in La Paz and employees of the national railway and airline, who could more easily obtain the documentation required to travel abroad. Several of these employees set up their own storerooms, where they collected duty-free products bought in the United States and Chile to resell behind closed doors, mostly to popular traders and peddlers.

Already in the 1970s some Taraqueños from Gran Poder were traveling to the Colón duty-free zone in Panama to bring in cheap commodities, and the opening of the Iquique duty-free zone in the north of Chile in 1975 was a further step toward the consolidation of this commercial district of La Paz. The Iquique duty-free zone in the Chilean desert was part of a strategy by the dictator Augusto Pinochet to promote economic growth and institutionality in a sparsely populated area of the country—disputed by both Peru and Bolivia—after the decline in the mining of local deposits of saltpeter and phosphates. In the Iquique duty-free zone, Taraqueño traders would buy in large quantities from wholesalers, who would load the goods onto an entire sealed truck entitled to free circulation across Chilean territory and tax exemption until it reached Bolivia. Taking advantage of porous borders and Aymara networks in Chile, popular traders in the Eloy Salmón began adapting the *pasanako* to the new circumstances. They started pooling their capital, sharing the costs of transport, and placing large joint orders with Iquique's "capitalists" to gain access to discounts and be able to fill the truck. In a few years, they had managed to displace foreign wholesalers running import houses in La Paz. From then on, they were the ones who defined the forms and rhythms of supply and distribution.

Inevitably, the Eloy Salmón markets and the Gran Poder neighborhood took on a character that transcended the strictly ethnic Taraqueño networks of the early years. A series of new actors ranging from truck drivers of rural origin to Chinese entrepreneurs in the duty-free zone of Iquique provided the economic networks with a new scope. Gran Poder traders had managed to transform a marginal neighborhood into the city's main commercial area for manufactured goods. Even today, however, this commercial heart of the city remains identified as a dangerous and coarse neighborhood neglected by official institutions because of its association with informality, drunkenness—connected to popular religious celebrations—and a general failure to abide by "shared norms," meaning the norms of the white-*mestizo* middle class, which, interestingly enough, in Bolivia are the minority's norms. Although the commercial high street of *Zona Sur* is lined with flowerbeds and impeccable sidewalks taken care of by the municipality, Gran Poder remains largely neglected by the improvement projects of local and national institutions despite the daily inflow of national and foreign consumers. At the same time, this lack of consideration or disdain by official institutions has been strategically used by local traders to assert their territorial control over the area by repaving the sidewalks and renovating the lampposts by themselves, consequently denying the municipality from interfering with their organizations and activities. The institutional disregard of these popular urban sectors and their ability to engender an economic ferment that neither the state nor the large enterprises were able to create has been strategically used by local economic actors to delegitimize official attempts to impose socioeconomic rules and standards.

The characteristics of Gran Poder also partly apply to other markets on the *ladera*. Located ten or fifteen minutes' walk up the slope from Gran Poder, the Huyustus market is the largest wholesale market (in terms of flows) for manufactured goods in the metropolitan area of La Paz and El Alto. Now well connected with Chinese enterprises, networked with Iquique's Arab and Far-Eastern entrepreneurs, and linked to retailers in Brazil, Argentina, Paraguay, and Peru, the Huyustus market barely existed in the early 1980s. A neighborhood that thirty years ago was lacking sewerage and paved streets and traversed by a fetid river collecting all kind of waste is today a commercial area renowned among economic consortia in Guangzhou—although much less "renowned" in the *Zona Sur* residential neighborhoods of La Paz.

Until the early 1980s, the Huyustus was identified as an area where salty high-plateau cheese was sold by Aymara women. At that time, groups of rural Aymaras, mostly from the region of Pacajes on the import route from Chile, began flocking to the city by train to sell commodities. Some of them had been employed by established traders to bring imported goods over the border, avoiding customs. Others provided traders with intermediate storage spaces for smuggled goods and received a payoff in kind. On Saturdays, urban consumers could be found lining up at the train station, waiting for the commodities brought over by the Pacajeños (Tassi et al. 2013). Gradually, they found a space for their business on the marginal, unpaved, and foul-smelling Huyustus street, a few blocks away from the train station. In a few years, they literally changed the urban geography of the area and the Huyustus was transformed into the most "attractive" wholesale commercial hub of the city, displacing traditional traders in the nearby Miamicito, who had been comfortably accommodated in a covered and unattractive market built by the municipality.

The competition from the already established Gran Poder retailers forced Huyustus traders to combine retail with wholesale trading. This implied having large amounts of capital available, which among rural Pacajeños was often achieved through forms of commercial cooperation to import in large quantities and generate economies of scale.

Aymara Traders in the Amazon Basin

In the past decade, the town of Cobija on the border with Brazil in the Bolivian Amazon region has started expanding, turning into a crucial commercial enclave and duty-free city controlled by Aymara traders. In the case of Cobija, most traders in manufactured goods come from the community of Orinoca—the birthplace of President Morales—in the barren highlands. The pioneer trader in Cobija was the Orinoqueño Patricio Villca, who in the 1970s reached the Amazon basin by boat to trade steel pots and pans (Tassi et al. 2013: 120). At the time, Cobija was a small town rapidly decaying after the rubber boom. Patricio Villca founded a commercial cooperative of Orinoqueños. Through the *pasanako*, they brought kin, relatives, and friends from the highland community and sponsored their commercial activities. They quickly displaced the Lebanese, Italian, German, and Jewish traders who had settled in the region during the 19th century to cater to the often-bizarre consumption style of the rubber barons. Today, the "Orinoca clan," as they are dubbed by local people, operate a capillary control of commercial spaces in a border area where real estate prices are the highest in Bolivia (Carlo et al. 2013). This enables them to avoid the incursion of local and Brazilian businessmen who have lately begun to smell the commercial potential of this duty-free city on the border with the Brazilian states of Acre and Rondônia.

Aymara traders provide food and goods to the remote towns and cities of the Northern Amazon region of Bolivia. After being bought in Iquique or loaded up in the city of El Alto, goods begin a five-day trip along dangerous unpaved roads with no facilities and no state presence. In these extreme conditions, the combination of a lack of infrastructure and legal insecurity makes the entry of formal enterprises and conglomerates unviable while strengthening local informal actors and unofficial forms of institutionality (Tassi et al. 2013: 143). The narrow mountain roads that lead down from the Andes to the Amazon basin are built on the side of precipices that drop thousands of feet. According to locally and informally defined regulations, trucks descending toward the Amazon must drive on the left to keep a closer eye on the precipice. Such unofficial regulations and institutionality make the incursion of unaware Brazilian truck drivers in the area virtually impossible.

El Alto: The "Merchant City"

As we have seen, in the popular urban markets of La Paz and Cobija, incoming Aymara traders have been contending with local, non-Aymara, and established social groups for social and economic spaces. In El Alto, a city that remains composed mostly of Aymara migrants from the high plateau, the competition for commercial spaces takes different forms. In the past few years, an unexpected shift of popular entrepreneurs from La Paz toward El Alto has materialized, tilting the traditional balance of power and economic weight between the two settlements. El Alto has been consistently represented as a large and uncontrollable slum (Davis 2006). Some thirty years ago, pressured by the demands for autonomy from local organizations in El Alto and the inability to provide basic services to a growing migrant population (Lazar 2008; Poupeau 2010), the Congress decided that the two cities should become administratively separate. Lacking the hierarchical spatial structure of other Bolivian colonial cities as well as their *mestizo* population, El Alto enacted a reinvention and adaptation of forms of spatial and social organization drawn from rural communities, outlining counterintuitive practices of making the city and affirming citizenship (Arbona 2011). Having grown in a disorderly fashion through popular initiatives, El Alto now appears to provide popular entrepreneurs from the *hoyada* with land and larger spaces for commerce, proximity to thousands of other family-run enterprises, weaker official control and regulations on trade, and more possibilities for autonomous organization, as well as a closer affinity between Aymara traders and municipal authorities.

Whereas in La Paz popular markets were established in marginal and far-off neighborhoods high up the slope, in El Alto—traditionally referred to as a slum or a marginal settlement—the popular economy acquired an interesting centrality, both in the urban landscape and in the definition of the social and economic space. Banks, mobile phone companies, and insurance companies that only recently have realized the commercial potential of the "slum" are often relegated to peripheral parts or second floors of the commercial areas, which remains heavily controlled by traders' guilds (Arbona et al. 2015). Internationally renowned as the heart of the political revolts of the 2000s, El Alto has now turned into the center of a popular economic movement, introducing the country to modalities of economic operation that often escape the control and understanding of official institutions.

The Asodimin wholesale grocery market in El Alto is an example of these dynamics. Run by traders who have gradually "migrated" from smaller retail markets in La Paz, rural dealers on the import route from Chile, and former tenants of food shops in more central areas of El Alto, the Asodimin market is a new commercial establishment installed in a neighborhood slightly off the beaten track although close to El Alto's new bus terminal. This association of wholesalers took up a collective loan for several million dollars and collectively acquired the land on which they constructed various blocks of buildings from scratch, including shops, banks, stores, dwellings, party venues, and plenty of other spaces and services required for wholesale trading. In a context and area where the institutional presence is weak, the association has taken charge of paving the street, installing electricity, and bringing public transportation to the neighborhood. At the beginning, tensions arose between the traders and the neighborhood committee, but the scale of the investment helped to placate the conflicts. Before handing over the maintenance of the streets to the municipality, traders named the main street after the president of the association, reasserting a certain degree of administrative autonomy over the market (Tassi et al. 2013).[3] The message sent by this type of initiative defies conventional institutions and lays out a statement of autonomy, making visible the ways in which interstitial Aymara institutions may replace conventional ones in the provision of basic economic and administrative rights and services to citizens.

There are some common patterns in the formation of popular markets. First, they outline a tendency to occupy marginal urban areas in a collective fashion through the work of communities, cooperatives, trade unions, and associations, displacing old settlers and introducing new forms of institutionality on their own terms. The technique of gradually occupying the sidewalk before renting shops is still in full swing in the city center of La Paz itself. Two blocks away from the city's central square (*Plaza San Francisco*), clothes producers from El Alto descend every morning to sell their products on the sidewalk. The assertiveness and magnitude of their "occupation" has forced formal businesses to close their shops, creating further space for the inflow of new producers. These forms of occupation of commercial space by popular sectors are coupled with ritual activities, such as dance parades and musical events, asserting—often in a threatening fashion—their control of urban spaces traditionally a prerogative of formal businesses, the middle class, and officialdom. On the one hand, these ritual events help to mark a territory, and on the other hand, they emphasize the contrast with conventional forms of institutionality.

General narratives about the development of commerce suggested a progressive absorption of street sellers and popular traders into larger firms (Geertz 1963) and covered markets. This was supposed to be followed by the transformation of markets into supermarkets that managed to sell at favorable prices thanks to their economies of scale, optimization of the division of labor, and reduction of human capital. In the Andes and in countries with a high percentage of indigenous population, the market has been seen as a means to reproduce unequal forms of integration of these "backward" sectors into both the modern economy and the nation, simultaneously granting them citizenship while stripping them of their indigenous practices and identities (Seligmann 2004; Lazar 2008). In fact, indigenous peoples have been seen as subjects as long as they are integrated into predefined patterns of development and change (Andolina et al. 2009). In our case, Aymara traders have been the ones creating markets in the spaces and interstices of the conventional economy, transforming marginal neighborhoods into attractive commercial hubs. Not only has this produced the emergence of forms of institutionality that mainstream economic analysts had failed to take into account, but also it has guaranteed local actors the possibility of defining the socioeconomic rules for these spaces. Instead of an instrument vertically channeling traditional indigenous actors into modern economic forms, the local market with its own practices of socioeconomic control and regulation can operate as a tool to consolidate and expand local ideas and strategies.

Regulation from Below

Interstitial economic spaces like the ones generated by popular traders do not necessarily imply unregulated economic activities or antisocial forms and practices. In the case of Aymara traders, the forms of exclusion from the formal economy, their spatial segregation, and the chronic lack of a regulatory framework from above are being addressed through complex strategies of socioeconomic regulation from below. The popular markets we have previously described are interspersed with a multiplicity and variety of often-overlapping local institutions operating at different levels, from the union to the neighborhood committee, from the religious fraternity to extended kinship networks. These frameworks comprising different relational structures allow for both horizontal cooperation among members of the same union or market and vertical articulation between suppliers and retailers (cf. Guaygua and Castillo 2008; Samanamud et al. 2007), thus ensuring the functioning of the whole commercial chain (Tassi 2012a). In a context where the presence of official institutions is weak and both the police and the official authorities are often kept at a distance to prevent them interfering with local political arrangements, it is this variety of overlapping relational structures and institutions that regulates access to the markets and deals with forms of crime and antisocial behavior.

We have already observed how, in several markets, access to commercial spaces was initially guaranteed to kin members through forms of rotating loans, which also allowed the guild, family, or community to strengthen its presence in a hostile urban environment. Today, in the markets with a longer historical tradition such as the Eloy Salmón or Huyustus, the traders have become the owners of local properties and strengthened their mechanisms of control of commercial spaces. Some of them have adapted their dwellings to the requirements of shopping arcades and begun to rent out retail spaces. This has magnified their ability to discern potential new allies for controlling local commercial spaces. In the case of the Eloy Salmón, it has become almost impossible to rent a shop in an arcade or put up a stall on the sidewalk unless one has family or *compadrazgo*[4] connections with some of the "founders"[5] or has shown oneself to be a person worthy of respect and loyalty in the activities of the renowned religious fraternity of Eloy Salmón traders. So-called *simpatizantes*—participants in the fraternity who are not members of the trade union—may be able to gain access to a space in the market by taking up the role of fiesta steward and sponsoring the fraternity during the religious celebrations of Gran Poder (Tassi et al. 2013).

In El Alto, where the presence of the official authorities is even weaker, the role and importance of trade unions is generally magnified. The federation of traders in El Alto provides trading licenses, is in charge of the maintenance and organization of markets and retail spaces, and takes care of cleaning the commercial streets (Lazar 2008, 2012). As is common in most popular markets, the federation and/or the local trade union allocate commercial spaces and sales spots to their members but may also revoke "licenses" and charge fines to those merchants who do not open their stall regularly or do not participate in the social and political activities of the guild. In so doing, the federation replaces municipal and state authorities in the provision of basic socioeconomic services and also acquires an authority and legitimacy comparable—or locally superior—to those of the state and the municipality. These popular organizations literally become the "state" in an ongoing process of extension of different forms of local authority, covering over the "holes" in state authority (cf. UNDP 2007).

Popular markets have become spaces where local guilds not only administer forms of control but also occupy domains and functions that had been neglected by the official institutions. Among the self-attributed powers of popular trade unions, another crucial element is their capacity to expel members, generally on the basis of a collective decision taken to evaluate forms of "disloyal competition" or antisocial behavior. The punishment for disloyal competition can be applied to members of the union who practice forms of contraband and sell at lower prices or strike deals with foreign companies to displace local union members. In these cases the person found guilty of disloyal competition can be physically expelled from the market. In the past few years, the threat of physical expulsion has become irrelevant in the case of the entrepreneur or investor who does not run a space in the market but participates in forms of wholesale trade and distribution. This has been dealt with by producing sophisticated forms of exclusion that make it difficult for the investor to participate in the supply and distribution networks.

These dynamics should not induce us to believe that Aymara trade unions are monolithic institutions little inclined to change and largely homogenous. The Huyustus, with a number of traders not exceeding 5,000, is divided into more than forty associations (Barragán 2006). These reflect a division by product or business category, the provenance of the traders or different waves of migration, and the specific zone, side, or street of the market they occupy. In more central areas of La Paz, trade associations are also divided by "shift," with different groups of street sellers taking turns (morning, day, afternoon, and night) to occupy the same commercial space. We encounter a similarly complex form of organization in the religious fraternities, each of which is divided into "blocks" (*bloques*) that simultaneously express the heterogeneity and the unity of the "traders' family." On the one hand, these divisions into blocks and associations facilitate the possibility of creating alliances with other groups, regrouping according to different criteria (age, friendship, product category), and pursuing independent business opportunities separately from the ones defined by the head of the family. This is usually seen as a necessary expression of difference within a guild, stimulating forms of collaborative competition within the traders' family and increasing the possibilities of forging links with external actors. On the other hand, these divisions enable coexistence among different generations, lineages, and gender groups that are often reunited in the same federation. In other words, this multiplicity of blocks and associations gives the trade union a certain flexibility and the possibility of a concomitance of different codes and practices with an apparently monolithic system aimed at controlling a specific territory.

Trade unions and religious fraternities are generally concatenated with other local institutions such as the neighborhood committee (*junta de vecinos*), which mainly oversees commercial activities to ensure that they are fairly run, promotes the rights of traders, and upholds the safety of the district. These committees were introduced by the Popular Participation Law in 1993 and still maintain an ambiguous status, somewhere between an administrative unit and a popular council. In 2003, the Gran Poder Committee was composed of thirty-eight different secretariats, each in charge of a different field of "business" (*asuntos*) and reelected every one or three years (Tassi 2010). In practice, every family in the neighborhood had a member holding a post in this popular network, potentially enabling members of the family to have a direct influence on the local political decision-making process.

Similarly to trade unions and religious fraternities, a popular tribunal (*Tribunal de honor*) operates within the neighborhood committee and is in charge of sanctioning, regulating, and finding solutions to any conflicts. In 2012, a Gran Poder trader found a neighbor stealing from his goods store (Tassi et al. 2013: 126). Rather than reporting the theft to police and taking the thief to court, the trader decided to resort to the neighborhood committee. From the point of view of the trader, the committee was thought to be more effective: it operated according to local codes and practices and it had a better understanding than the conventional justice system of the moral and social implications of the act being judged for the local community. In addition, the committee held both the legitimacy and the capacity of coercion to cast a verdict over the frequent cases of theft in the neighborhood. In its final deliberation, the committee decided that the neighbor found stealing would be expelled from the neighborhood unless he produced the stolen goods and returned them to the trader by a set date.

Generally, important deterrents of criminal activities in the market areas are the forms of definitive exclusion from the associations and networks on which capillary social and economic relations are founded. An accusation of theft in the Huyustus or Asodimin markets may activate forms of social isolation and even annihilation, often inducing the actor to undertake a necessary relocation to another neighborhood or city. In these circumstances, the threat of measures such as exclusion from the neighborhood or from the guild may prove more effective in producing a certain behavior than the official political apparatus whose coercive functioning is not always predictable.

This complex organization and sophisticated practices of neighborhood safety, social security, and conflict resolution avoid the intervention of official authorities in the internal equilibrium of the traders' organizations and also generate a sense of safety in marginal areas of the city often referred to by the middle class as "red zone" districts. Particularly after the neoliberal reforms imposed on Bolivia since the 1980s (Gill 2000; Postero 2013), we have witnessed a process of withdrawal of official institutions from marginal neighborhoods and a limited capacity to provide basic social and economic services. Counterintuitively, this is paralleled by the penetration of the urban fabric by popular guilds and committees that had not been dismantled by the structural adjustment measures.

In Buenos Aires, the Bolivian popular entrepreneurs of the *feria* La Salada,[6] who had survived the 2001 collapse of the banking system thanks to their habit of keeping savings at home, reacted to the withdrawal of the official institutions by creating their own popular clinic, a rehabilitation facility for young thieves and addicts, a school, and a security system for the market. They also made various forms of investment in the municipality's infrastructure projects. In this way, these marginal economic actors/migrants managed to negotiate forms of citizenship and socioeconomic participation on their own terms with local authorities traditionally hostile to their presence in the country.

Ritual Institutionality

The ritual and the religious fields are other crucial domains allowing the sedimentation of the interstitial institutions on which popular trade is founded. In fact, among popular sectors, ritual activities such as dance parades take on the role to materialize unconventional forms of expression of status and economic success, given popular traders' exclusion from the mainstream channels of social mobility (Soruco 2012). In such a context of persistent discrimination from the urban middle class and mainstream institutions, ritual activities turned into powerful tools to defiantly reassert traders' sociocultural difference and their nonmodern practices and beliefs. On the one hand, these practices reenacted a historical and ontological difference between popular sectors and the urban middle class, provoking the latter to withdraw from the traders' newly conquered spaces. On the other hand, they also provided spaces for resocialization, enabling the consolidation and expansion of the traders' social and economic networks.

Performed for Catholic saints[7] and images, ritual activities such as dance parades have become structuring events of the local ritual calendar. The dancing and the magnificent display of fabrics, dancing gear, and costumes were conceived of as offerings to local saints supposed to be witnessing these lavish performances (Nash 1979). To magnify the performance of plenty, dozens of traders' guilds from a variety of markets and product categories would get together in these events, reiterating their social and economic bonds and materializing an iconic challenge to formal institutions in terms of both proper religious practice and control of spaces.

Most popular markets are associated with a specific Catholic saint or virgin. In a syncretic assemblage of Catholic and Andean practices and beliefs, the Saint is invested with the power to protect local traders and to make fecund the ground on which the market is built. This generally means that the Saint guarantees the attraction of customers and the circulation of goods and capital. In the 1980s, when La Paz municipality attempted to resettle the Eloy Salmón traders about half a mile up the slope in a newly built market equipped with shops and modern facilities, the traders rejected the offer, arguing that it would be both a risk to move to a new "ground" and a lack of consideration for the local Saint—the Holy Trinity—that had provided them with wealth and plenty for decades.

The Saint's intercessions must be reciprocated. Although traders would perform offerings to the Saint and other deities on an individual basis throughout the year, the main collective celebration is the Saint's "birthday." At the end of May or beginning of June, the Gran Poder dance parade (*Entrada del Gran Poder*) in honor of the Holy Trinity transforms the west slope and the city center of La Paz into the theater for one of the largest religious celebrations on the continent. The *Entrada del Gran Poder* mobilizes not only an incredible number of people and tens of thousands of devotee-dancers, but also an amount of material resources that would seem to exceed the possibilities of this institutionally neglected area of the city. From butchers to grocers, from truck drivers to appliance traders, more than sixty popular guilds involved in the urban economy and organized into religious fraternities snake down the traditionally indigenous side of the city, starting off in the highest and poorest neighborhoods. At a slow pace, the parade then enters the commercial *barrio* of Eloy Salmón, filled with high-tech shops and flanking the Sanctuary where the image of the Holy Trinity, also known as the Lord of Gran Poder, is taken out of the church to receive the dancers (*folkloristas*). After snaking across the *barrio*, the parade reaches the hotels and handicraft shops of the tourist area of the city and eventually flows into *Avenida Mariscal Santa Cruz*, the main street at the bottom of the Andean canyon where La Paz stands.

With a mixture of pride and excitement, Carlos Estrada remembered vividly how in 2001 the parade was hindered by the authorities from reaching the center of the city as a sign of mourning for the death of Víctor Paz Estenssoro, one of the founding fathers of the modern Bolivian nation. In a blast of fury and joy, the dancers in their heavy costumes broke through

Unión comercial fraternity in the Gran Poder dance parade (note the rattle in the shape of a container ship).

police lines and barriers and invaded the main street, which was jammed with traffic. The audience supportively joined the parade and the dancers "took possession" of the city center. On the one hand, these parades expressed social and economic affirmation by suddenly making visible—in their magnificent costumes—those indigenous urban sectors to which the elites had repeatedly turned a blind eye. On the other hand, they asserted in a more or less metaphorical way traders' control of central urban territories and spaces of officialdom to which they had been historically denied access (Albó and Preiswerk 1986; Guss 2006; Himpele 2003; Tassi 2010).

Ranging from political indigenous forms and organizations to symbolic and religious codes, a multiplicity of elements overlapped and converged in the spatial control of the markets and of urban commercial spaces outlining a polyphonic organizational system structuring and regulating the economy. In 2012, my godson at the age of ten was named *pasante* (fiesta steward) of one of the most renowned traders' fraternities for the year 2025. Although disparaged and misunderstood by official institutions, this barely formal and scarcely visible world had consolidated a solid institutionality showing a capacity to reproduce itself and its power structures with a firmness and coherence that force us to rethink its supposed "improvisation." Deemed by the municipality highly disordered, feudal, and improvised (Aramayo 2014), Aymara commercial and religious organizations revealed a degree of sophistication and a capacity to reproduce themselves by generating solid referents for the new generations that official institutions simply could not (Tassi et al. 2013; see also Chapter 5). In their social, religious, and economic structures historically anchored in local codes and traditions, Aymara traders were anything but improvised, suggesting an incapacity or refusal of mainstream institutions and white-*mestizos* to envisage modalities of organization that did not reflect their own.

Rather than being absorbed or replaced by supposedly dominant powers or more modern and effective institutions, these popular religious fraternities were expanding in a capillary way. Subsidiary groups of Gran Poder fraternities were springing up in El Alto and Santa Cruz for the celebrations of the *Virgen del Carmen*, in Buenos Aires among Bolivian migrants for the fiesta of the *Virgen de Copacabana*, or in São Paulo for the patriotic celebrations of August 6. The international expansion of religious fraternities facilitated forms of "reciprocal exchange" where Gran Poder traders would travel from La Paz to Buenos Aires to honor agreements with friends and *comadres* by participating in their social and religious events. The religious and kinship connections often spilled over into economic domains, weaving trading partnerships between Eloy Salmón traders and Bolivian migrants in Buenos Aires working in La Salada.

If religious fraternities accomplish an important social and economic role, to the point where members of the same fraternity refer to each other as *comadres* and *compadres* or use the name of the fraternity to refer to a common familial origin, traditional ritual specialists (*yatiri* in Aymara) are often the fulcrum around which important economic alliances are shaped. Traders, truck drivers, and bus companies resort to ritual specialists to perform offerings to the earth—*Pachamama*—the *Tío* (cf. Taussig 1980), and other cosmological forces to avoid goods being confiscated by customs, attract customers, and avoid accidents or complications on the journey. Groups of the *yatiri*'s "clients" or "patients" get together on special occasions such as New Year's Eve or the beginning of August—the *Pachamama* month—to perform lavish communal offerings (*mesas*). On these occasions, while their offerings are being burned, the participants share meals and drinks as if participating in a common banquet with cosmological forces. These are fecund moments where clients come to share, talk, and explicitly verbalize their most intimate desires, namely, the requests (*pedidos*) they put forward in their offerings.

This uncommon reciprocal sharing of private aspirations and personal secrets engenders forms of pathos and trust among clients. It was during a New Year's Eve offering that Rigoberto, a trader of secondhand American shoes in the *feria* 16 de Julio in El Alto, negotiated an agreement with the owner of a bus company for the transport of goods. Because the import of secondhand clothes and shoes has been banned by the government, Rigoberto had suddenly found himself and his trade "illegal" and was experiencing notable difficulties in the import and transport of goods either from the Iquique duty-free zone or from warehouses in Oruro. During the offering, Rigoberto negotiated with the owner of the *Exaltación* bus company for his goods to be transported twice a week in the hidden compartments of the company's buses in exchange for a substantial payment.

Yatiris not only bring together and engender socioeconomic communities of actors communally participating in popular economic forms, but also the ritual work of *yatiris* penetrates deep into the very heart of the global economy in which popular traders are involved, playing a regulatory role and helping to strengthen the solidity and institutionality of their practices. A few months ago, on a cold Monday morning, I was walking with my father, Carlos, toward the Eloy Salmón to help him open and set up the shop. Once we reached the shop, we realized that the three locks of the outer door had been removed and the door forced with a crowbar. My father threw a quick glance at the goods inside the shop and, after thirty seconds, turned to me and said bluntly, "It's the flat screen televisions." He grabbed his mobile phone and made a call. For a moment, I thought he was reporting the theft or calling one of his several friends and/or *compadres* who serve as high-ranking officials in the police and the army. Instead, he called Paulina, a young but popular *yatiri* from El Alto in her thirties, to inquire about the theft. After a quick description of the details of the robbery, she read the cards for my father while on the phone and gave him the names of two people who needed to be questioned to get information about the theft. Carlos hung up on Paulina and made a rapid series of phone calls to mobilize his social networks and "encircle" (*cercar*) the two suspects. The following day, the thieves had been identified and Carlos then had to begin the tough negotiations to retrieve the merchandise or its value in cash.

Andean religion provides another structure, codes, and beliefs to strengthen and complement the framework that regulates, coordinates, and allows the functioning of this interstitial popular economy. The anecdote of the robbery gives us an idea of how a series of Andean codes and beliefs have penetrated the administration and conceptualization of this popular although global economy. Not only have Andean religious forms found new meanings and values in the flows and dynamics of the global economy, but also they have been able to resignify conventional practices and inscribe on them new connotations. Most of the traders who resort to *yatiris* are importers who frequently travel to Iquique and to China for business. Nevertheless, they do not hesitate to resort to a *yatiri* to clarify a mysterious robbery or, as in the case of Silveria, to forecast the outcome of an investment. Once again, tradition, local codes, and beliefs are used as tools for understanding and shaping the traders' own forms of participation in the global economy and modernity.

A different set of tools—organizational, ritual, and economic—are simultaneously mobilized by Aymara traders to deal with external threats and dominant powers, as well as to consolidate their control of the locality. In the case of the global economy, indigenous codes and religious practices are used to generate spaces of autonomous decision making and to anchor locally a series of broader economic processes by enveloping them in local forms and meanings, tuning them to or even forcing them to operate according to local logics and cosmological principles.

Exclusion by Inclusion: The Relationship with and Appropriation of External Actors

Popular institutions such as the neighborhood committees and the federations of brotherhoods are complexly structured organizations governed by presidents, secretariats, statutes, norms, and tribunals, apparently reflecting and imitating mainstream state institutions (Barragán 2006). However, as we have previously observed, those same popular institutions are often in charge of keeping the state and the municipality at a distance as well as limiting police access to their businesses and markets.

Forms and practices of appropriation of official religious and political institutions have generally been associated either with practices of concealment or with imitation. On the one hand, scholars (Rivera 1996) have tended to emphasize how the reproduction of official forms and structures of regulation in popular and interstitial institutions is the consequence of a subaltern desire to imitate the established powers, the rich and the powerful, which would symbolically provide a gateway to access the magical realm of the modern. On the other hand, it has been seen as a cosmetic operation aimed at disguising—and concealing from the eyes of the authorities—practices, beliefs, and institutions that remained "indigenous" at heart (Montenegro 1982). What we are witnessing among popular traders is a genuine appropriation and resignification of the forms and structures of the officialdom, from tribunals to Catholic iconography, turning them into strategic tools to consolidate and expand their own kind of institutionality. It was through the decisions and strategies defined during guild assemblies that traders in both the *feria* 16 de Julio in El Alto and the Huyustus market resolved to confront the dragnet put up by customs police to confiscate commodities imported illegally. In other words, the appropriation of mainstream modalities of organization is used to reassert popular traders' autonomy and even to confront official institutions.

The relationship with external economic actors is often based on similar strategies of appropriation. In the past few years, the popular markets of La Paz and El Alto have become appealing commercial spaces for foreign brands as well as Chinese and regional investors. Local traders have been obliged to decide how to relate to these external actors who were bearers of both opportunities and threats to local power structures that had been consolidating gradually and against the odds. The popular markets that enjoyed the most potent forms of economic success and growth had paralleled their consolidation as attractive commercial hubs with the effort to verbally and visually downplay their achievements to preserve local forms and institutions and avoid attracting attention to their informal activities. However, Chinese investors and foreign brands were not completely rejected. In fact, they were often controlled or coopted into the traders' own system. Given the capillary control of commercial spaces in popular markets, Chinese investors were often unable to gain access to a selling space to retail their products directly. However, they were offered the possibility of using the local chains of supply and distribution based on ethnic networks and reproduced through ritual activities (Tassi et al. 2012) for their goods to access to local markets.

In a context where local traders were not interested in setting up subaltern economic partnerships with foreign entrepreneurs but rather sought to expand their own forms of institutionality and their independent businesses, such articulations of popular markets with global actors were viewed locally as possibilities for expanding their structures of power. In other words, instead of threatening forces endangering culture and locality, foreign brands and investors become instrumental tools to reproduce local networks, forms of control, and belonging.

Although I will address the relations between local traders and foreign actors in more depth in subsequent chapters, it is worth clarifying the traders' ingenious subaltern strategy—what I call "exclusion by inclusion"—aimed at safeguarding their local control and primacy despite their subaltern condition. If we take, for instance, the religious fiesta of Gran Poder, probably the most important celebration in the country in relation to popular trade, we observe that the participants in this popular fiesta have gradually included a number of foreigners and members of the traditional elites—referred to as *profesionales*.

Once disparaged by the middle class for its indigenous and primitive character (Albó and Preiswerk 1986), in the past few decades the Gran Poder dance parade has increasingly included members of the urban middle class willing to develop an attachment to a festive and folkloric cultural capital and ultimately connect to a country they have not quite felt was theirs (Abercrombie 1992). Popular fraternities tend to grant highly visible roles to members of the traditional elites who participate in the fiesta's dance parade. Whereas *profesionales* tend to dance in the first rows of the fraternity, performing their own steps (*figuras*) and wearing costumes different from the rest, established traders (*antiguos*) tend to prefer the last rows of the fraternity for their proximity to the music of the brass band and to prioritize uniformity and collectivism, in both the steps and the costumes (Himpele 2003). Although publicly welcoming middle-class *profesionales* in their fraternities, senior traders are often privately scornful of the former's emphasis on individuality and difference interpreted as distinctive signs of their arrogance and frivolity.

The participation of the middle class in a popular or indigenous fiesta has certainly magnified its visibility and acceptance in the national media, making it more digestible to the urban elites and allowing it to penetrate social spaces and imaginaries once disparaging of these improper and "uncivilized" cultural manifestations. However, rather than softening differences, this process has reproduced different codes of understanding of and participation in the fiesta. Despite their visibility in the dance parade and their aspiration to play a more central role in the organization of the fiesta, middle-class *profesionales* remain practically excluded from the decision making concerning the fiesta and the fraternity. In other words, not only are traders' fraternities utilizing middle-class members to legitimize their "informal" organizations and religious practices and project the image of a popular sociocultural system aspiring to be granted national recognition, but also it is the traders who define the rules and forms of participation of external actors, inducing them to believe they are at the core of the fiesta although actually they are relegated to a marginal and even scorned position. In this case, we are dealing with radical and ingenious forms of appropriation of the other, which imply an inclination to include together with a simultaneous tendency to exclude.

Although the market presents other forms and levels of complexity, there are a series of resonances in relation to the fiesta. A number of foreign brands and enterprises participate in the Gran Poder markets. Despite their flashy neon-lit signs, however, the capillary control of commercial spaces by local traders forces those brands and companies to conform to a series of locally defined economic practices (Tassi 2012a). A few years ago, large electrical goods brands such as Samsung and LG began asking some of the local shops for exclusivity in exchange for attractive compensation. This practice clashed with the local tendency to stock a large variety of products to attract customers from different social layers. So, several traders decided to enter into agreements with both Samsung and LG (and sometimes Sony too) for "exclusivity"! In other words, they received compensation for exclusivity from both LG and Sony while continuing to sell both brands and simply removed or swapped the neon signs when an employee or manager of the foreign firm visited the shop.

Recently, mainstream brands such as Samsung and Sony have been granted the possibility of opening up their own showrooms in the Eloy Salmón. However, in their showrooms they are only entitled to explain the technical features of products; they are forbidden from selling merchandise and even from talking about prices. In fact, commodities can only be purchased from local retailers of the Eloy Salmón. In La Paz, Samsung keeps opening showrooms in strategic and elitist spots of the city. Even in middle-class residential neighborhoods, Samsung refers their clients to the popular shops of the crowded Eloy Salmón high up on the slope.

Through a detailed knowledge of territories and markets, culturally specific forms of organization, religious codes, and practices, Aymara traders not only manage to establish local forms of market regulation but also defy the mainstream practices of large brands and define the rhythms and local rules for foreign multinationals to operate. Eventually, large brands such as Samsung and LG adapted to local practices of diversification, exclusivity, and territorial control as Aymara traders' capacity to operate locally exceeded their own market knowledge, organization, and ability to operate.

Conclusions

In third world countries, informal and popular economies have been seen as a consequence of the excess of bureaucracy, rules, and institutions and the simultaneous inability of such institutions to enforce the rules (cf. de Soto 1986, 2002). This state of affairs was said to generate weak, improvised, subsistence economic forms living off the crumbs of the official economy given their chronic lack of capital, access to technology, and specialized know-how (Long and Roberts 1984). Aymara traders have generated a framework of social, religious, and economic organizations and institutions to sustain, regulate, and limit an economic endeavor that had been traditionally excluded from the formal regulatory framework, concealed and rejected by officialdom, and barred from an egalitarian access to the market. It was through this interstitial framework and their subaltern resourcefulness (Escobar 2001) that they began first to confront official institutions and then appropriate and overwhelm them, producing their own forms of accumulation, know-how based on local knowledge, and modalities of accessing the market on their own terms.

At a time when global economic processes were encouraging forms of deterritorialization and disembedding from local places, spaces, and practices (Harvey 1989), Aymara traders were opting for forms of reterritorialization based on a firm control of commercial spaces through a framework of overlapping institutions often generated by historically rooted sociopolitical practices and strategies. Conventional narratives and economic analyses have characterized popular economic actors as "improvised" and as lacking mature institutions, a well-educated professional body, institutional memory, and consolidation through collective processes (Wanderley 2003). It was through their interstitial institutional framework, simultaneously anchored in cultural, religious, and economic dimensions, that Aymara traders were able to establish a space of negotiation between internal and external, local and global forms, displacing official authorities and turning a condition of social and economic exclusion into one of self-affirmation.

Through a similar exaltation of underprivileged economic actors, in the 1990s international development agencies began promoting the individual capacities that small and informal entrepreneurs were developing in the interstices of the global economy (Narayan 1999; Schneider 1999; World Bank 1997, 2000). Under the label of "social capital," such efforts were often aimed at reducing the interference of a dysfunctional and overbureaucratized state in the economic endeavors of private citizens (de Soto 1986, 2002) and promoting the penetration of neoliberal forms in third world local spaces.

This sudden refashioning of local microenterprises from obstacles to modernization and development into activities worthy of credit and institutional support did not last long. In the following decade, international development agencies started complaining about the lack of a solid regulatory environment for their investments in the developing world (Hart 2007). Suddenly, large multinationals found themselves bypassed by informal actors who were evading regulations and utilizing local and often informal resources to reduce prices. Carlos Forment (2014) argues that both the World Trade Organization and the European Union are today waging a crusade against the mostly Bolivian microentrepreneurs in La Salada market in Buenos Aires, threatening the Argentinean state with canceling the agreements on trade tariffs if it does not address the informal practices, exploitation, and counterfeiting going on in La Salada. Once again, when local institutions and interests do not match or abide by international regulations often designed to protect the interests of large enterprises, the development police begin flexing their muscles.

In Bolivia, Aymara traders are penetrating spaces and territories traditionally controlled either by transnational capital or by its local allies. In so doing, they have attracted widespread criticism from national and international media. However, their capacity to root their socioeconomic penetration in the interests and aspirations of historically sidelined local actors and their provision of basic services that neither foreign capital nor conventional institutions were able to provide, together with their reinvestment in the country, has gained them an important level of legitimacy outside of formal circles. Despite the media campaign depicting them as smugglers and antisocial, through their own discourse and media they are positioning themselves as an "asset" for the country.

In this chapter I have mostly analyzed the tendency of traders to consolidate forms of local institutionality by appropriating, digesting, and resignifying dominant institutions and their forms. In the next chapter I will address how this local institutionality has enabled links to be forged with a variety of equally interstitial and translocal actors, outlining a complex trading system of unexpected dimensions.

CHAPTER 2

Kinship Networks as Chains of Supply and Distribution

In his works, Arturo Escobar (2005, 2008) emphasizes that when local and indigenous groups are faced with politicoeconomic forms of deterritorialization engendered by global processes and flows, they tend to produce a series of subaltern strategies aimed at redefining forms and practices of relocalization. Among these strategies, Escobar mentions the "politics of scale," namely, the tendency of indigenous subaltern groups to operate at different sociopolitical levels. Forms and practices of relocalization are shaped by the ability to function, organize, and move in circumscribed local spaces and simultaneously by the capacity to forge strategic new alliances at a wider national, global, or translocal level.

In the previous chapters, we observed how a historically and geographically fragmented state, produced by different and often contradictory processes of revolution, liberalization, and recolonization (cf. Rivera 1993), had engendered discontinuous forms of operation over the territory. This "state with holes" (UNDP 2007), whose legal, ideological, and bureaucratic arms are unable to reach and function in certain remote areas or marginal urban neighborhoods, had fostered a series of local and interstitial forms of institutionality able to replace the state and organize political and economic structures filling the holes. In truth, the holes were also produced by the dual structure of the Bolivian economy (Laserna 2005; Molina 2013), where an extractive industry with high levels of productivity and modern technology coexisted with a labor-intensive, small-scale economy with incipient know-how but was unable to generate synergies with it.

Rather than being dysfunctional or normatively threatening to the functioning of the economy and the nation, these parallel structures in the holes of the country appeared to outline a plurality of social relations and organizational capacities, shaping both economic possibilities and novel ways to think of the country (UNDP 2007). Whereas Chapter 1 focused on how these institutions have grown in the interstices of the state, in this chapter I show how the holes are interconnected and how forms of extraofficial mobile institutionality have been shaped and developed along routes and networks linking and filling the holes.

Filling the Holes: Cultural Forms and Practices of a Mobile Institutionality

In Bolivia, the responsibility for connecting the different ecological and economic spaces during both the colonial and the republican periods has often fallen on the shoulders of indigenous lineages. Since the colonial administration barely managed to control urban settlements and the mining enclaves (Klein 1995), the indigenous lineages that often possessed an extensive knowledge of the territory and controlled the means of transportation became instrumental in the practices of distribution and supply (Glave 1989). Through caravans of llamas, a system of rural footpaths, and a series of outposts for replenishing supplies (*tambos*) scattered across the territory, indigenous highlanders maintained control of the transportation of coca leaf from the tropical plantations to the mines of the high plateau, wine from the interandean valleys to the urban centers, or even mercury from Huancavelica (Peru) to the silver mine of Potosí. Such a "production of circulation" (Glave 1989: 50) created a system of "travelers" (*sariri* in Aymara, *trajinantes* in Spanish) managing the exchanges between highly differentiated climate zones in the Andean territory.

The highland economies have been defined by peculiar patterns of settlement, practices of exchange, and circulation of products determined by an environment characterized by stark changes of climate across minimal variations in altitude (Murra 1975 [1972]; Lehman 1982; Masuda et al. 1985). Andean lineages, families, and kinship networks lived scattered across multiple territories and ecological niches to maximize their access to a variety of products and reduce the risks of a climatically vulnerable region. Murra (1975 [1972]) coined the metaphor of the "vertical archipelago" to characterize this system of scattered settlements ranging from the Pacific to the lowlands across the Cordillera, where colonists from different highland kinship networks and lineages intermingled. Settlers were seen as living like "islands" in "multiethnic" neighborhoods alongside islands placed there by other groups.

Each year after the harvest, highland llama herders would travel down to the valleys, coast, and lowlands to take part in exchange relations with their kin and other exchange partners with ties to the lineage. This system of transversal exchange (Renard-Casewitz et al. 1986) produced practices of multiple domiciles within the family and the lineage and a heightened degree of geographical mobility among Andean settlers, but also forms of direct access by the family/lineage to a variety of products from different regions (Salomon 1985). These dynamics consolidated an Andean modality of inhabiting the environment by traversing it as well as a network of rural footpaths marked at intervals by shrines and ceremonial sites engendering sacred connections among the diverse territories linking the path (Platt 2009). Sites of restocking and storage turned precursors of the contemporary market, the *tambos* constituted crucial reproductive and sacred sites embodying the convergence of the different paths, territories, and veins of the nation (Arnold and Yapita 1998). Travelers themselves did not perform a merely economic function because their repeated acts of traversing were thought to activate fecund relations between the spirits of different territories, which regenerated the cosmological forces of the whole landscape (Harris 1989; Arnold and Yapita 1998).

As a result of these social, cultural, and morphological dynamics, the Aymara sociopolitical structure was defined by a high degree of decentralization and by interspersed groups, sometimes located a few days' journey away from their settlement of origin, articulated by changing economic and political alliances (Platt 1987). In this context, interecological and interethnic networks became crucial for the survival, reproduction, and extension of such a system. Instead of an enclosed community with a predefined and circumscribed territory, closed circles of relatives, and ancestral unity, the ecological vulnerability forced Aymara social structures to make repeated and continuous attempts to annex new territories and expand their networks and crops. This outlined a tendency toward a constant renovation of the territory and paths, based on the enhanced capacity to appropriate external forces and resources (Arnold and Hastorf 2008).

Aymara modalities of sociopolitical organization and their socioeconomic structure became instrumental not only in the operation of the "ethnic economy" (Harris 1982) but also as crucial tools enabling the functioning of the mercantile economy in Bolivia (Harris et al. 1987). If, in the first place, the indigenous system of transportation and their networks enabled products to circulate (Glave 1989), it soon became apparent that their interecological alliances and networks of different economic spaces could work as tools to open up and connect national markets as well as to structure advanced chains of supply and distribution that were national in scope, in a context where the official economy was more concerned with foreign markets and the export of raw materials.

The Production of Circulation: Social Mechanisms in the Creation of Economic Networks

Such extended networks, indigenous forms of mobility, and practices of multiple domicile were often curtailed by the administrative require-ments of the nation-state and also by the requirements of modern ideas of development, which encouraged both more stable settlement patterns and adjustment to the economic modalities of the middle classes. How-ever, in recent decades a series of latent Andean practices and structures of mobility have been revamped to operate in a global economic scenario where mobility, flexibility, and simultaneous links to multiple markets are paramount.

Traders in the Huyustus market and the *feria* 16 de Julio not only present a series of social strategies and mechanisms to exert control over local commercial spaces but also constantly operate to consolidate and expand multiple economic networks that range from border towns and high-plateau *ferias* to Chinese industrial hubs and Chilean harbors. For the type of "informal" trade I have been describing, the work to create economic networks is often twofold. On the one hand, it implies the ex-pansion and diversification of the social and economic possibilities of the local trader. On the other hand, it requires setting up and investing in new forms of institutionality to enable the solidification of chains of supply and distribution, allowing trade to operate safely in contexts where the presence of official authorities is weak and their capacity to enforce commercial regulations is limited or arbitrary.

Developing connections with other markets can take two different forms. The first and more conventional one is through building partner-ships with actors both at the end of the supply chain and in intermediate locations to control and provide services to the distribution process. The second option is through traveling. Traders in the *feria* 16 de Julio, held on Thursdays and Sundays, would spend the rest of the week traveling to different market locations. In the case of the Huyustus market, which is held daily, traders would rely on members of the family taking weekly trips to a variety of commercial locations across the country or region.

Vertical Alliances

Despite the stereotypical representations of the Aymara as locked into forms of sectarian corporatism (Schulte 1999) or engaging in resistant practices of radical ethnic trade unionism, the process of expansion of Aymara traders toward other cities and markets required their organizations and forms to be flexible enough to allow multiple articulations with external actors and organizations. In addition to the horizontal relations among members of the same guild we observed in the previous chapter, a series of vertical alliances among actors at different levels in the chains of distribution and transversal partnerships with members of other guilds now comprise the complex scenario of popular trade. A variety of economic actors—ranging from relatives in the countryside controlling the trade route to border policemen, from peripheral intermediaries to retailers in market towns, from truck drivers to Chinese producers—are weaving extended and fragmented networks connecting the main urban markets with other national and translocal spaces.

The Aymaras played a historically important role in connecting different ecological and economic spaces thanks to their ownership of the means of transport (Glave 1989; Medinaceli 2011). From running llama caravans across the different ecological niches of the Andean territory, some of them turned into truck drivers articulating the ethnic with the mercantile economy (Llanque and Villca 2011), whereas others became "travelers" connecting multiple regions and markets.

Nowadays, Aymara traders/travelers (*viajeros*) play a key role in the practices of wholesale distribution in the major cities of Bolivia and the borders with neighboring countries. After traveling the whole night, they begin wholesaling at dawn (hence the names *mañaneras* or *madrugadoras*— early-risers) before the retailing activities of the local markets start. Once they are done selling, they move to other markets and regions, thus linking spaces as diverse as the puna regions of the Cordillera and tropical cities in the lowlands. In fact, this mode of trade requires forms of articulation with multiple markets and also multiple forms of belonging to different trade associations to access commercial spaces as diverse as the biweekly market in the highland border town of Desaguadero and the textile producers' market in the booming tropical city of Santa Cruz. These multiple connections to both market places and guilds appear as the reactivation and expansion to a national level of a network of itinerant and intercalated rural *ferias* that for centuries had remained under the control of Aymara lineages and part of the so-called indigenous economic space (Langer 2004). A traditional economic modality and structure such as the *feria* was reactivated and expanded in its reach and scope to cope with the rapidly changing demands of global markets as well as the increasing flexibility they require.

Aymaras from the high-plateau village of Sica Sica have specialized in the import and wholesale of machine tools and electrical artifacts. Initially, they established their own shops, both in the *Isaac Tamayo* street in the Gran Poder neighborhood and in the Huyustus. In the 1990s, thanks to their connection with China, they created their own brands of tools produced in the Zhejiang region as well as perfectly counterfeited Argentinean and Brazilian electrical equipment. Their Chinese-produced brand, "Huyustools," achieved a regional distribution, conquering important

Shrine of the Lord of Gran Poder erected by Aymara traders and travelers in a market in Santa Cruz (Bolivian lowlands).

market shares in Peru, Argentina, and Chile. Their distribution capacity increased dramatically at the same time, extending from Gran Poder to the lowlands, from Santa Cruz to Buenos Aires. These forms of expansion managed to establish a powerful network of concatenated actors across the distribution routes—from Shanghai to towns on the border with Argentina—as well as a system of Sica Sica "ethnic islands", engendering both economic synergies and ramifications of their celebratory activities. As a consequence of this process of geographical expansion and "conquest," Sica Sica traders have been establishing shrines in the new locations (see Arbona et al. 2013: 59) and begun spreading their festive celebrations across multiple cities within the region.

In the case of Sica Sica wholesalers, they have been building their network by conquering spaces and through forms of cooperation with other guilds and actors, thus widening their chains of distribution. Another way to establish socioeconomic alliances beyond one's own guild is through collaboration with other trade unions that specialize in a different product category. If we take, for instance, the cohesively organized mechanics' workshops of El Alto, the local guild has also encouraged links with auto parts traders, tools importers such as the Sica Siqueños, and also truck drivers' unions. The combination of often family-based modalities of guild association with more vertical and heterogeneous ones is reproduced through forms of fictive kinship and generally responds to a need to facilitate and speed up the placement of products, services and commodities. However, these kinds of vertical interguild articulations are also key in generating effective integrated processes of information circulation, including producers, traders, and users, which are instrumental in the consolidation of forms of know-how based on local specificities.

In El Alto the articulation among the local guilds of truck drivers, mechanics, and auto parts importers has produced a strategic economic microsystem operating under the radar of the law, which has been instrumental in displacing the competition of the technologically more advanced Chilean neighbors. The auto parts importers' and mechanics' neglect of international standards of production together with local truck drivers and their representatives' ability to deal with the fuzzy norms of the Bolivian customs, traffic laws, and shipping forwarders in the Chilean ports wove together a powerful although informal system of articulated actors paradoxically more suitable to the infrastructural limitations and possibilities of the region where Chilean truck drivers were unable to operate. In fact, it was almost impossible for a highly technologically advanced Chilean truck to travel to La Paz across mountain regions without specific truck services, deal with the convoluted and unwritten rules of Bolivian customs, and resort to counterfeited or artisanally produced spare parts from El Alto mechanics and auto parts importers in case of a mechanical emergency. In other words, the Bolivian interguild alliance made it impossible for the highly regulated Chilean transportation system to operate along the strategic commercial route between Iquique and La Paz, favoring the incursion of Bolivia's popular economic actors in a geopolitically sensitive region.

The truck drivers' guilds are strategic allies for Aymara traders, since they handle full truckloads of the trader's commodities, to the value of several tens of thousands of dollars, on the basis of a mere verbal agreement. But most of all, truck drivers' guilds have a certain familiarity and, in most cases, *compadrazgo* bonds with customs authorities and highway policemen. In other words, truck drivers can be instrumental actors in undertaking negotiations with officials and reducing the costs and times of import procedures as well as the number of bribes.

Freight transport enterprises and truck drivers' cooperatives never travel with an empty truck, so when they arrive at their destination they must find or wait for a load before they can go back. This system implies that drivers maintain a detailed and constantly updated knowledge of the commercial activities going on at the start and end of the route as well as in the towns along the route. Their control of the route and their capacity to connect to a multiplicity of commercial networks make truck drivers crucial administrators of the forms, costs, and rhythms of the local distribution.

The different guilds of truck drivers have opted for modalities of organization by type of transport (i.e., dump trucks, freight trucks, or smaller vehicles referred to in Bolivian Spanish as *alzapata* and *pachajcho*) and/or by route of operation. The latter form of organization has been instrumental in generating forms of control of the territory in areas of the country where official institutions were cautious to venture. Truck drivers' unions operate across regions, borders, and sparsely populated areas of the country, incentivizing both the provision of mechanical and food services and the consolidation of forms of institutionality in remote areas. Until 2012, the national representative of the confederation of truck drivers, Julio Ramírez, held weekly meetings with the state-run company in charge of the construction and maintenance of the road infrastructure (ABC, *Administradora Boliviana de Carreteras*) (Tassi et al. 2013). Ramírez provided ABC with strategic information about the existing routes in the country and the state of road infrastructure, particularly in remote regions of Bolivia. Once again, the expertise of popular guilds exceeded the often-poor knowledge of the country by official institutions but also outlined a system where interlinked popular sectors once excluded from processes of institutional decision-making are now turned into strategic actors able to define the forms and modalities of transformation of the country.

The alliance of traders and truck drivers' guilds requires a system of careful regulation that, as is usually the case (see the following sections), remains embedded in a system of *compadrazgo*, the exchange of presents and favors that inscribes the relationship in a wider domain of relations and actors. In fact, the deal between trader and driver is never a linear or individual transaction between "free" economic actors because it constantly overlaps with a system of connections and forms of protection and control, both expanding and regulating the framework of popular trade.

Furthermore, as we have seen in the previous chapter, these economic relations continuously overflow into cosmological domains and link with cosmological forces. A few months ago, the truck carrying the cargo of an Eloy Salmón importer was attacked on the road from La Paz to Santa Cruz and a washing machine was stolen. The importer's wife blamed the event on her husband for not being generous enough (*mich'earse*) with the truck driver and not offering him sufficient beer and pleas. Simultaneously, the truck driver was blaming the event on himself because he had lately been thinking of buying a new truck and neglected the old one, forgetting to pay "him" with offerings and endow him with *cariño* (affection). This would have induced the old truck to take revenge on the driver or to give "himself" into the hands of robbers.

A multiplicity of codes, practices, and beliefs intervenes in these interstitial domains, extending economic transactions and relations well beyond mere commercial convenience or specific individual action. It is also through these codes, beliefs, and forms of communication between beings and cosmological forces, objects, humans, and spaces that holes can be filled and connected.

In the articulation of different spaces and the connection with networks and economic actors outside local markets, structures such as the *bloques* and the trade associations provide both the significant degree of flexibility required for establishing multiple economic articulations and the spaces granting forms of independent organization and decision making. Just as religious fraternities are internally divided into *bloques* or smaller and more flexible sections able to mobilize and move around more quickly and effectively, trade unions are similarly composed of a set of different trade associations. Although both are hierarchically linked to the "mother organization," *bloques* and trade associations enjoy a degree of independence and flexibility. In the Andes, forms of social organization such as the *ayllus* are often defined in terms of their filial and fraternal relationships with other territories, spaces, and organizations to signal reproduction and highlight the simultaneous sense of integration/descent and the circumscribed autonomy of younger siblings and progeny (see Chapter 5).

Bloques and trade associations can participate in social events and economic spaces that are not controlled or organized by the fraternity or the trade union. They may also develop networks and relations according to their own socioeconomic strategies and interests, as long as they do not produce forms of disloyal competition within the mother organization. This highlights the simultaneous centripetal and centrifugal tendencies within this kind of grass-roots organization (Arnold 2008). There have been several cases where, as a consequence of an excessive concentration of power in one fraternity or trade union, initiatives have been taken by

Bloque "Los Mantenidos" belonging to the Butchers' fraternity.

bloques or associations to fragment the mother organization, split its power by setting up a new fraternity or trade union, and reestablish a horizontal distribution of power and a socioeconomic equilibrium that remains poised on a thin line between concentration and decentralization (cf. Platt 1987).

It is interesting to observe how the geographical expansion of religious fraternities underlined by fraternities' mottos such as "Traders without borders" or "From Bolivia to the world" is constantly paired by an emphasis on or reference to the specific area, region, or even *ayllu* in which the fraternity originated. In the case of the fraternity *Central Sica Sica*, which, as we have seen, includes some of the most intrepid traders with a scope of operation ranging from China to São Paulo, from the plateau to Santa Cruz, the name of the four *ayllus* comprising the town of Sica Sica appears on the banner of the fraternity. Interestingly, in the dance parades in Santa Cruz and São Paulo it is also possible to notice *bloques* with different items of clothing as an explicit reference to their specific *ayllu* of origin. The religious fraternities and the *bloques* are key organizational structures that make visually evident the combination of an expansion toward translocal spaces but also the anchoring in specific localities. Although global development is often associated with deterritorialization and the dissipation of traditional ties and forms of belonging leading to a moral and social destructuration, what we see here is how the combination of resilience and flexibility, anchoring and networks of local structures make them into strategic tools to think and outline other forms of modernization and globalization.

Reinvesting in the Social: Strategies for the Expansion of Economic Networks

In spaces as diverse as El Alto, the border with Peru, and China, the otherwise weak relations among different and remote actors and entrepreneurs forming a chain of distribution appear to be regulated by a system of preemptive and unexpected favors oiling the smooth functioning of trade, creating forms of forced reciprocity and moral debt on which the commercial exchange is founded. A large importer from the *feria* 16 de Julio in El Alto who is a member of an urban fraternity may decide to participate with her extended family as a *bloque* in the celebrations of the patron saint festival in a border town where a local retailer or a relative is fiesta steward. This would bring the local steward not only prestige for being able to "attract" members of a renowned urban fraternity but also a substantial inflow of cash because each person in the *bloque* would pay the

Fiesta stewards in the fiesta of Gran Poder.

steward a sizable contribution toward the costs of the bands of musicians and the costumes for the fiesta. These kinds of favors are rarely paid back in cash, but they have more or less implicit costs. The border town retailer might have to increase her stock of commodities bought from the urban importer or provide a storage space in her border town to help the importer bring in her commodities. These mechanisms of "reciprocity" were instrumental in creating the conditions for developing chains of supply and distribution in a context where mainstream institutions were only intermittently present.

Ariel Loza is a fraternity founder originally from an Aymara high-plateau community who has established his business selling and producing clothes and dancing gear for ritual celebrations in the lowland city of Santa Cruz. Ariel's son Pablo lives in São Paulo running a textile workshop and he is a well-established member of the Bolivian migrant community that on August 6 performs a sumptuous dance parade in the neighboring country. Ariel's brother, Miguel, works in El Alto in the clothing manufacturing business, and his goddaughter and his nephew are installed in two rising towns in the lowlands. All of them work to open markets for Ariel's business in culturally and economically different parts of the country and the region, thus consolidating a family network that is constantly producing and circulating socioeconomic knowledge and information about multiple markets and different types of demand. Ariel gets supplies for his workshop from El Alto, Brazil, and China and he, in turn, "exports" his dance costumes (*trajes*) and gear to the Bolivian migrant community in Brazil, to southern Peru, and to a series of economically ascendant "intermediate towns" in the lowlands. Not only has Ariel managed to turn local practices of religious celebration into an "export" business but also he has established a spread-out economic network into which he "reinvests" about $15,000 every year in religious, social, and familial activities because it constitutes both a social and an economic asset.

Entrepreneurs such as Ariel are often caught up in a network of religious activities and social events that dot the cycle of their everyday life. Every Saturday evening and Sunday they find themselves participating in multiple events ranging from baptisms, weddings, and celebrations of high school graduations to patron saint festivals and fraternity receptions and anniversaries. Such events imply not only an investment of time in social relations but also a sound endowment of economic resources toward fiesta stewards or bridegrooms that will be carefully reciprocated by the recipient(s) in other festive opportunities. These dynamics weave a system of relations, favors, and opportunities based on credits and debts providing local entrepreneurs with the necessary safety net, mechanisms of social control and protection, and "juridical security" for their business to operate in a context of exclusion from the conventional legal framework.

Clientelization

Probably the most characteristic social mechanism structuring commercial relations in the Andes is the so-called *relación de casero* (clientelization, or a relationship born out of frequent commercial transactions) between buyer and seller, wholesaler and retailer. This type of commercial relationship can be the product of preexisting social and kinship bonds and it continuously overflows into noncommercial domains. Particularly among popular sectors of the urban population, the act of buying is never a simple economic transaction (Tassi et al. 2013). Where and from whom to buy is an act that is carefully pondered and strategically defined. Sometimes the goods required can be bought from a specific *comadre* or from a friend, although their quality and price might not be as good as in another establishment. This decision is often taken with a view to establishing or consolidating strategic bonds with those sellers and with the expectation that that subtle courtesy might be reciprocated in the future—either through consenting to sponsor the baptism of a son/daughter or through the consolidation of a preferential commercial bond. Although price is certainly a variable taken into account before deciding where to buy, consumption—rather than simply being the conclusive step in a linear and impersonal commercial process—also constitutes a reinvestment in the social network or in its expansion.

One feature that characterizes the Andean *relación de casero* is the *yapa*, an Aymara word referring to the additional quantity of product that the seller adds to the volume of goods purchased once the transaction is complete (cf. Angé 2011), thus sanctioning the agreement reached between buyer and seller, reproducing the bond and encouraging future transactions. The logic of the *yapa* is not rooted in the momentary convenience of the act of purchase or in the preemptive offer of two bags of rice for the price of one. The *yapa* is subsequent to the economic agreement between buyer and seller and constitutes an investment in the temporality of the relation by generating a social/moral "debt" enticing the buyer or the seller to "come back," namely, to develop and maintain a preferential social/economic relation in the future. If you are caught by your *casera* with goods bought from another merchant, you can be referred to as a "traitor" or a "backstabber," which, although sometimes expressed with irony, can be particularly loaded words in Aymara circles.

In the process of purchase and sale among *caseros*, a series of ritual conventions are integrated into the practice. In fact, the act of commercial exchange is regulated by a set of ritual acts and rules that extend from the domain of gift-giving. For instance, in the practices of "offering" (*invitar* in Spanish, *wajjtaña* in Aymara), when you offer a drink to a friend, you should never pour or serve it with your left hand because the supposed process of imparting *cariño* (affection) through the beverage implied in the action might be reversed into disrespect and offense. In the same way, when you receive your purchase from your *casera,* she will always hand over the goods with her right hand, respecting similar affective conventions at the moment of the exchange and reaffirming the gratitude of the seller and the loyalty of the buyer, as well as engendering a certain overlap between the domain of the gift and that of commodities. When paying your *casera*, you must be careful in the way you handle money. Before handing them over, banknotes must be folded with the head on the inside and passed across showing the open side of the bundle of banknotes to your *casera*. In that way, banknotes take the form of a hungry open mouth stimulating the processes of social and economic reproduction.

Luck is another constitutive element of *casero* relations. Julio Ramírez, an established union leader of truck drivers, would only buy spare parts for his trucks from a secondhand seller in the neighborhood of *Santiago II* in El Alto. Sometimes he would wait for weeks for a specific replacement part to arrive at the shop of his *casero,* arguing that products brought from him tended to last longer and not to break down in remote and unpopulated areas of the route he was covering. Similarly, my mother, Marta, would only buy potatoes from her *casera* Andrea, a reseller of products from the fertile valleys east of Lake Titicaca. She would say that Andrea's potatoes "endure longer" (*aguantan más*) in the sense that products bought from her would be able to cover the food necessity of the family for a longer amount of time compared with potatoes bought from other sellers.

Relations between wholesalers and retailers and between producers and distributors in popular trade are often based on a similar *relación de casero.* Among emerging traders who have recently gotten involved with commerce, the way they manage the relationship with importers or producers is often a determining factor in their commercial success or failure. A series of strategies are continually reproduced to feed forms of reciprocity with their suppliers and to stabilize their position within the flow of commerce. Rigoberto Ali—a secondhand shoe retailers in the *feria* 16 de Julio—once he had chosen his *caseros*/suppliers in Oruro, maintained his commercial preference for them even at times when local competitors could offer him better prices. He also plies them with apparently selfless presents of food such as fish from the lake or special bread from La Paz— food exchange being a primary means to consolidate bonds. Through these explicit acts of siding with and supporting his *caseros*, Rigoberto constantly reinvests in durable commercial relations and in making his position in the chain safer and firmer. As a reward for these dynamics of preemptive favors, he is now able to choose the best products from his *caseros*/suppliers, rather than buying sealed bales, as is common in the secondhand clothes business, and access forms of preferential treatment in seasons of high demand and scarcity of products. Today, Rigoberto has gained enough trust from his suppliers to be able to buy on credit. Despite a higher interest rate, Rigoberto prefers to take private loans from suppliers. Besides guaranteeing access to capital, loans of this kind become crucial in ultimately securing Rigoberto's position within the flows of commerce (Tassi et al. 2013: 172). It is now in the interest of the supplier to favor and support those traders to whom they have lent money as a strategy to stabilize their practices of distribution. Thus, the economic interests of these *caseros* become entwined. Once again, proficiency in the local codes and manners becomes a strategic instrument to expand traders' radius of operation, build networks, and participate in the flows of commerce.

Practices of clientelization, loans, and preemptive gifts are all strategies to make an economic relation between a faraway supplier and a retailer "settle" (*asentar*). *Asentar* a relation is a form of sanctioning, cementing and widening it beyond the mere economic interest. In most cases, however, the settling of an economic relation overlaps with the ritual and religious field. Fictive kinship (*compadrazgo*) is a key tool to sanction economic relations among business partners. First, the relation of *compadrazgo* activates a rather material—or cosmological—bond between the godmother and the godchild because the former is supposed to *gotear* (drip onto) the latter elements of her character, physical features, and even food preferences. In other words, *compadrazgo* engenders a twist or a ramification of blood kinship producing, more than a bond, an overlap between the original and the fictive family. Second, *compadrazgo* brings together and intertwines the social networks of the two families, heightening the possibility of reciprocal social control. At weddings, all godfathers and godmothers are asked to sit together at the main table. If, on the one hand, these practices are intended to expand the social network of the guests, on the other hand, they are also thought to create multiple sets of bonds among members of the two families that may be strategically useful in moments of crisis to "fence in," pressure, and control a potentially disruptive member.

In a context of scarce and inefficient official controls over economic practices, the sanctioning of a business partnership becomes a paramount endeavor that is often produced by a concomitance of social, religious, and cosmological dynamics. Recently, Rigoberto agreed to establish a commercial partnership with Hilarión, an importer from El Alto who has long-established economic ties with a series of Chinese producers. Whereas Rigoberto has a perfect knowledge of the type, models, brands, and colors of shoes suitable to the different niches of the Bolivian and regional markets, Hilarión holds the capital and the contacts to have shoes produced in China according to local preferences and have them imported in large quantities in a container. After arduous negotiations and reciprocal although unexpressed distrust, Rigoberto and Hilarión agreed to work in partnership for a three-year period, defined their respective percentages on the profit, and decided to have their verbal agreement and economic *compadrazgo* "blessed" with a Mass in the Sanctuary of Gran

Poder. On a sunny Saturday afternoon, Rigoberto and Hilarión turned out at the Sanctuary wearing impeccable suits and followed by an entourage of relatives, *compadres*, and friends. In front of their "extended" families and the Lord of Gran Poder (*Tata*), to whom both attributed their economic success, Rigoberto and Hilarión had their partnership sanctioned, but not before "libating" it (*ch'allar*) with dozens of crates of beer right on the corner of the Sanctuary.

Aymara Chains of Supply and Distribution

Used as tools in the regulation of economic activities and in consolidating the economic network, the above-mentioned social mechanisms have not dissipated with the incursion of the global economy. Forms of clientelization and preemptive gifts have begun extending both nationally and beyond national borders to create translocal islands of institutionality where trade could occur. However, in different social and geographical contexts, the diverse relationship with local populations outlined different modalities of engaging with economic networks. Paradoxically, the interstitial economic relations and networks developed by Aymara traders have positioned Bolivia as a new center of regional forms of supply and distribution.

Economic Complementarity with Peruvian Kin

One of the most common forms of international clientelization for Aymara economic actors is that with fellow Aymara traders on the other side of the Peruvian border. These international but intra-Aymara bonds are the consequence of either the same families living on both sides of the border or trading partnerships developed either in the markets of El Alto—an appealing marketplace for Peruvian entrepreneurs—or in the border town of Desaguadero. Flows of both people and goods across the border are traditionally tolerated as a consequence of the imposed national frontier that divided Aymara territories and families (Barragán 1990). Today, for instance, more than 30,000 Peruvians from border regions are said to be living in El Alto. Lately, a series of Peruvian-run tinned-food businesses have sprung up in El Alto, producing jams and tinned fruits and vegetables with a "Made in Peru" label while making a significant saving on production costs.

Twice a week, popular traders and producers from La Paz, El Alto, Oruro, Cochabamba, Santa Cruz, Arequipa, and Juliaca converge at the *feria* in Desaguadero, an Aymara border town on the shore of Lake Titicaca known as a major commercial gateway for trade between Peru and Bolivia. This rural-fair-turned-wholesale-market today generates a volume of commercial transactions estimated to be worth around $5 million per day (Rivera, in Soruco 2012). Desaguadero is the meeting place for *caseros* from both sides of the border.

El Alto producers wholesale their leather jackets or counterfeited jeans to Peruvian traders-turned-*compadres* who, after smuggling the jackets into the neighboring country using a series of false or recycled receipts, ship the goods through safe channels and routes to the Lima markets controlled by fellow Aymaras. In Peru, Aymara traders (*Puneños*) have a similar reputation for high entrepreneurial abilities, a disposition for geographical mobility, and an intuition for commercial deals. On the Peruvian side, the commercial control and the presence of the Aymaras extends from Juliaca to Cuzco, from Arequipa to Lima (Aspilcueta 2007). This implies that Bolivian products are distributed to Peruvian markets by means of Peruvian Aymara socioeconomic networks whose members are linked to Bolivian popular economic actors through economic and *compadrazgo* relations.

In a symmetrical manner, Peruvian canned food, cotton, and detergents are bought in Desaguadero, mostly by Alteño traders, and redistributed to the entire country, from the main cities to the border towns with Argentina and Brazil. As mentioned previously, the heightened Alteño geographical mobility has been instrumental in finding new market niches for fine Peruvian cotton in the warm tropical regions of the Bolivian lowlands, the border towns with Brazil, Paraguay, and Argentina. The golden rule is that while Bolivian Aymara traders are in charge of distributing Peruvian products imported semiformally into Desaguadero through local but extended networks, Peruvian Aymaras control the distribution of Bolivian products on the other side of the border.

Because of cultural complicity between Peruvian and Bolivian Aymaras, these commercial practices of exchange are constantly paired by spectacular forms of sociocultural exchanges. Bolivian brass bands are repeatedly invited to religious fiestas and civic celebrations in southern Peru, whereas Peruvian highland orchestras are a must at wedding ceremonies, baptisms, and *cabos de años*[1] on the Bolivian side of the border. Bolivian traders travel repeatedly with *bloques* to the fiestas of *compadres* and commercial partners in southern Peru, engendering forms of social debts that are expected to be repaid through economic or social favors by Peruvian counterparts. The economic and spatial expansion is constantly paired by a social and cultural occupation of spaces and routes, consolidating and reproducing local codes and practices.

The regional networks of Aymara traders present a series of resemblances to the regional ethnic-based economic chains in West Africa. After the creation of institutionally weak nation states and despite the process of severing the scattered and extended lineages, ethnic-based networks—such as the Housa (Grégoire 1993) or the Malian traders (Lambert 1993)—reemerged both as crucial structures in the processes of supply and distribution and as trading communities exploiting the economic discrepancies between the different countries of the region. Often established on shared local codes or religious forms, as in the case of the Mourides of Senegal, such networks extended regionally and internationally, consolidating chains of supply and distribution structuring local economies. Rather similar to the Aymara, as we shall see in the next chapter, those same Malian traders were running shipping companies in Shanghai supplying the main commercial hubs of West Africa (Li et al. 2007).

From the Pacific to the Atlantic: Penetration and Mobility of Aymara Traders in the Lowlands and Brazil

Although in a different cultural and social environment, similar modalities of small-scale trade over long distances are reproduced in the towns on the border with Brazil. In Cobija and Guayaramerín, local highland traders have established forms of clientelization with Brazilian *sacoleiros*, street peddlers, and stall owners from cities and towns in the Brazilian interior (cf. Rabossi 2012). Taking advantage of the Cobija duty-free zone and the tax exemption for purchases below $300 per person, Brazilian *sacoleiros* organize bus trips to the border, hiring people who pretend to be casual tourists while in reality purchasing what the *sacoleiros* have ordered. In addition to allowing reciprocal practices of contraband and economic ventures under the radar of the law, the relations between traders and *sacoleiros* activate translocal alliances blurring frontiers, linking fragmented global spaces and consolidating networks of translocal spaces in these often neglected Amazonian regions (cf. Ribeiro 2006).

Highland traders who have settled in the Amazon basin work the legal and economic discrepancies between the two countries. Some of them travel repeatedly to Brazil's production hubs on the Atlantic coast to purchase goods to be resold at the border. The relation with Brazilian entrepreneurs, traders, and *sacoleiros* is generally different from the division of distribution routes and the forms of economic complementarity we observed in the relation with Peruvian Aymaras. Whereas Lima's markets were a prerogative of Peruvian Aymaras, in the case of Brazil, Aymara traders operate as far as the Atlantic coast. In the past few years, forms of clientelization have developed between the Orinoca clan and Bolivian Aymara migrants who have established textile workshops in São Paulo (Hinojosa and Guaygua 2015). Aymara entrepreneurs running textile workshops in São Paulo wholesale garments with a "Made in Brazil" label to Orinoca Aymara traders, who then resell them in Cobija to Brazilian *sacoleiros* and tourists, taking advantage of Brazil's heavy tax discounts on commodities destined for export.[2]

Although supplying relatively small markets[3] in a remote part of the region, through their commercial flows the popular traders in the Amazon basin have created complex and unexpected connections between Pacific harbors on the coast of Chile and China and Brazilian cities on the Atlantic. The same family would run simultaneously binational enterprises operating on the Bolivian and the Brazilian sides. On the Brazilian side, they would entertain commercial relationships with their *caseros* in the cities of the interior and with *compadres* particularly in São Paulo and the Atlantic coast, and on the Bolivian side they would resort to relatives or travel repeatedly to El Alto, Oruro, and Iquique for their supplies (Tassi et al. 2013).

This is happening at a time when the economic integration of the Atlantic and Pacific coasts has become a recurring preoccupation of regional powers. The Initiative for the Regional Integration of South America committee has been promoting mega-infrastructure projects run by large conglomerates and multinational companies in ethnically and ecologically sensitive areas of the region (i.e., the Amazon basin). Using counterintuitive routes, the existing infrastructure, and locally available resources, Aymara family-run businesses are generating highly sustainable forms of commercial integration "from below" and simultaneously producing forms of institutionality in neglected remote areas.[4]

These wide-ranging networks and forms of clientelization also perform the role of managing and updating economic information, a crucial task when operating simultaneously with a variety of countries and currencies. In his work on the bazaar economy in Sefrou, Clifford Geertz (1979) emphasized that one of the major problems of this type of markets with nonhomogeneous products and prices was access to information. In the case of Aymara trade, the networks and the extended and multiple forms of clientelization allow for an impressive flow of information through often informal and unconventional channels and routes. In remote and marginal areas such as the ones I have described, large companies exploiting natural rubber, coffee traders, and landowners had traditionally benefited from local people's lack of access to legal and economic information because they were able to freely impose prices for labor and goods. The heightened mobility of traders, their reticular forms of clientelization, and a specific culture in managing information about different places (see Chapter 6) have given them the capacity to operate simultaneously in a variety of translocal markets, sometimes even displacing conventional economic actors not used to such levels of dynamicity and mobility.

The Aymara Economic Islands in the North of Chile

Despite the recent ban on selling used clothes and the Bolivian authorities' crackdown on illegal imports, the trade in secondhand garments provides a useful tool to visualize the complexity of Aymara economic networks that have turned into genuine chains of supply and distribution involving a variety of different actors. Secondhand clothes are usually either unsold garments or used clothes collected by charities, mostly in the United States, which are then shipped to the South (cf. Brooks 2013). The port of Iquique in the north of Chile is the gateway for secondhand garments. They are stocked in a part of the duty-free zone where they can be bought either in sealed bales—at a price of $100–$120—or per unit. From Iquique, bales are shipped to the Bolivian city of Oruro, either by truck or semihidden in the luggage compartments of buses, along an unpaved mountain road via the high plateau border town of Pisiga.

Iquique has enjoyed a privileged connection with the Bolivian Aymara border regions for centuries (Llanque and Villca 2011; Medinaceli 2011). Caravans of llamas from the highlands of Oruro would travel seasonally to the Chilean mining enclaves on the coast. They would deliver a variety of potatoes, quinoa, and coca leaf but also alpaca textiles and chinchilla fur. They would come back bringing dried meat, fish, and flour for their own consumption as well as charcoal, wine, and Arica textiles that they would later barter or trade in other regions of Bolivia. Since the early 19th century, this ongoing trade has been producing a permeation between the practices of the Aymara ethnic economy (cf. Harris 1982) and the capitalist economy and commodities of the Chilean harbors and coastal towns. Llama herders from the regions of Sabaya and Litoral had been tracing a network of routes and contacts throughout Chile and strengthened their relations with Chilean Aymaras on the other side of the border. Their privileged connection with Chile made the Sabaya Aymaras the natural intermediaries for bringing in the latest commodities and technologies from Chile.

By the time of the decline of the Chilean mining enclaves and the inauguration of the Iquique duty-free zone in 1975, Sabayeños had converted their traditional means of transport into modern trucks and established practices of monopolistic control of incoming trade from Chile to Oruro. Right in the city center of Iquique, Sabayeños had managed to establish an "ethnic island" (cf. Murra 1975 [1972]), an urban area controlled and run by Bolivian Aymara settlers providing services specifically designed to meet the needs of Bolivian traders and truck drivers. As described in an earlier work,

> [t]oday, the smells, accents and aesthetics of the renowned Calle Esmeralda in Iquique remain powerfully reminiscent of the Bolivian highlands. A variety of Alteño travel agencies, Orureño restaurants and Cochabambino hotels have penetrated the area around Calle Esmeralda, becoming attractive points of reference for Peruvian and Paraguayan traders operating in Iquique. This has turned the area into an open air market where commercial and social activities potently intermesh. Even Chilean taxi drivers had to adapt to this overflowing social and economic ferment and to the conventional practices of Aymara traders: instead of using the taximeter, they shout out reduced fares for "shared taxis" between Calle Esmeralda and the duty free zone. (Tassi et al. 2013: 144, my translation)

Similar to Taraqueños and Pacajeños in La Paz, highland Sabayeños still constitute one of the most powerful trading groups in Oruro today. Probably the leading Orureño entrepreneur and former president of the San José Football Club, Walter Mamani, is an Aymara Sabayeño who has made his fortune in the business of secondhand garments. After purchasing goods in Iquique, Sabayeños would use contacts with friends and relatives on both the Chilean and the Bolivian side, either for providing a series of intermediate storage spaces close to the border or for transport along alternative routes avoiding the customs controls. Sabayeño traders' detailed knowledge of the border areas and paths, together with the protection they were granted by local communities fiercely engaged in keeping the authorities at a distance, granted them a comparative advantage in this tax-free import of goods. Once they reached Oruro, the bales of garments would be carefully selected by means of an impressive infrastructure of warehouses, stores, and labor. The selection would produce four different types of clothes, divided according to quality. After the garments are repackaged, some of the quality clothes are sent to the border with Peru, Argentina, Brazil, and high-end boutiques in La Paz and Santa Cruz. Others are sold either on the market or directly from the stores to local retailers who hide the clothes in the luggage compartments of buses and negotiate with policemen at the checkpoints. In the *feria* 16 de Julio in El

Alto, the unions of clothes retailers have on several occasions protested against any attempt by the customs police to check the merchandise and hindered their access to the market.

Whereas Pisiga and the Sabaya region constituted the gateways through which Chilean commodities from Iquique would make their way into Bolivia via Oruro, the border town of Charaña, inhabited by Pacajes Aymaras and on the railway line from the Chilean port of Arica to La Paz, has for years been the main entry point for commodities destined for La Paz. Even today, the fraternity of the Huyustus traders is called "The Travelers to Charaña" since most of these trading families traveled weekly to Chile via the Charaña border for the supply of commodities. They often resorted to Aymara *compadres* on the Chilean side of the border and the most adventurous reached Arica by train where, once they acquired the products, they had them repackaged by Bolivian residents to reduce volumes and escape customs controls. On their nocturnal journey back to La Paz, the travelers chewed coca leaves and smoked cigarettes to keep sleep at bay and to draw protection from saints and spirits. When crossing the border by train, the train slowed down before the customs post to allow traders to unload commodities that local porters would ship across the border by mule.

These dynamics wove together a complex system and a chain of actors involving Bolivian settlers in the Chilean town of Arica, railway workers, customs policemen in Charaña, *piloteros*, storekeepers, and retailers in rural towns as well as traders and shopkeepers in La Paz.

Redefining National Structures of Supply and Distribution

As hinted at previously, Bolivia's economic structure has been often characterized by the mix of disarticulated economic enclaves unable to generate synergies between themselves and also by an insurmountable gap between a capital- and technology-intensive primary economy oriented to the export of raw materials and a labor-intensive "informal economy" of small and microentrepreneurs (Wanderley 2003). In such a context, laws, public policies, and official institutions privileged and promoted the export of raw materials to foreign markets and incentivized the adoption of foreign economic models to the detriment of a local informal economy that needed to be absorbed by large firms and channeled into the right track of development (Casanova 1988; Doria Medina 1988; UNDP 2005). The focus on export and external economic dynamics produced a certain disregard toward internal economic infrastructures and markets as well as an institutionalized lack of awareness of the basic quantities, rhythms, and practices of local supply.

The features of Aymara trade and its networks outlined previously add up a series of counterintuitive elements to such economic analyses. In the first place, Aymara traders had been able to consolidate their presence in multiple remote areas of the country, borders and precarious and isolated roads filling up the holes of the country, economically reconnecting the periphery with the main economic hubs and attenuating the sense of separations among the different regions of the country. Aymara traders rendered visible the emergence of a series of new economic axes connected to the provision of foodstuffs linking the Amazon basin with the Southern valleys or the Pacific with the Atlantic. But also, they outlined a connection between the informal economy of El Alto with the highly mechanized and export-oriented soy production of the lowlands, with Alteño mechanics producing trailers, presses, and mechanic supplies for lowlands agribusiness.

Interestingly, Aymara traders' ability to produce articulations across markets and regions thought to be economically incompatible was not based on conventional marketing recipes but on kinship alliances, family networks, and forms of "social investment" in local actors and institutions. These provided Aymara traders with a comparative advantage in relation to foreign and formal companies—but also official institutions—when operating within the local infrastructural possibilities and limitations, adapting to the local circumstances, and functioning with existing resources. Besides, these networks linking multiple markets and actors—from truck drivers to border policemen—activated sophisticated circuits of strategic information about possibilities and volumes of supply, costs, and demands. Aymara traders not only found themselves in a privileged position for managing and defining practices of local supply and distribution, often displacing the municipality, but also fundamentally were able to define the forms and rhythms through which the economy functioned.

Once culturally and economically articulated with Brazil and geographically and politically disconnected from the Bolivian centers of power, these Amazonian border towns have today been reconnected to the national economy by means of highland traders' networks that are now in charge of the distribution of groceries, garments, and electronics. Interestingly, the multiscale enterprises and the interstitiality of Aymara traders allowed them to shape a national "economic axis" alternative to the official economic backbone that revolved around the cities of La Paz, Cochabamba, and Santa Cruz. Such economic structures and networks not only appeared to make the national economy more complex, generating unexpected synergies between economic spaces that were considered socioeconomically incompatible, but also began to outline an economic system that was national in scope, rooted in the country and not subjugated to the interests of foreign oil companies. Albeit through often-secondary routes and unofficial networks, now it was popular economic actors connecting the different economic hubs, weaving chains of supply and distribution, and developing economic partnerships and institutionalities in remote regions of the country.

These networks, which make use of a variety of actors and groups as well as intermediate settlements along often-neglected routes, based their effectiveness on the capacity to reduce costs by resorting to resources already existing in the territory and the work of multifunctional actors able to engage with the mobility of trade while simultaneously consolidating local forms of institutionality. In this context, besides being unable to afford the multiple costs of accessing these trade routes, large firms are hampered in their operations by a lack of knowledge and information about multiple local markets that popular actors have developed domestically and empirically.

The capacity to operate in the interstices of the economy, the heightened geographical mobility, and the extended networks linking multiple actors and places enable traders both to escape forms of political and economic control from mainstream institutions and to function at a fast economic pace. In a time when governmental and nongovernmental institutions are struggling to understand and implement suitable economic policies in a context of social and political transformations, Aymara networks and mobility endow them with a capacity to constantly get a sense of the country and its economic mood. In fact, as we will also see in Chapter 7, the effectiveness of these multiple articulations engendered circuits of knowledge, information, and connected actors, which displaced the role of the state in economic planning.

What we observe in the case of Aymara traders is a concomitant expansion of their institutionality and their economic reach toward other regions and spaces. This tendency counteracted one of the main problems of the contemporary economic and democratic crisis—particularly in Europe (Habermas 2013)—where the national economies' expansion on a global scale is not paralleled by a concomitant expansion of social and political institutions and popular sovereignty. This gives rise to an increasing disconnect between solid and interconnected global forces and popular sovereignty, exacerbating the inability of the latter to influence global decision making on economic matters.

Conclusions

Bolivia's commercial history has been characterized by and founded on the export of raw materials, from silver and tin to oil and gas. This incentivized the consolidation of an economic structure that neglected the internal market as much as local structures of supply and distribution (cf. Rojas Ortuste 2009). This was partly amended by the 1952 revolution with the state's attempt to regain control of the economy and to invest in infrastructure, know-how, and state-run companies. If at first the revolutionary project was engulfed by the interests of local bureaucrats who used state resources and favors to their own benefit, the neoliberal era dealt a final blow to the nationalist aspirations, widening the gaps with the developed world in terms of industrial knowledge, infrastructure, and public services and exacerbating the economic separation of the different regions. Paradoxically, a series of small entrepreneurs and traders, highly independent and receiving no benefit from state policies, were the ones forging potent though interstitial economic links across the markets of the region and reinvesting locally, building on and reproducing a series of already existing resources and capacities. Their heightened mobility and flexibility not only responded to the requirements of an increasingly globalized world but also built on indigenous structures and practices of multiple domicile based on the articulation of a variety of (socio)ecological zones.

Conventional ideas of development founded on the requirement to generate economies of scale to produce for export or on the import of foreign technology and industrial knowledge to jump-start the economy are repeatedly paralleled by the emergence of a series of local capacities and know-how. Despite its capillary and extended reach, this local knowledge and entrepreneurial activity operates within local infrastructural limitations, economic possibilities, and resources, with the potential to outline practices of economic organization and capital accumulation anchored in the local territory and reality.

The combination of a deep-rooted knowledge of the local territory, culturally specific institutions, and a capacity for geographical mobility and relocation were key elements feeding one of the most surprising achievements of Aymara traders, namely, their articulation with Chinese family-run consortia.

CHAPTER 3

The Chinese Connection:
An Interstitial Global Economy
"under the Radar of the Law"

R amiro Yupanqui first traveled to China in 1994 when he was twenty-eight. At the age of twelve, Ramiro quit school to work in his sister's bakery in the neighborhood of San Pedro on the western slope of La Paz. He was still a teenager when he concluded his first business deal. On the week of the All Saints festivity when the production of bread and pastries massively increased because of the feeding of "visiting souls," Ramiro resold eighty hundredweight of the bakery flour at twice the price. He invested the profit from the deal to travel to Chile for a month, where he repeatedly visited a renowned video games workshop to learn the tricks of assembling and repairing electronic devices. He jotted down in his notebook electronic circuits and codes, characteristics of the electronic components, and the addresses printed on the cardboard boxes of the Taiwanese and Chinese factories providing accessories.

Back from Chile, Ramiro started his own business in his parents' garage, assembling coin-operated video game machines using old TV screens, recycled wood planks, and electronic components brought over from Chile. Right after the hyperinflation crisis of the 1980s, with tens of thousands of workers on the street, Ramiro's was a pioneering and immediately successful business. A few years later, together with Eloy Salmón Choque, his brother, and mother, Ramiro traveled to China to buy video game accessories and technology. The plan was to share the costs and space of the container among the four. At a time when China was still an unknown world, Ramiro's electronic know-how was a valuable commodity because it enabled him to evaluate the quality of the products and avoid fraud. Ramiro did not speak a word of English, but he was able to successfully negotiate with producers and freight forwarders by typing prices and quantities on a calculator. The gang of four followed the route and contacts of other Paceño traders and visited the addresses on the cardboard boxes from the Chilean workshop. However, they engaged in private and individual negotiations with the producers to avoid conflicts and competition over selling strategies. Eventually, they placed a few common orders from four different family-run consortia (*consorcios familiares*), reaching a volume of commodities that could barely fill one small container. At the time, Ramiro could not even imagine that the trip and the business deals with unassuming Chinese entrepreneurs would dramatically reshape his economic and social life.

In the Chinese ports and production hubs, small firms and freight forwarders have established connections tangential to the official economy with kinship networks of Aymara traders, their translocal islands, and commercial strategies. With the consolidation of their bonds with China, Aymara traders were not only taking their elaborate chains of supply and distribution and the investment in their own institutional forms to a new level, but also outlining modalities of interstitial interaction of cultural, economic, and geopolitical relevance.

The Chinese Transformation and Globalization from Below

The latest macroeconomic analyses of the relations between China and Latin America have begun to reflect a certain apprehension as China appeared more and more as an awakening giant, or monster, with the potential to engulf local economies (Gallagher and Porsekanski 2008: 185). If in the beginning China's demand for raw materials to feed its impressive industrial growth and expansion was seen as a blessing for most Latin American countries, more recent and more cautious analyses have begun emphasizing the penetration of a greedy Chinese finance in the region (Gallagher et al. 2012), together with a series of investments uniquely concerned with raw materials. Although there were substantial differences from country to country (León-Manríquez 2010), China was beginning to be seen as deepening Latin America's dependence on primary commodities (Gallagher and Porsekanski 2008), accentuating concerns about the regional "resource curse" and deindustrialization (Gallagher and Porsekanski 2009) as well as about a chronic trade deficit.

But macroeconomic analyses often failed to grasp the counterintuitive dynamics and developments of an economic underworld that directly linked family-run Chinese workshops and Latin American popular entrepreneurs (cf. Aguiar 2012). China was meant to play a crucial role in the economic processes of globalization from below, becoming the source of most small commodities flowing into Latin American, African, and South Asian markets and replacing the United States as the main foreign supplier of consumer goods. A series of reasons have been adduced to explain this state of affairs. Mathews and Alba Vega (2012) mention the abundant and cheap labor force and the work discipline of Chinese factory workers. But there was also a tendency to specialize in commodities that, although they were not particularly glamorous or fashionable, displayed an acceptable quality and appealing price for third world consumers.

Besides a series of economic contingencies that had led China to play a crucial role in the processes of globalization from below, there were a variety of historical and structural features that appeared to facilitate China's role as the world's supermarket and as the supplier of consumer goods for emerging markets. Lin (2011), for instance, points to a deep-rooted *shanzhai* culture—a history of local imitation of conventional commodities that dates back to the 1940s, when small entrepreneurs from Shanghai taking refuge from the civil war in Hong Kong produced and sold unauthorized goods. Other examples are the highly networked and mobile Zhejianese (Xiang 2005) and Fujianese (Chu 2010) migrant entrepreneurs generating innovative and far-reaching forms of articulation between local structures and global possibilities and specializing in the production and trade of "small commodities" (Plietz 2012).

Alan and Josephine Smart (2012) have suggested the seminal role of Hong Kong's small and medium enterprises and "petty capitalists" in fueling the rise of China and its role as the world's manufacturer. This type of actors, simultaneously involved in self-employment and investment, interstitially positioned between capital and labor, market and community, and tied to the Guangdong economy, found themselves operating with a comparative advantage in relation to large enterprises in the fuzzy institutionality of reform China. Relying on their knowledge of both global markets and local conditions, languages, and customs, Hong Kong petty capitalists took advantage of the possibility to strike deals directly with local authorities such as township and village officials, often disregarding formal rules of investment and becoming instrumental in establishing their factories in rural townships in the Pearl River Delta. However, China's official economic policies that sought to promote "national champions" and large global brands and specialize in solid high-tech products were soon to become detrimental to small investors and migrant entrepreneurs.

In the early 1990s, the Guangdong region and the Yiwu fair were the preferred destinations of the pioneering trips of Huyustus and Eloy Salmón traders such as Ramiro. Located on the west coast south of Shanghai, Yiwu was "a world-scale low-price wholesale showroom specializing in the sale of 'small commodities'" (Plietz 2012: 27) such as socks, underwear, toys, costume jewelry, and appliances. In the 1970s, the Chinese attempt to promote forms of industrial specialization through the doctrine of "one town one product" generated a series of small industrial towns often networked through kinship bonds, each specializing in the production of a different type of commodity. With the liberalization of the 1980s, a variety of local producers from the Zhejiang region began coming together with the encouragement of local authorities in the trading city of Yiwu, a small commercial city that by the 1990s had evolved into a wholesale supermarket for traders from the developing world (Plietz 2012; Simpfendorfer 2011).

The articulation of small enterprises mostly run by entrepreneurs of rural origin made the Zhejianese city of Datang the producer of 60% of the world's socks (Sun 2008). Around what were once artisanal workshops, whole "trading cities" were developed that provided the necessary infrastructure, services, and commercial coordination to receive international orders and distribute them among the thousands of local family-run firms. Interestingly, such forms of economic development did not rest on the concentration of capital, but rather allowed family-run enterprises to subsist in a context of rapid market expansion.

The region of Guangdong in the south was host to China's first special economic zone, transforming it into the symbol of Deng Xiaoping's turn to the export economy epitomized by the glowing progress of the cities of Shenzhen and Guangzhou. Their specialization in light industrial and electronic goods (Siu 2007) made it another attractive spot for Aymara traders. The region had benefited from its long-lasting connection with Hong Kong, a major source of investment into China, feeding both an extraordinary demand for labor and the largest inflow of temporary migrants from Chinese regions as diverse as Sichuan, Hunan, and Hubei. However, the increasing demand for labor brought about by the influx of new investments following the opening of the special economic zone clashed with the attempt of the Chinese state to regulate and control the residency of its citizens. Often living illegally in the cities of Guangdong without access to housing, migrant workers found a suitable space to live in the so-called urban villages (*chenzhongcun*)—settlements within the city under the control of village committees that maintained an ambiguous residence status and where the city authorities had limited jurisdiction. It was this socially and legally ambiguous set of conditions that played an important role in fomenting interstitial industrial enterprises (Bach 2010), considered by some (Wang et al. 2009) strategic for the industrialization process.

Already in the mid 1980s, collective farms in the Pearl River Delta had begun turning into joint stockholding companies, with villagers as shareholders and profiting both from housing rented to migrants and light industries built on the collective land. Particularly in Shenzhen, the villages' proximity to Hong Kong had fomented a series of economic links and smuggling practices across the porous border. In fact, most farm families in the area had relatives overseas, either in Hong Kong or in other countries in the region (Wang et al. 2009), expanding their clan-like structure through a series of global business networks. It was this peculiar mix of medium-size family-run enterprises globally articulated through transnational networks of information and relations, goods, and capital that made these firms flexible, effective, and attractive to Aymara traders.

After preliminary trips to the Yiwu and Guangzhou fairs, Aymara traders soon began expanding their radius of operation. Thanks to the know-how of their sons and daughters studying in China or to the Chinese diaspora in Bolivia (mostly from Fujian) who spoke the language and had friends or relatives in the Chinese manufacturing centers, Aymara traders began establishing direct bonds with family-run enterprises (*consorcios familiares*). Located in the booming cities of Shenzhen and Guangzhou, the *consorcios familiares* were often run by the sons and daughters of villagers and migrants who had set up their own workshops or factories, either investing capital provided by overseas relatives and/or—after acquiring the necessary know-how—spending years working in larger compounds. As suggested by Luo Youmin (2012) in the case of Guangzhou textile workshops,

> some people got their own spinning machines and set up workshops in the household. Some workers stole samples from the factories [state-run enterprises] and produced the cloth at a faster rate than the collective factories and launched it into the market even a week earlier. Compared to the collective factories whose bureaucratic system was complicated, the workshops were more flexible and segmented in market. (92)

As in the case of Aymara traders, Chinese *consorcios familiares* appear either to revive or "return to" a series of traditional socioeconomic structures—kinship, clan—overlooked or disparaged by conventional institutions to meet the demands of modern global flows or to take full advantage of their possibilities (Ong and Nonini 1997). Even the requirements of mobility, flexibility, and diversification brought about by a gradual shift in the global economy toward smaller and more adaptable firms are mapped onto local forms, networks, and institutions that were forecast to fade away with the advancement of globalization and modernity.

Far Away but So Close: Socioeconomic Complicities between Aymara Traders and Chinese Family-Run Consortia

When talking about Europe and the United States, Ramiro often referred to these regions as economically and creatively exhausted. According to Ramiro, the exhaustion was a consequence of their lack of creativity when compared to China's capacity to continuously put new, inventive, and cheap commodities on the market and also of their inability to interact with and understand the ferment of new economic actors from emerging markets. Ramiro would defiantly refer to Europe and the United States as the "old world."

For semiformal, popular entrepreneurs such as Ramiro, trading with China offered a series of comparative advantages in relation to trade with the old world. The first advantage was in terms of accessibility (Simpfendorfer 2011). It was simple and quick for a Bolivian trader to get a visa to travel to China—either for tourism or for business: no long and repeated lines from the small hours of the morning, no trick questions in the interviews, and no sense of humiliation when dealing with the embassy authorities. The Chinese visa would be ready one or two days after the presentation of simple and straightforward documents that were easy and cheap to obtain. This suggested that China was actually eager to receive local small traders or "tourists." This openness toward foreign entrepreneurs was also reflected in the "flexibility" in export paperwork required of foreign traders such as Ramiro. Several importers of information technology from the United States had moved either to importing hardware from China that would be later assembled in Bolivia or to buying finished products from retailers in the Iquique duty-free zone because the access and export procedures in the United States were considered too burdensome for small, foreign entrepreneurs.

Despite their rural background and often poor schooling, Chinese producers had a clear understanding of the needs, problems, and typology of the trade in small batches practiced by the Aymara. In some cases, traders would need to squeeze their purchases into one or two suitcases that would then be shipped by "safe" couriers, avoiding going through the United States and therefore reducing the risk of controls. In other cases, they might require identical copies of Argentinean electrical/electronic components, including the engraved inscription "Made in Argentina," at one-third of the price of the original. In addition, these small-scale traders would either need to share the container space or fill it up with a variety of products instead of just one product, as in the case of mainstream importers. The links and kinship bonds between Chinese *consorcios familiares* and local freight forwarders were instrumental in facilitating the shipping requirements of Aymara traders.

The Chinese *consorcios familiares* provided Bolivian traders with a network of contacts and specialized semiformal services ranging from packaging to logistical support, from counterfeiting to assistance with export procedures. Besides these networks of relations and under-the-counter services, the real plus of *consorcios familiares* was their flexibility and ability to readjust production to the requirements of Aymara traders operating in a relatively small market. In contrast to large manufacturers who would often impose standardized products, *consorcios familiares* maintained an impressive receptiveness to the demands of traders acquainted with the requirements of local markets and social sectors.

The other deliberate policy of Chinese producers and forwarders was their willingness to dispatch orders and containers to the most remote ports and customs posts on the planet (Tassi et al. 2013). Whereas freight forwarding companies of the old world would only operate on mainstream trading routes with fewer bureaucratic complications and higher profit margins, Chinese forwarders would often cover intermediate and small-scale routes in third world countries. In Bolivia, this meant that Chinese goods would be able to reach directly a series of intermediate cities that had been booming in recent years because of the revenues from natural gas and the high prices of minerals and agricultural products. Although the three cities of the "central axis" (La Paz, Cochabamba, and Santa Cruz) had been regarded as regional economic hubs through which wealth and commodities would trickle down to the rest of the country, the more capillary form of distribution of Chinese forwarders would benefit a series of local actors and towns, reducing their dependence on these three main cities.

In addition to the willingness of Chinese family-run consortia to negotiate with the unconventional requirements and forms of the Aymara economy, a specific kind of complicity between Aymara traders and small Chinese manufacturers materialized in their scant access to formal education, rural origins, and extended and often international family networks. In La Paz, for instance, Chinese importers and investors were mostly operating and living in the popular neighborhoods on the western slope of the canyon, sharing a series of social spaces and services from markets to restaurants, street stalls to *colectivo* buses associated with the popular and urban indigenous sectors. This posed a challenge to the traditional spatial divisions of the city with its hierarchies and differentiations among indigenous, creole, and foreign spaces. Unlike most foreigners (if we exclude Peruvian migrants in El Alto), Chinese importers appeared unusually comfortable in finding a space to operate their business in the cheap and compact housing of the slope, bargaining for vegetables in the crowded and "unhygienic" popular markets, and moving in those highly dynamic but apparently disordered neighborhoods where foreigners and white-*mestizos* clumsily wandered like "bees without a queen."[1]

More or less willingly, Chinese investors were coopted into the Aymara ritual structure. After collecting his consignments from customs, Mister Qu, a middle-age entrepreneur known as René who resides in La Paz for most of the year, has his "new" commodities "blessed" (*ch'allar*) with alcohol and decorations by local business partners or employees before they distribute them to the local shops. The *ch'alla* is a propitiatory ritual libation where Aymara traders share decorations, food, and drink with their goods to extract from them the highest possible profit but also to "grow together" with them, engendering a communion of destinies and an unexpected interlocking (cf. Allen 1988) between trader and commodities. On a couple of occasions I have witnessed Mister Qu being literally dragged by his employees and the local distributor to take part in the *ch'alla* of new incoming commodities, unwillingly ending up sitting on a beer crate and "drinking with the commodities" in his warehouse surrounded by goods piled on their storage racks. These practices reinforced the association of Chinese entrepreneurs with a specific sector of the urban spectrum from which the elites repeatedly tried to differentiate themselves.

Among popular sectors, a series of recent events are hinting at an increasing interest in, appropriation of, and articulation with Chinese culture.

Andean–Chinese architecture in the Nueva
Alianza-Asodimin market, El Alto.

On the popular TV channel RTP (*Radio Televisión Popular*), the daughter of
Comadre Remedios, a renowned Aymara presenter from El Alto, runs a
weekly TV show about Asian trends, music, cultures, and cuisine. Mainly
aimed at young audiences, Sekay TV also addresses issues of Asian religion,
spirituality, and language in an explicit attempt to generate forms of cultural
articulation between Bolivia and the Asian world. In the neighborhood of
Villa Esperanza in El Alto, a number of Chinese pagodas have spontane-
ously sprung up as decorative elements in public spaces and side streets.
Although they might be a reference to the powerful "Chinese connection" of
local traders, the pagodas are used according to local requirements as spaces
to shelter from the rain, to chain dogs to scare strangers, and even to hang
out clothes to dry.[2] Silvia Rivera (2010b) mentions a textile trader importing
fabric from China who, while fiesta steward (*pasante*) in the high-plateau
town of Guaqui, provided all members of his fraternity with a rattle
(*matraca*[3]) in the shape of the typical and folkloric Chinese peasant to be
displayed during the dance parade. In fact, in the religious celebrations of
Aymara traders, both on the invitation cards and on the dance costumes—
seen as the repositories of local tradition—there has been a mushrooming of

Chinese ideograms and symbols, hinting not only at the Aymara connection with China but also at their appropriation of foreign elements to amplify their ritual system.

The Kinship Mode of Production

Despite the language barrier, the common rural origins and the experience of exclusion from the formal economy appeared to function as bonding elements between Aymara traders and Chinese producers, fostering forms of reliance on their respective traditional institutions, structures, and practices. Similar to urban Aymaras, Chinese small-scale entrepreneurs were often involved in processes of urban migration from other regions and would settle illegally in interstitial urban districts, constituting transitional zones of ambiguous institutionality in processes of rapid transformation of the metropolitan space. Without the benefit of formal administrative support and protection, these actors—often organized by region of provenance—tended to reproduce their own territorialized space in the "urban villages," weaving together informal service networks, establishing market niches, and engaging in collective action to protect their businesses from the intervention of the state (cf. Xiang 2005: 2). Similar to what we have observed in the previous chapters concerning Aymara traders, Chinese entrepreneurs were often forced by forms of social, political, and economic exclusion to consolidate their own forms of institutionality and self-administration (see Chapters 1 and 2). This was constantly associated with practices of sidestepping the state and avoiding contact with it, which consolidated into genuine strategies to circumvent the obstructing actions of formal institutions.

In the previous chapters I emphasized the importance of relations, networks, and forms of clientelization (*relación de casero*) among Aymara traders in a partly informal and concealed economic system. When it comes to the modes of operation of small family-run Chinese firms, a similar system of "circles" and "connections" is embodied by the concept of *guanxi*. A vast literature on the subject has mushroomed in recent years, outlining a system of personal connections defined and regulated by unwritten social and cultural codes, together with honor-based and hierarchical relations of indebtedness (Vanhonacker 2004; Kipnis 1996, 1997; Wank 1996, 2000). *Guanxi* is defined by practices and ritual etiquette through which relationships are "cultivated" and it was originally based on structures such as the family, kinship, and regional filiation. This system of relations often spilled over into economic practices, playing a central role in the assignation of jobs (Knoke 2012) and in generating forms of trust in a context of ambiguous institutionality.

As in the case of the Aymara's, the literature on Chinese kinship networks has been swinging between a tendency to romanticize such bonds or highlight their colonization of the economic field (Pinheiro-Machado 2011) and one that characterized these networks as a way of disguising economic interest as reciprocity (Gao 2011). Particularly in the region of Guangdong, the economic transformations of recent decades have produced a series of radical swings of attitude in relation to kinship bonds. During the years of the cultural revolution, the artisanal and family-run enterprises mostly dedicated to the production of silkworms and often complementary to agricultural activities were the object of a series of reforms aimed at transforming local artisanal enterprises into collective cooperatives and state-run enterprises, severing agriculture from industry and curtailing old feudal traditions—read religion and kinship. With the gradual dissipation of planned policies, the liberalization of trade and production during the 1990s and the emergence of a series of private industrial workshops, the ancient kinship structures reemerged with the task of playing a new role as the socioeconomic backbone of the new economy.

> People generally had the feeling of "return," that is, from a strict constraint under the planned economy to the traditional community's livelihoods and lifestyle, and a return from the national collective life to the life of individuals, families, communities and social relationships. (Youmin 2012: 93)

Not all of these family-run businesses were successful: some fell victim to competitive markets, whereas others were forced to merge with larger and more powerful companies. However, these historical tendencies strengthen the idea that local and flexible cultural networks may represent an effective response at a time characterized by variability, heterogeneity, and mobility. As happened for Aymara traders, this state of affairs reversed the modernist association that identified kinship networks with a remote, localized, and bygone past because they were now seen as crucial tools to cope with the demands and challenges of a modern global economy.

Entrepreneurs with *guanxi* are connoted by a "thick background" (Xiang 2005: 16), namely, people with wide circles of influences and connections. Xiang affirms that despite their lack of official recognition, "big players" with *guanxi* become instrumental arbitrators guaranteeing the reliability and smooth running of economic transactions between partners who are often far away although they belong to the same regional diaspora. Rather than linear and individual connections, this type of bond was essentially "viewed and acted upon as managing clusters of relations" (Xiang 2005: 16) and therefore able to "redress and penalize actions of other parties" (18), stabilizing unofficial forms of control and regulation of economic activities.

In the Interstices of the Global Economy

As in the case of Aymara guilds (*gremios*) and their networks of *compadrazgo*, these social circles, relations, and structures functioned as proper institutions regulating economic transactions and also replacing the state that appears to be challenged in its centralized structure by more mobile and dynamic social institutions. These features tend to outline an economic system operating "under the radar of the law" (Mathews and Yang 2012) in the interstices of the global economy. Whereas Chinese producers elude brand and quality controls and evade production standards and rules of copyright, Aymara traders circumvent customs controls and operate in a series of popular markets where they themselves regulate crime and access. Although informal practices can be observed both at the beginning and at the end of the chain, there is an intermediate part—shipping and transit through ports—that remains governed and monitored by international conventions (cf. Nordstrom 2007). This leads to unexpected articulations between formal and informal practices within global trade flows. In fact, from the time of their production in the Chinese workshops to their consumption in the Bolivian market, the commodities undergo several metamorphoses, shifting repeatedly from licit to illicit circuits, from the informal to the formal economy, and vice versa (Pinheiro-Machado 2008: 126; Neuwirth 2011).

The complicity of operating in the interstices of the global economy and being excluded from participation in the official institutions and economy has engendered a series of extraeconomic practices cementing the articulation between Aymara traders and Chinese family-run consortia. In the case of Aymara traders, in a context of absence of formal contracts, limited proficiency in the local language, and distrust in the authorities, it became crucial to establish certain levels of trust, particularly since they tended to place orders worth tens of thousands of dollars. So they resorted to their most consolidated strategies of reciprocity and gift-giving such as offering preemptive favors and presents to the Chinese entrepreneurs and forwarders and making repeated purchases from the same supplier, even when the prices offered by the competition were lower, thus building up an idea of preference, bonding, and indebtedness. Once again, another "traditional" tool—the logic of the gift (Mauss 1990)—operated as a regulating mechanism at the heart of the global economy.

Traders were particularly attentive in identifying what their supplier might require from Bolivia or what kind of commodities easily accessible in Bolivia were highly appreciated by the Chinese. So, for instance, after an informal conversation with the Chinese supplier about the possibility of a business trip to Bolivia, Ramiro would show up next with a letter of invitation from a Bolivian institution needed to get the visa. Or, in the case of a supplier's brother who could not get a license to open a dentistry practice, a trader resorted to sending him the necessary degree in odontology from a Bolivian university.

Through these practices of reciprocity and selfless actions, Aymara traders attempted to engender a sense of indebtedness in their Chinese counterparts to reduce the risks of fraud, get special treatment from their *caseros*, and even gain access to forms of credit from producers. When visiting China, some traders would stay at the home of their suppliers or freight forwarders, saving money on food and accommodation and enjoying the full Chinese hospitality while gaining access to their hosts' intimate sphere, a practice that was also viewed by traders as a possibility to raise the level of control over the family-run consortia.

Thanks to these practices of indebtedness, the sons and daughters of Aymara traders living and studying in China would find attractive jobs in the freight-forwarding companies, dispatching containers to ports and customs throughout Latin America (cf. Li et al. 2007). Such arrangements appeared to be convenient both for the Aymara "residents" in China—because they would gain expertise in the shipping business—and for Chinese forwarders, who gained firsthand knowledge of the tricks of local customs. This alliance further encouraged practices of underinvoicing that were convenient for both parties because they allowed them to reduce the amount of taxes to be paid to the Chinese IRS and to Bolivian customs, respectively. The consolidation of the Chinese connection together with the entry of their sons and daughters into the shipping business has led a group of Aymara entrepreneurs to begin contemplating the joint purchase of a container ship (Alfonso Hinojosa, personal communication).

The Overlap of Chinese and Aymara Institutionality

The complicities, commonalities, and alliances between Aymara traders and Chinese producers not only gave rise to unconventional economic practices but also engendered an overlap and interaction between Bolivian and Chinese relational circles and networks. Although Aymara traders had been wary of marrying their sons and daughters into the families of the urban elites—either for fear of discrimination or because of the latter's antagonism toward the traders' socioeconomic structures—matrimonial alliances have been springing up between Aymara traders and Chinese producers. Traders' sons and daughters living in Guangzhou and Shanghai were the most exposed to this kind of alliance because they have been acting for years as economic and cultural intermediaries between China and Bolivia. On the one hand, they were alerting relatives in Bolivia about new products suitable for the local market and fostering the penetration of the traders into new areas and domains of the Chinese economy, such as shipping. On the other hand, they constituted an important source of information for Chinese producers and entrepreneurs venturing into unknown markets. However, both the Aymara and the Chinese have a reputation for being strict and traditional when it comes to matrimonial alliances.

In 2012, Justina Aguilar's son David married Meixuan, the daughter of the owner of a medium-size electronics workshop in the Tianhe district of Guangzhou. Originally from an Aymara community on the Tiquina Strait (the strategic point for crossing over to Peru on the shores of Lake Titicaca), Justina is a global trader exporting coarse alpaca wool to China, where she has it threaded and woven before she reexports it to Europe. As often happens among younger generations, David did not specialize in the same line of business as Justina. He preferred to diversify into electronic products and accessories, some of which he assembled in El Alto, although taking advantage of his mother's circles and connections in China. Meixuan is the daughter of an entrepreneur whose family migrated to Guangdong from Wenzhou in the eastern Zhejiang Province during the 1980s but still maintains a strong connection with Zhejiang migrants across China and overseas. Although she is only twenty-three, she speaks Spanish, English, and French and deals with clients from four different continents, thus helping to expand her father's enterprise portfolio significantly.

The wedding was celebrated both in China according to the Confucian tradition and in Bolivia in keeping with Catholic ritual. The social and economic "trickle-down" effects of the wedding were immediate. As per the Aymara tradition, during the wild three-day wedding celebrations the *compadres* and *padrinos*[4] (or relatives) of the bride and the groom were granted specific spaces for mingling and bonding where social interaction overflowed into commercial matters. This not only created a prompt consolidation of bonds of multiple qualities between the two families but also fostered an amplification, overlap, and integration of the various networks and circles to which the two families were connected.

Chinese entrepreneur dancing with Aymara traders.

This interpenetration of different circles and networks becomes a tool to guarantee certain levels of control and safety in an interstitial context overlooked by formal institutions and to allow commerce to occur. In 2010, two Aymara traders were swindled by a Chinese freight forwarder with whom they had engaged in business relations for years. They had placed a series of orders to different consortia and they had dispatched the money to the freight forwarder for him to pay each supplier and collect the goods, simultaneously saving time and money by avoiding multiple payment transactions. It was a large order by local standards because the traders had managed to fill the space of two large containers. After weeks without news about the shipment, the traders began inquiring.

The freight forwarder had lost a considerable amount of money on a bet on the quarterfinals of the football World Cup in South Africa between the Netherlands and Brazil. Brazil was the safe bet, but unfortunately for the freight forwarder, the Dutch staged a miraculous comeback and went on to win the match. Having lost tens of thousands of dollars, he was unable to deliver the goods to Bolivia and went into hiding. The two traders decided to travel to Guangzhou. They went to the forwarder's office, they informed the family and the suppliers what had happened, and, eventually, because the forwarder did not show up, they stood at the gate to the forwarder's company office and outside his house door, holding placards denouncing the swindle in Mandarin and English. The traders were touching on highly sensitive issues: honor, reputation, and nonfulfillment—all elements affecting not only the individual forwarder (Xiang 2005) but also his wider circles and connections, who felt threatened by the possibility of losing business with the Bolivians. The traders had only been there with the placard for a few minutes when the forwarder arrived, explaining that he would ask for a loan from the head of a local consortium to gradually indemnify them. The traders' reaction was similar to what they would have done in a marginal popular market on La Paz's western slope: instead of denouncing the offense to the local authorities, they activated social mechanisms such as circles and networks that regulate the economy and redress and penalize "antisocial" actions.

The overlap, interlocking, and interaction between Chinese and Aymara networks not only wove together an interstitial global economy and institutionality whose meaning and scope had been largely ignored, but also held a powerfully symbolic meaning for these actors. Considered vestiges of a rural localism and backward past, preventing the city from developing in an orderly manner and therefore marginalized, transformed, and screened out from official urban spaces and the formal economy, these economic actors had consolidated impressive global networks and become important players in the dynamics and transformations of the urban space. Destined naturally to become the losers in the unequal "progression" toward the global economy and left largely to their own devices, both in China and in Bolivia these actors transformed marginal urban spaces in emerging industrial or commercial areas by erecting markets and buildings (known in China as "handshake" or "kissing" buildings) with concrete shells on the ground floor for shops and workshops (cf. Bach 2010: 429). On the one hand, these dynamics spelled out the exclusive or unequal nature of processes of modernization and "integration" with the market. On the other hand, they suggested a remodeling of these spaces of exclusion often based on local devices that outline proactive ways to participate in and experiment with the global economy.

In Bolivia, the strategic alliance between Chinese family-run consortia and Aymara traders came to highlight important challenges to conventional economic knowledge and socioeconomic hierarchies between urban economic experts and Aymara traders of rural origin. The formal associations of entrepreneurs in La Paz connected with the urban elites promoted a type of articulation with China aimed at attracting investment by large Chinese firms. As we have seen, Aymara traders were not only exporting Bolivian products and outsourcing to China to reexport to a third country; they were also utilizing Chinese technology to manufacture goods locally and export these goods themselves to the region. While the Bolivian entrepreneurial elite continued to foster interventionist economic models that could improve and modernize from the outside a backward and unsuitable production system, Aymara traders forged multiple and more horizontal alliances with foreign partners in the attempt to consolidate and expand the local economic structure. In so doing, Aymara traders developed a much more intimate knowledge of global flows and processes, their dangers and possibilities, inequalities and interstices, and eventually much more grounded politicoeconomic tactics to deal with them.

A New Type of Consumption

The social and cultural symmetries and overlaps between Chinese family-run consortia and Aymara traders seem to also extend to a series of economic domains and practices. The translocal circles described in the previous sections appeared to materialize interstitial but global economic modalities. In fact, in the convergence between the inflow of Chinese goods and the increased purchasing power of the local popular sectors, a new type of consumer goods seems to be taking shape. Rather than goods of well-known brands, certified products, and the latest available technology, the popular sectors have been aiming at Chinese commodities with lower prices and acceptable design and performance (Mathews and Yang 2012), which often meant brandless goods or imitations of the mainstream brands.

Aymara traders found in these cheap and copied commodities an opportunity to compete with conventional traders, both national and foreign, that had traditionally neglected products and forms of consumption suitable to popular sectors. In fact, several Aymara traders used cheap Chinese commodities strategically to create their own market niches, displacing conventional traders and enterprises.

Most importers from the Eloy Salmón and the Huyustus markets had created their own brands of electronics produced by *consorcios familiares* in Guangdong and Zhejiang according to the requirements of local consumers, with their own logo stamped both on the product and on the box (Tassi et al. 2012). For an Aymara trader, the creation of his/her own brand, often coinciding with the setting up of an import firm, was generally seen not only as a personal achievement but also as a possibility to define your own marketing strategies and typologies of product, avoiding the interferences of mainstream trademarks in relation to production standards and commercialization. Electrical goods traders would provide their Chinese partners with the design of specific accessories and technical improvements to be implemented on the final product. *Consorcios familiares* were keen on these suggestions because they allowed them to enhance the product and expand their market.

Local popular consumers have a particular skill for immediately identifying and recognizing both the technical characteristics and the appearance of a brand or product to the point of stupefying the external observer (see Chapter 5). The consumer had a clear understanding that popular local brands of electrical goods produced in China were "fake"—they are commonly referred to as "copies"—however, popular consumers did not stigmatize them. This multiplication of brands encouraged the local consumer to question not only the value and authenticity of the "original" (Juan Manuel Arbona, personal communication) but also the aura of allegedly unachievable technological features of conventional brands that could be reproduced by entrepreneurs with hardly any formal schooling.

For a large portion of popular sectors, well-known and original brands are not necessarily a symptom of status or an expression of modernity and participation in the global flows. Despite their economic achievements and to differentiate themselves from the middle class, traders would not position themselves as consumers of mainstream brands. In fact, they would often employ disparagingly the word *jailón* (a Spanish transliteration of the English words "high" and "long") to strategically emphasize the concern with brands and the performative consumption patterns of the high class as well as their foreignness in relation to local forms and practices.

Most mainstream trademarks have neglected the specificities of local trade and markets, based on the assumption that third world local consumers would imitate and mold their practices of consumption to the patterns defined by first world middle classes. In fact, trademarks were often reluctant to invest resources in research and new products to satisfy the demand of local markets with supposedly scant purchasing capacity and little prestige. The complicity between Aymara traders and Chinese family-run consortia brought onto the market new products that were suited to the aspirations of a type of consumer acting outside of the radar of mainstream trademarks and fostering local economic logics.

In several cases, the availability of cheap materials from China encouraged traders to set up light workshops in El Alto to carry out the last tasks in the production process before the end commodity. Several aluminum pot importers distributing their products to the retailers of popular markets began installing their own workshops to cut and laminate aluminum imported from China and create their own brands of pots made in Bolivia. Silveria had begun importing motorcycle parts from a producer friend in China. She had calculated that in a large container she could barely fit ninety assembled motorcycles, but she could fit three times more bikes in a disassembled state. Besides, importing disassembled motorcycle parts enabled her to save almost one-third in customs taxes. Silveria's nephew, Vladimir, had set up a small assembly workshop with five or six workers and created a flashy brand with the family name on it saying "Made in Bolivia." He fantasized that TV channels would come to publicize the first brand of Bolivian motorcycles and the workshop producing them and that President Evo would inaugurate his workshop in the same way that he goes to consecrate newly installed state-run factories and enterprises across the country.

In the 1970s, middle-class Bolivian traders imported parts of Ford vans from the United States that they would later assemble in the country. However, far from substituting Ford with a local brand, they would simply save on the labor costs required in the assembly operations, selling and marketing the vans as a legitimate and authentic Ford product. In the past, large brands and enterprises such as Ford were often able to impose certain forms of consumption from above because of their control of the market, availability of resources, and marketing capacity. What we are observing now is the strengthening of a commercial sector that, through a series of alliances with Chinese family-run consortia, has been able to define their own marketing strategies and rhythms of supply, to add the brand at different stages of the chain of production, and to foster local patterns of consumption, thus democratizing access to commodities for a set of consumers whose aspirations had traditionally been neglected (Tassi et al. 2013: 175–176).

Studies on consumption practices have often highlighted a series of unexpected meanings, resignifications, and rationales involved in the act of consuming conventional commodities and brands (cf. Miller 2012, 2009). What I try to suggest here is a proactive effort by these popular sectors to make commodities more accessible and suitable to their needs and aspirations through the proliferation of local brands as well as through strategic and horizontal alliances with Chinese family-run consortia.

The Other Path(s) of Globalization

The symbolic importance and practical impact of Chinese *consorcios familiares* for the Bolivian popular economy is effectively illustrated by the case of Bolivian fabric importers. The area of La Paz and El Alto is renowned for its festive and ritual activities where popular sectors "premiere" (*estrenar*) their uniform and individually tailored suits and *pollera* dresses every year. In addition to indicating belonging to the same guild or fraternity, such uniform outfits assert a collective expression of status according to local codes and aesthetics clearly differentiated from the style and taste of the urban elites. This feeds a complex system of popular tailors, *pollera* designers, and fabric sellers located in urban areas such as the western slope of La Paz or the 16 de Julio in El Alto, supplying a variety of customers ranging from rural settlers to Aymara migrants in Buenos Aires and São Paulo.

Until a few decades ago, the material for *polleras* and suits was imported from Europe by a German dealer who brought over suitable fabric available on the market (Diego Muñoz, personal communication). With the boom of Chinese family-run consortia, popular Paceño designers began sketching fabric patterns that were either sent over to the *consorcios familiares* to be produced or digitized by members of the local Chinese diaspora in La Paz and sometimes by intermediaries in Iquique. Simultaneously, in China the sons or daughters of Bolivian traders would monitor the newest types of fabric coming out on the market, sending photographs and samples home. In September in La Paz, stewards of the Gran Poder fiesta begin approaching fabric importers and designers to choose and negotiate the type of fabric, the color, and the patterns of the outfits to be premiered during the celebration of the Holy Trinity the following May or June. The orders they place are usually massive. In the case of the largest fraternities, the fabric required amounts to 500 suits, 1,000 *pollera* skirts, and 1,000 shawls (women wear two different types of dresses—*paradas*—during the celebrations). The negotiations over the fabric are generally quick and take place in a completely secretive environment with the participation of the steward's family, the importer, and mutually trusted tailors and designers. The outcome of these negotiations defines the popular fashion trends for the following year. Usually before December, the order,

Premiering dancing outfits in the Gran Poder festival. Photo courtesy of Juan Yupanqui Rodríguez.

patterns, and fabrics are forwarded to the Chinese producers, who return the end product by the following May.

The urban Aymara world, with its traditional and distinctive taste for quality fabric and decorative patterns, has paradoxically found an ally in the Chinese *consorcios familiares*. Clearly, it is not all rosy. Several local entrepreneurs (particularly clothes producers) have found themselves competing with Chinese commodities produced on a larger scale and with lower costs. However, Chinese producers were offering Aymara traders the possibility to reproduce local aesthetic forms and to generate "alternative fashions," in contrast to traditional importers who tended to bring over the conventional modern trends from Europe.

This situation leads to a paradoxical or maybe just counterintuitive articulation between local and global spaces where the affirmation of Andean practices and symbols par excellence—such as the *pollera* skirt—is engendered through transnational alliances. But this is also a situation where a symbol of oppression and exclusion par excellence such as the *pollera* skirt is turned into a fashion item, defining other possibilities of being Bolivian that do not imply renouncing local ethnic self-representation (cf. Van den Berghe and Primov 1977) and demonstrating a pattern of social affirmation on their own terms.[5]

A similar example is provided by the emergence of neo-Andean architecture, particularly in El Alto. Although inspired by strongly Aymara, pre-conquest motifs and patterns and transformed into a unique modality of social and status expression by ascending Aymara entrepreneurs, the neo-Andean architecture relies heavily on materials produced by Chinese *consorcios familiares* (Arbona et al. 2015). Most of the neo-Andean architects not only have their decorations produced by Chinese *consorcios familiares* but also import plaster sheets for ceilings and walls that are reconditioned and embellished in their local workshop to better fit Aymara aesthetics. In other words, Chinese products, elements, and patterns are introduced into the local expressive system with the intention of amplifying a local cultural horizon.[6] If Chinese products and commodities are often represented as displacing local economic forms and cultures, what we observe here is a tendency to appropriate them in (re)defining and expanding a cultural horizon that is distinctively "Andean" or even "Aymara."

These apparently marginal dynamics and alliances have important economic and even geopolitical consequences. In the mechanics' workshops of El Alto, local manufacturers take advantage of the flexible production systems of Chinese family-run consortia by sketching technical improvements to be implemented both on tools such as drills and grinding wheels and on metal products used in the assembly of trucks. Such technical improvements are negotiated with the Chinese manufacturer by fellow Aymara importers who also test the interest of other workshops in the new tools or products to make the technical improvements cost-effective. In this way, foreign technology is adapted to local knowledge and to local specificities and limitations (Arbona et al. 2015), such as the requirements imposed by a rough road infrastructure that demands special shock absorbers for trucks or resistant wheel rims. The direct link between small Chinese manufacturers and local workshops highlights an interstitial possibility of ceasing to think of technology and know-how as universal commodities trickling down from the more to the less advanced in a linear process of uniformization of knowledge. In fact, through their connections with Chinese family-run consortia, popular economic actors manage to develop and extend local forms of know-how and enterprise, complexifying the assumption of China as the powerhouse responsible for the deindustrialization of Latin America.

An important geopolitical consequence of the direct link between Chinese family-run consortia and Aymara traders is a series of new trade routes and practices that circumvent Miami and its role as an intermediate hub between South East Asian companies and Latin

American retailers (cf. Rabossi 2012). For the former, Miami constituted a safe and secure point for the sale of their goods providing specific services for foreign investors, guaranteeing clear commercial
regulations and the capacity to enforce them. Many Asian companies
preferred to limit their commercial operations to Miami instead of
dealing directly with Latin American retailers in their own countries,
given the "uncertainty" of doing business locally and their lack of familiarity with local customs.

Simultaneously, Miami represented a first world attraction for Latin
American middle classes lured by the lifestyle and economic opportunities of the north. These middle classes operated as intermediaries between
Asian companies and Latin American retailers, usually because of their
capacity to understand and cope with the two different ways of working
and socioeconomic dynamics. In addition, these intermediaries acted as
key—although often informal—financial operators with the ability to provide credit services to Latin American retailers and to collect their payments, thereby facilitating the Asian companies' business. This often
resulted in the emergence of a series of "gate openers" in Miami defining
which Asian products would be marketed in which Latin American country (David Zung, personal communication).

Similar to the case of Singapore (Tagliacozzo 2011), Miami and its
intermediaries, as well as Taiwanese and Hong Kong companies, began
losing part of their business because of the direct connections between
Latin American retailers and small Chinese producers. On the one hand,
this appeared to transform the practices of doing trade between Latin
America and Asia, highlighting new dynamics, services, and synergies.
On the other hand, small economic actors operating globally such as
Aymara traders or *consorcios familiares* now appeared to have a say on
the type of products, trade routes, and business agreements involved in
global flows.

The heightened velocity of this interstitial global economy (cf.
Pinheiro-Machado 2008) was either the cause of or an instrument enabling Chinese family-run consortia and Aymara enterprises to cut
off, in some cases, established intermediaries. The often-informal arrangements of their enterprises enabled them to skip lengthy and
formal bureaucratic processes. Instead of operating through the official business networks, they often preferred to invest in personal and
trusted relations that, given their flexibility, guaranteed a heightened
velocity of response and a faster access to strategic information often
denied to them by official business circles. Eventually, their capacity to

circumvent both bureaucratic procedures and barriers of access facilitated international operations and reduced the costs of transactions.

Thinking the World from the Margins: Change and Continuity in an Interstitial World-System[7]

One of the key tensions throughout this chapter is the concomitance between a series of culturally specific practices and a variety of new commodities and markets that either presuppose forms of cultural expansion or challenge cultural integrity. In particular, how is the annexation of new territories, frontiers, and commercial partnerships into the orbit of Aymara traders conceptualized, understood, and signified?

The question that I am interested in here is how the Aymara have been reading and understanding the process of expansion of their radius of operation to the manufacturing centers of China, but also how they have proceeded to resignify spaces and sociocultural practices that were supposed to disappear with the advancement of modernity. Traders' participation in the global economy and their Chinese connection are paired by forms of simultaneous revival or consolidation of traditional practices and structures. These operate either as instruments of protection against uncontrollable external processes or as tools enabling them to cope with the mobility and flexibility demanded by global capitalism. These modalities of continuity within change (Robbins and Wardlow 2005) outline a specific conceptualization and transformation of, as well as connection to, external processes, which often crystallizes in the ritual practices of Aymara traders.

One of the most important religious festivals for urban Aymara traders, particularly those in the Huyustus market, is the Sacred Heart of Jesus, celebrated in the border town of Charaña in the high *puna* on the border with Chile, about a seven-hour bus ride from La Paz.[8] As we have seen, Charaña is the border town through which most of the commodities coming in from Chile are smuggled into the country by intrepid traders. The image of the Sacred Heart of Jesus itself arrived by train from Italy to Charaña in a wooden box, but it was treated by customs authorities as contraband and therefore confiscated. As in the case of many other images in the Andes, the Sacred Heart constituted the link and pathway that articulated the local world with the center of Catholicism—the Pope, Rome, and its political and economic power more widely (cf. Sallnow 1989). In Charaña, it is common to hear people addressing the Saint as a "stranger" (*forastero*). This is not only because the image originally came

Bolivian customs in Charaña. Note the Sacred Heart Chapel with the silver cross next to customs on the right-hand side of the barrier.

from Italy but also because it constantly negotiates with people and goods coming from other parts of the world.

People say that the house of the Saint is the border (*su casa frontera es*) and a chapel of the Sacred Heart is located on the exact borderline between the two countries, facing the customs barrier, as if the Saint were in charge of opening and closing the way through. During the 2010 festival, urban traders brought from La Paz a replica image of the Sacred Heart wearing military uniform since the Saint was in charge of patrolling the border.

The practices around the Sacred Heart of Jesus on the Chilean border give us a hint about the question of how Aymara traders reconcile manufactured commodities produced on a large scale in China coming into the country across the border and entering ethnic circuits with clearly defined religious patterns such as the ones I have described. Having become a protector of importers and smugglers—people in both Charaña and La Paz affirmed that failing to celebrate the Saint would lead to being detained by customs and having your goods confiscated—the Saint was the element enabling the articulation/transition from one domain to the

Image of the Sacred Heart with military uniform.

other and connecting different zones/countries and economic logics. As we have seen, sanctuaries signaled the passage (and integration) of different ecological zones. In the case of the Sacred Heart, the sanctuary embodies the passage and integration of different ontological domains and the articulation of the local with the global while simultaneously being an instrument of protection, expansion, and appropriation of foreign wealth and power.

One of the fundamental principles of the Aymara cosmology is to continuously "link up" with different spaces and territories to expand their contacts, trade networks, and spiritual pathways. The Aymara tend to perceive these acts as spatial and cosmological extensions, forms of physiological and physical "growth" of bodies, spirits, and territories that are accompanied by a series of often complex strategies—political, economic, and religious—to establish and consolidate control.

Material and technological transformations among successful Aymara traders, as well as the expansion of their radius of operation, are continuously paired by an expansion of cosmological forces. I have explained elsewhere how this is not a process of reflection (Tassi 2013), as Plato would have it, but rather a consequence of the ongoing communication and exchange between material worlds and cosmological forces. Today, for instance, the *Pachamama* is thought to be the mother earth and owner not only of rural produce but also of urban houses—originally made from adobe, therefore of earth—and consequently to control the real estate market and protect the presidential palace. In the case of the *Tío* (Taussig 1980), the God of the underground, from being the simple owner of raw materials it has become the entity in charge of money and controlling bank vaults and also the owner of cars and electronic commodities such as computers, flat-screen televisions, mobile phones, and refrigerators. Mass-produced objects are here integrated into a local system of production that is based on the continuous and fluid connection, exchange, and reflection among the human, divine, and material worlds (see Chapter 4).[9]

These practices outline a model of social transformation where the changes in artifacts, spaces, and territories produced by the Aymaras' involvement in the global economy and their Chinese connection are paired with a degree of creative continuity and expansion of cultural forms. Global artifacts and transnational spaces are not only resignified but also anchored into preexisting forms, beliefs and practices, networks, and institutions, "expanding" them and magnifying their reach and meaning. Thus, trucks replace llamas as a means of transport and flat-screen televisions replace potatoes as the new commodities, but they eventually remain embedded in ritual forms and structures, generating a sense of continuity within change. As we have already observed in the forms of appropriation of urban commercial space, these modalities of transformation engender practices of appropriation of external, "foreign" elements, spaces, and powers that are meant to consolidate and expand existing structures and practices.

Conclusions

If modernity and development for indigenous peoples had once been framed in terms of rupture or as a "new dawn" of freedom from the constraining chains of tradition (cf. Keane 2007), the relations between Chinese family-run consortia and Aymara traders outline modalities of modernization and development that feed on traditional structures, practices, and institutions but are also anchored in strategies of stretching those interstices to which they have been relegated both by dominant global forces and by mainstream institutions. In fact, Aymara traders' engagement with Chinese manufacturers takes to its geographic extreme the articulation of interstitial translocal spaces I have described previously. Interestingly, Aymara traders conceive of such transformations not so much in terms of modern "development" but as forms of geographical expansion and prolongation of those same economic, social, and institutional interstices they already inhabit. As we have seen here and will expand on in the next chapter, with varying degrees of success, global artifacts and Chinese connections are perceived as tools in a constant battle to access the market on their own terms.

CHAPTER 4

"Revolving Capital": Aymara Cosmoeconomics in Global Trading Practices[1]

In the previous chapters we observed how a series of historically rooted Aymara social structures and organizations have been able to guarantee ingenious forms of regulation and control of access to the market and more recently to keep at bay state authorities and foreign entrepreneurs who may obstruct the functioning of the local power structure. This same local institutionality, strategically articulated with global flows and partners and organized according to culturally specific patterns, has also been instrumental in enabling the continuous production of ideas about the economy and the market, value, and wealth. Without underestimating the capacity of the global economy to produce forms of exclusion and subordination, in this chapter I will explain how the Aymara have continued to produce conceptualizations of exchange, wealth, and relations that resulted in the carving out of creative spaces and economic techniques, highlighting a pattern of participation in modernity and the global economy that is conspicuously Aymara.

The Social Meanings of the Market and Trade

In Europe, the "commercial revolution" and the rise of powerful families of traders such as the Medici in Florence or the Doria in Genova were associated with cultural and social processes of secularization and rationalization (Le Goff 1980, 1982). Merchants' accounts, bookkeeping, and calculations were instrumental catalysts in the societal transition toward recording information by means of writing and in the emergence of instruments of calculation such as abacuses and counting frames. The spread of international trade was the turning point in the transition from religious education to secular schools (Le Goff 1982), which responded to the knowledge needs of a guild requiring detailed and reliable cartographic and geographical information, language, and calculation skills. But probably the most significant transformation in these new trends was the gradual abandonment by the church and religion of its role of defining the rhythms and the boundaries of social life and its withdrawal to a transcendent spiritual domain (Dumont 1977). Jacques Le Goff (1980, 1982: 132–133) brings up the question of time and the trader's need to measure time as opposed to the Church's lax attitude about this domain, conceived as a prerogative of God, and its calendric system based on mobile festivities without fixed references. This implied a shift in the regulation of urban life where the secular clock of the city council (often managed by trade guilds) replaced the church clock.

In the Southern Andes, the precolonial lack of trade and markets (Murra 2002) was replaced by forms of "direct access" to a variety of products guaranteed by kinship networks and settlements located in different ecological zones (Salomon 1985). In a northern peripheral area of the Inca Empire identifiable as the current border between Ecuador and Colombia, Frank Salomon (1986) mentions the existence of a system of long-distance traders referred to as *mindaláes* dealing in sumptuary goods and politically sponsored by the aboriginal lords they supplied. *Mindaláes* specialized in the acquisition of lowland and distant products of markedly exotic origin while groups of smaller traders employed by local chiefs dealt with nonsumptuary goods, generating an exchange of the surpluses coming from different ecological zones. This economic structure produced a system of local markets (*tiangueces*), typically located at the border between ecological zones, where a variety of goods from the highlands and lowlands converged. Inevitably, such a configuration reflected the system of shrines and ceremonial sites related to passes and striking features of the landscape, where political authorities and travelers used to perform sacrifices and pour libations to ensure the fertile relations between lowlands and highlands (Platt 2009). Like shrines and sanctuaries, *tiangueces* play the role of connecting different ecological zones, plots, and families scattered around the territory and ensure a fecund relationship and articulation between these spaces and people. Such territorial connections and relations were in fact associated with reproduction—both material and cosmological—to the point that exchange and transactions across these spaces acquire a generative power.

The economic role of *mindaláes* remained entrenched in cosmological meanings, ceremonial practices of exchange, and forms of redistribution of wealth so as to build political influence. In the Southern Andes, the absence of markets before the Conquest (Murra 2002; cf. Salomon 1986) made the *tambo* into the main economic institution. The *tambos* were state-administered stores of products disseminated across multiple ecological niches. Local groups would provide labor for running the *tambo* in a system that reciprocated the provision of work for the state with an important degree of autonomy and the recognition of local authorities (cf. Harris et al. 1987). The *tambo* constituted the articulation of a network of stone paths, stores, and taverns disseminated throughout the territory, allowing the connection of different ethnic domains and ecological zones and the circulation of products and people. As the space embodying such circulation, the convergence of different places, and the articulation of local chiefs with the wider state, the *tambo* was invested with a particular cosmological power that was constantly fertilized and reproduced through ritual. This system of paths for the circulation of goods and people worked like arteries, allowing the movement of the body state (Arnold and Yapita 1998). In other words, the *tambo* was a kind of transplanted epicenter (Arnold and Yapita 1998) of different territories enabled by the convergence of different groups and of productive forces—identified with pack animals and goods but also spiritual forces that still today are acknowledged as the protectors of trade centers and markets.

Such configurations point to a conceptualization of an economic space such as the *tambo* and successively the market as exceeding its circumscribed location and its mere economic function, continuously transcending into social and religious domains as a center of convergence of cosmological forces with a performative meaning. As we shall see, the idea of wealth likewise acquires the connotation of a process that includes forms of personal growth and accumulation but also implies spatial/cosmological extensions that go beyond the self and articulate with other domains (cf. Munn 1986). In the previous chapters we have seen how local beliefs and practices operate at the heart of the global economy. Rather than being overcome by rational economic knowledge, ritual and ritual specialists (*yatiri*) had become valuable tools to strengthen local institutionality and to deal with risk and novelty in the complex field of the global economy. In fact, *yatiris* have undergone a process of refinement and specialization. Those who were able solve robberies, predict the outcome of investments abroad, and effectively speed up the growth of local businesses would put together rosters of hundreds of "patients." Simultaneously, cosmological forces were also transforming and expanding their scope of operation to secular, economic, and mundane domains from which an increasingly transcendent church had withdrawn.

The Economic and Religious "Spheres"

In the Andes, relations between local animism and the Catholic religion have often been tense and contradictory.[2] The overlap I have described between religious and economic values and practices in the forms of Aymara trade has been traditionally and instrumentally utilized by the custodians of urban propriety and morality (read the church, official institutions, and the middle class) either to downplay Aymara traders' economic achievements or to question the authenticity of their religious practices. In both cases, the articulation of economic and religious elements was identified with an unaccomplished stage of modernization. In La Paz, the economic emergence of Aymara traders has been paralleled by the expansion of their ritual cycle and practices and by a mushrooming of their religious celebrations and dance parades. Such an expansion in the popular neighborhoods of the city has been so blatant and powerful that it has started threatening some of the most deep-rooted conceptions and spatial hierarchies erected by the white elites and conventional institutions.

The ritual excesses and performances of abundance during the urban dance parades went largely unappreciated by the urban elites and the Catholic Church as they clashed with the sense of propriety, parsimony, and moderation (Le Goff 2003), which supposedly embody the fundamental values of the Christian middle class. Besides, when judged from the perspective of the market, where audacity, self-interest, and the maximization of profit are paramount values, those performances of abundance were seen as a loss of important reinvestment capital and a symptom of an inability to reinvest rationally.

At a time when these emerging popular sectors were usurping the role of the church in the definition of the ritual calendar, the Catholic clergy has discursively begun attributing a kind of incompleteness, unviability, and limitation to the religious practices of Aymara traders. Not only are the latter seen as fomenting an atavistic form of popular religion (cf. Orsi 2005), which beyond mere appearances remains animist at heart, but also they do not seem to grasp the basic dogmas of the Catholic doctrine. For instance, popular traders are considered devoted churchgoers who fail to understand the motives and the rationale of the Mass. They attach great importance to the priest's blessing with holy water, to ostentatious dance and musical performances for the Lord, and to the food offerings they make to him, but they do not quite seem to grasp, or to practice, the official rituals of the Catholic religion. According to the clergy, the subtle and counterintuitive nature of dogmas such as the Holy Trinity and Communion are commonly "distorted" or "misunderstood." For instance, to believe that Christ is actually "represented" in the wafer—as several Catholic priests suggest—requires such a sophisticated leap of faith that most urban indigenous people are put off by the challenge.

Interestingly, Aymara traders perceive a risible sense of incompleteness and limitation in the practices, systems, and discourses of the "enlightened" urban elites and the official church. As recounted by Don Daniel, a *yatiri* and a leader of a butchers' trade union, one of the main drawbacks of the Catholic God is the fact that he does not possess money (*Dios no tiene plata*) (cf. Taussig 1980). Some years ago, when working in an Aymara community by Lake Titicaca, I noticed that a similar sense of incompleteness was often attributed to traditional Catholic figures. Jesus, for instance, was central to the calendric system and religious activities of the community. However, it was often mentioned as a downside that Jesus died without having left any progeny. He did not marry and reproduce. To account for God's incompleteness, Don Daniel explained that God's most powerful angel, which he called *Sat*, was the owner of money. If the Catholic doctrine had created a sense of antinomy between the law of God and the law of Sat(an), these two figures coexisted harmoniously in the thought and practice of most urban dwellers.

One of the favorite anecdotes of my fieldwork is the pilgrimage of some friends, traders in domestic appliances, to the Sanctuary of the Virgin of Urqupiña (Virgin of the Mountain), also known as the "moneylender Virgin" (Giorgis 2004). As modern pilgrims, they traveled to the Sanctuary of Quillacollo by airplane and, as is typical of such pilgrimages, they "borrowed money" from the Lady. This money was actually stones dug up from the ground around the Sanctuary and brought back home, where they were carefully stored and looked after so as to speed up the process of their materialization into real monetary wealth. The following year, on the day of the Virgin of Urqupiña, my trader friends traveled back to Quillacollo, with their hand luggage filled with stones, to return the money to the Virgin. As in a proper financial transaction, they returned the money, after a year of loan, with the necessary "interest," which consisted of real money deposited in the Sanctuary.

Among Aymara traders, money and its circulatory capacity, conceived of in terms of not only reproduction but also interest and debt (cf. Harris 1989), become relational tools to connect with both social[3] and religious domains. On the one hand, these dynamics compel us to acknowledge how global economic practice, thought to be purified of a remote past, is still imbued with nonmodern forms and beliefs (cf. Maurer 2005). On the other hand, we are forced to look at Aymara traders' worldview as an economic project per se rather than an unaccomplished and volatile stage in a linear transition towards "real" capitalism and modernity. The contrasting worldviews outlined above tend to highlight different understandings of the relationship between the economy and religion, the market and morality, cosmology and modernity. The usual boundaries and oppositions that late capitalist societies tend to create between the different moral values of public and private spheres—the latter associated with family, solidarity, religion, and charity and the former with competition, self-interest, profit, and commodities (Carrier 1995; Parry 1986)—are

"Cash box" in an electrical goods shop in the Eloy Salmón.

constantly blurred by Aymara traders' practices. In their indigenous economy gone global, not only do kinship networks and religious values permeate economic domains, but also economic values, financial interest, and money transactions enter the sphere of the family and religion without necessarily deconstructing it.

Aymara Cosmoeconomics: The Concepts of Circulation and Abundance

One of the most recurrent features of ethnographic descriptions of the Andean region has been the portrayal of an interconnectedness, or rather a fluid enlacement, among the features, qualities, and appearances of sacred, human, and material worlds. Bastien's (1985) description of the *Pachamama* (the Andean Mother Earth) as a hungry human body carved on the landscape suggests a physical and immanent relation between the nonordinary domain and the human. The *Pachamama* is not only materially fed but also asked for permission whenever the plough or bare hands "touch" her body/ ground. Economic activities such as agriculture, therefore, cannot be simply conceived of as economic means to guarantee people's material survival; rather, they are inherently interwoven with the expression of people's identity and with the necessity to make the earth live (Gose 1994). Similarly, religious practice and ritual ceremonies may be associated with or aimed at the production or "multiplication" of the family business, while relations and exchanges with spiritual forces may be framed in economic and financial terms such as "paying," "loan," or "interest."

For Aymara traders, relations with the divine are mostly mediated by a series of complex food and material offerings, feeding being both a way to placate the insatiable hunger of God and spiritual forces and a tool in communicating a request, because such offerings imply an explicit invitation to reciprocate the gift. As much as dancing, offering still implies a reciprocal dynamic where the worshipper offers (*convida*) or pays (*paga*) something to the spiritual forces and at the same time "shares" (*comparte*) with them. Sharing is here intended in a literal sense as a communication of powers and bodies among celebrants and spirits and is expressed by the action of eating, drinking, or smoking "together with" such forces as they come to consume the offering.

The Material and the Spiritual in Ritual and Economic Practice

The most common form of offering is the so-called *mesa*,[4] a round plate piled with a number of sweets of different shapes (*misterios*), fruits, herbs, colored wool, and llama fat—or even fetuses—wrapped with a sheet of paper and a woolen ribbon that is arranged by a *yatiri* on a bed of firewood. Sweets with different drawings, forms, and meaning are both instruments that satiate the hunger of the spiritual forces and specific references to the desires/requests (*pedidos*) of the worshipper. Requests might be "strengthened" by placing a carbon-copied sheet of paper with a written list of *pedidos*, a practice reminiscent of bureaucratic documents and forms of interaction/communication with formal institutions. The carbon-copied paper can be spread with honey on its written side to sweeten up the requests and "attract" the spirit before the *mesa* is burned.

Traders tend to place in the *mesa* sweets in the form of U.S. dollars, cars, airline tickets, well-furnished shops, or even banks, but also ants and flies. On some occasions I have witnessed live flies and ants, stuck in honey in linear sequences, being incorporated into the *mesa* with the intention of attracting customers "like flies" to the shop of the trader "paying" (*pagar*) the offering. The gustatory appeal of the sweets and honey is complemented by the smell of herbs such as the *q'oa* but also by a set of aesthetic

Mesa sweet (*misterio*) representing people lining up in a bank to withdraw money or collect a loan.

patterns generated by abundant, circular, and colorful wools together with shiny coils of silver paper intended to attract spiritual forces.

In Aymara, the word used to refer to this ritual event is *wajjta*, the same term employed when feeding your livestock or buying a drink for a friend. When I asked Don Daniel whether the offering performed and burned or the *pedido* communicated to the spiritual world was reflected back onto the material world, he replied sardonically that it was a matter not of reflection, but of digestion. Through a physiological process, the food/request offered activated through the body of the spirit a physical transformation of the material world. Not only is the *mesa* an instrument of world-making (Devisch 1993), but also the exchange between the worshipper and the spirit is envisioned as a form of cosmological transformation and creation (cf. Harris 1989).

Robert Randall (1993) observed not only a series of correspondences between the human body and the body of the *Pachamama* but also a certain kind of communication between them. For instance, the stimulation of the human body by means of alcoholic drinks and food is understood as having a similar stimulating effect as the feeding of the *Pachamama* with *mesas* or libations, therefore stirring her (re)productive capacity. Quoting Pachakuti Yamki, Randall describes the work of a kind of "Ambassador of the Inca" (the *Qhollaq Ch'away*) that was sent to eat and drink with local chiefs. Given the *Qhollaq Ch'away*'s capacity to eat and drink in large quantities, the growth of local production would be stimulated. As Randall suggests, it is through the same physiological process—the feeding of the human body and the feeding of the *Pachamama*—that the reproduction and transformation of the cosmos is enabled.

During funeral wakes, for instance, traders would not pour libations to the floor (to the *Pachamama*), as they usually do on most ritual occasions. The libation to the ground is replaced by the simple act of drinking and eating. Because of the communication and sharing of bodies instantiated during the wake of a defunct relative or friend, it is by "offering" beer to your own body that you simultaneously produce an offer to the "body" of the soul. More than an overlap between spiritual and material domains, what seems to take place is a physiological communication between the human body and the spiritual body. By heightening and amplifying such communication, you link your *suerte* (luck) or *camino* (path) with the soul and activate a series of physiological processes—of "digestion" of foods and liquids—that can transform and produce the cosmos according to your *suerte* and *camino*. In contrast with the predefined destiny of Protestant ethics (Weber 1998), not only is one's destiny constantly redefined, but also one's *suerte*—or path—holds the power to transform the cosmos.

In the case of Aymara traders, such overlap and communication among corporeal and spiritual domains and between economic and physiological processes that activate forms of reciprocal growth extends to Aymara traders' relationship with their shops and commodities. In the Aymara tradition, Carnival coincides with the *Anata* festival when the *Pachamama* is blessed and thanked in the form of offerings, in the hope of being supplied with an abundant harvest. In the city, the blessing of the earth—the *Pachamama*—as a dispenser of produce is substituted by the blessing of any material item (it can be an office, a shop, or a workshop) that constitutes a source of income for the family or trade union and remains associated with—literally owned by—a cosmological force or spirit. For instance, for the thousands of minibus drivers in La Paz, the minibus represents a source of income to be blessed and thanked. From simply being a utilitarian instrument of money making, the minibus is transformed into an entity with spiritual and corporeal characteristics.

In February 2004, I was unexpectedly faced with the impressive blessing of minibuses at the *Cementerio* bus terminal. Twelve minibuses, all belonging to the same union,[5] had been lined up in three rows, all facing an improvised stage in the middle of the street where *morenada* music was being played on huge loudspeakers from a CD player. Music was played and beer was poured for the minibuses as they come to be treated literally as human/animal bodies[6] and attributed with humanlike qualities. Ethnographic works in the rural Andes have often suggested how music is supposed to fortify the spirit of people, animals, and crops, stimulating their growth and stirring their emotions (Arnold and Yapita 1998; Stobart 2000). The minibuses were arranged in lines—a regimentation reminiscent of religious dance parades—and successively blessed with petals and confetti on their roofs in a similar fashion to the blessing of stewards during a fiesta. Furthermore, flowers were tied to rear-view mirrors, an image powerfully reminiscent of the decorations secured on the ears of sheep and llamas during the mating season to stimulate reproduction. After a season of intense work, the minibuses were decorated, energized with beer and music, and thanked for their services. The event restored the forces and vigor of the minibus and made it ready for a new season of production.

Following an Andean pattern, modern objects, goods, and means of production in the urban context can be perceived as "functioning bodies" whose spirit is stirred by music and alcohol. All the Gran Poder traders would, without fail, bless (*ch'allar*) their shops, products, and commodities

at Carnival, playing music, drinking, and eating with them to heighten relations and consolidate bonds, suggesting an unexpected interlocking and
even communion (cf. Allen 1988) between trader and commodities. Rather
than the objectification of relations and the disembedding of the human
from the object produced by industrial production, the minibus and other
globally produced commodities remain included in networks of relations
and communications with other humans and objects as well as with local
cosmological forces. Minibuses and televisions need to be reenergized,
cheered by music, and resocialized by grouping them together with the
other "beings." Private wealth, individually owned items, mass-produced
objects, and global economic processes come to be framed in the terms of
the local system of "production," which is based on the continuous and
fluid communication, exchange, and feeding among the human, divine,
and material worlds.

Trade and Circulation as Forms of Production

As we have seen, the ideology of secularization and rationalization associated with modern trade and capitalism, leading to the confining of religion to a transcendent domain not concerned with everyday practice
(Dumont 1977; Le Goff 1982), is here counteracted by the radical imma-
nence of the spiritual dimension constantly involved in processes of production, transformation, and expansion of the cosmos. Therefore, the
material and the spiritual, the economic and the religious, are thought of
as physiologically communicating domains to the point that the economic
growth of Aymara traders activates a necessary spiritual growth reflected
in their geographical expansion of ritual practices and celebrations.

Platt (1992) suggests that Andean economies have been constantly
structured according to processes of circulation and transformation where
material and spiritual forces, economic interest, and cosmological (re)pro-
duction are intertwined. He points out that a system of circulation/trans-
formation existed during the Inca Empire when the services rendered in
the state-run corn plantations were reciprocated by the theocratic state
with the production of corn beer (*chicha*), a substance that held an association with spiritual forces. In the colonial era, such a circulatory system
endowed with religious connotations was fundamentally replaced by the
silver economy. The *Casa de la Moneda* (Mint) embodied not only a generative and reproductive establishment but also a processual stage in the
system of circulation and transformation, starting with the extraction of
silver by indigenous workers in the colonial mines and ending with the
distribution of minted silver coins by the theocratic state/*Casa de la*

Moneda. Mike Sallnow (1989) emphasizes how these processes of circulation ended up conjoining into actual chains of distribution connecting spirits, local indigenous authorities, and state institutions:

> Each year in the month of August when throughout the central Andes the Earth is believed to be open and alive, the mountains open their doors, load their treasures [gold and silver] on to their vicuñas and viscachas which they had changed into burros and mules for the purpose, and send it across the hills to their own chiefs. These in turn surrender it to the two most powerful mountain spirits of the region, who finally hand it over to the government of the republic. (219)

Rather than a process of increasing rationalization, global economic practices such as the exploitation of precious metals in highland mines can be framed in terms of an expansion of local cosmological forces and their relational scope. According to Don Daniel, the election of the Aymara president, Evo Morales, has intensified the relation and exchange between the Bolivian state and cosmological forces such as the *Tío*. In fact, the *Tío* holds a privileged relationship with the president. If the *Tío* pays the president through loans and/or tributes in the form of precious metals, the

"Office of the *Tío*."

president will have to redistribute—recirculate—the money in the form of infrastructural projects (*obras*), investments, and, most recently, royalties to the local communities from which the mineral/money originated. The process of nationalization of raw materials by President Morales—avoiding the outflow of minerals to nonreciprocating foreign conglomerates—and the scheme of redistributing the profits to local communities has reactivated fertile relations of exchange and circulation between the state and cosmological forces. Interestingly, Don Daniel does not talk about the state but speaks of the presidential palace functioning as a point of convergence or the "transplanted epicenter" of the country's diverse territories and of their respective exchanges. These processes of exchange are in themselves transformational.

In one large room of his house in El Alto, Don Daniel hosts the "office of the *Tío*" (cf. Taussig 1980), a space where he keeps four human-size images: the *Tío*—which he identifies with *Sat*—the *Tía*, and their twin sons, as well as their "*Casa de Moneda.*" On Tuesdays and Fridays, businessmen, traders, or fiesta stewards come to deliver expensive gifts to the *Tío* (note the Chinese silk robes in the "office of the *Tío*") and spend the night drinking and smoking with

The son of the *Tío* sitting on the "*Casa de Moneda.*"

him, more or less explicitly asking to be endowed with the money required for their investments or to cover their expenses for the fiesta. The *Tíos* are sitting on piles of fake banknotes, mostly U.S. dollars and old Bolivian currencies not in circulation any more. This is the "*Casa de Moneda*", which functions both as an expression of the *Tío*'s ownership of money and as a space where money "grows" and gifts are transformed into currency, which is then circulated and redistributed. Sallnow (1989: 218–219) suggests that indigenous peasants in Ayacucho (Peru) alleged that local cosmological forces owned underground machines to transmute offerings provided by worshippers into precious metals and money.

These circulatory processes linking spiritual forces with material processes of production often determine that products that have "circulated," as well as the profit in the form of money generated by such circulation, are referred to as "growing" and "giving birth" (Harris 1989; cf. Lederman 1991; Strathern 1988). In Aymara, when people refer to products that have traveled from the community to urban markets, they use the words *jiltaña* or *wawachaña*, "to grow" and "to give birth," respectively. Harris (1989) affirms that when a rural household buys alcohol in bulk in town to sell by the shot during fiestas, money is said to give birth (*wawachi*). These trading activities are not regarded as morally condemnable or detrimental to the social bonds of the community; rather, it is the contrary. As Harris (1989) suggests, the notion that profits are a form of giving birth and that they arise from the time and effort expended in travel and transport suggests that circulation and production are part of a single process and that we should be wary of separating them.

In orthodox Christianity, money and trade have often been seen as disruptive of social relations (Simmel 1990) and clashing with religious activities. Parry and Bloch (1989) outline a long European tradition ranging from Aristotle to forms of Christianity and, in a certain way, even to Marxist theory conceiving profit-oriented exchange as not only unnatural but also detrimental to communal and family bonds. Once objects become commodities destined for trade outside the community, they begin eroding bonds of personal dependence among community members. According to Aristotle (1962), for instance, money as an instrument adopted to facilitate trade can be a threat to the functioning of society, whereas loaning money with interest was a practice contrary to human nature. All these ideas denouncing trade as a form of producing profit without generating substance or, in the case of usurers, of making money even while asleep, therefore by manipulating time once a prerogative of God, appeared to be based on the religious premise that material production is the source of all value (Le Goff 1980; Parry and Bloch 1989). In a context such as the Andean world, where the community is spread across a vast and climatically differentiated territory rather than being a tightly knit nucleus, practices of circulation of products and exchange are envisioned as part of fertile flows connecting territories and generating "growth." Instead of decomposing the community (Bohannan 1959), money and trade are appropriated as tools creating links both socioeconomic and cosmological. Once again, circulation is envisioned as both an economic and a religious tool articulating and generating forms of communication among different territories, ecological niches, and spiritual forces and domains.

Abundance, Repetition, and Multiplication

The Aristotelian and Christian view of trade and money with their circulatory capacity, emphasis on exchange, and interest as potentially threatening the cohesiveness of society and an unmediated relation with God is constantly paired in the Western tradition by the opposed and irreconcilable liberal discourse of civilization (Parry and Bloch 1989; Harris 1989). From the perspective of liberal freedom, the market and money are envisioned as capable of extinguishing social hierarchies, traditions, and feudal systems of power. Money and the market not only disintegrate bonds of subordination to and dependence on the local authorities, but also free the individual from social structures and beliefs that have kept him tied to a specific locality. As we shall see (and in fact have partly already seen), in the case of the Aymara traders the emphasis on relations, connections, movement, and circulation as both economic and cosmological tools is complemented by the importance placed on locality and territory, which comes across in forms of commercial control of local spaces and spiritual practices grounded in specific locations.

In the discussion of Aymara socioeconomic institutions in Chapters 1 and 2, we observed traders' simultaneous tendency to generate strategies for the control of locality and tactics to develop connections and networks with external spaces. Aymara economic cosmology presents a similar tension between anchoring and movement. Whereas in the previous sections we addressed the idea of circulation as a tool engendering synergic and fecund articulations between different spaces and domains, I here delve into the concept of abundance as a manifestation tied to a specific place or person and equally able to instantiate communication with spiritual forces and activate forms of material and economic growth.

In the practices and ideas of Aymara traders, abundance is another crucial aspect bringing into a close concomitance economic and spiritual, material and physiological dimensions. An excess of matter has been often envisioned as an obstacle to social relations, to abstract thinking (Hall 1997), and to an unmediated communication with spirits (Keane 2007), and I will dwell here on the role of material abundance and its specific aesthetic patterns in activating and regulating exchange and communication between spiritual and material worlds. I will also address abundance as a force, an "iconic statement" that, given its capacity to attract physical and spiritual forces into relation, also allows for their simultaneous growth and reproduction.

The aesthetic of abundance is a visually astonishing characteristic of both popular markets and religious practices, to the point that terms such as "abundance," "plumpness," and "fleshiness" have come to identify the wealthy popular trader. The body is a crucial locus where the performance of abundance is enacted. First, the body is the place where the unsubstantial profit of economic activities is materialized into fatness and rotund bodily shapes, thus incorporated into physical form. Being fat among Aymara traders is often considered an expression of power, and a series of dress devices are employed to emphasize plumpness. Successful female sellers would wear traditional *pollera* skirts piled one on top of the other and stuff their undershirts with purses, money, and objects to amplify the volume of their bodies and convey an attractive feeling of abundance, roundness, and power. They would often use smaller-size open shoes—to produce the effect of a visible overflow of abundant flesh—and minute bowler hats to stress the size and fatness of the face.

Religious dance parades are another space where the material amplification of the body takes place, together with an unrestrained display of material plenty. Heavily costumed and masked, hundreds of identically dressed dancers devotionally parade across the urban landscape for the Lord of Gran Poder. The repeated visual abundance generated by these dancers, heavily decorated with precious brocade ribbons, pearls, and braids from the Far East, dancing in step with each other and in perfectly ordered rows and lines to the rhythm of large brass bands, is thought to create a tangible effect both in the body of the dancers and in the spectators. In addition, the circular path of the dance tends to heighten the roundness of the bodies, and the coordinated movements consolidate the potency of the performance. Dance can constitute another "pathway" through which contact and exchange with spiritual forces is instantiated because Saints and spirits are often thought to be witnessing or participating in the performance (Nash 1979). Events such as dance parades are thought to create material and sensorial amplifications where the material world appears as an ontological extension of the spiritual (Himpele 2003). As in the case of the *mesa*, the material abundance, the devotees' displays of joy, beauty, and material excess thrust into the festival, is thought both to activate a contact with spiritual forces and to constitute an offering whose abundance will be reciprocated by spiritual forces in the lives of worshippers—plus interest.

Material abundance works in a similar way to food offerings. At one and the same time, spiritual forces are visually attracted by the display of material plenty and "feed" on it, while at the same time sharing with the dancers not only abundance but also power. During one of the dance parades for the Lord of Gran Poder, which lasted for about five hours of uninterrupted dancing along a six-mile route, I was about to give up dancing because of the weight of the costume and the continuous oscillations that had become unbearably painful for my back. My fellow dancer, however, after forcing me to bolt down a considerable amount of alcohol, put on a straight face and commented seriously that I could not leave: I had to "exaggerate" if I wanted to attract the power of the Lord.

Much could be said here about Aymara traders' compulsive attitude and moral obligation to ingest food and drink in large quantities (see Allen (1988) and her idea of "forced feeding"), especially at fiestas. In 2010 at the end of a religious fiesta when everybody was already sick-drunk with alcohol, the local steward's daughters went around the hall for a few last rounds, holding a bottle of spirits in one hand and a lash (*chicote*) in the other. Those participants who refused to exaggerate with drinking were the objects of seriously painful whipping until they consented to bolt down the alcohol. As we have seen in the case of the Ambassador of the Inca—the *Qhollaq Ch'away*—exaggerating with food and drink is not only an auspicious performance inducing the reproduction of economic abundance but also an act of instantiation of that same abundance.

Counterintuitively, spiritual forces and gods are attracted by material abundance, which appears to be able to consolidate communication and exchange as well as to force them to reciprocate it. The butcher Justo Soria once revealed to me that the performances of material abundance during religious dance parades enable the saint to "reverberate" and "multiply" in every corner of the city, thereby reproducing and amplifying its reach and power across the urban landscape. Instead of clashing with religious morality, material abundance constitutes a force whose exaggeration and repeated and synchronized statements of material plenty during the Gran Poder parade enable the saint to grow (*jiltaña*) and reproduce its power and presence.

Visual plenty can be engendered by a specific pattern of repeated sequences of abundance through hundreds of heavily dressed dancers moving synchronically in ordered lines. These patterns of "repetition" embody crucial Andean ideas about reproduction (Platt 1996; Ferraro 2004) because they conjoin into actual iconic statements (Allen 1997) stimulating processes of multiplication. In his ethnographic analysis of Quechua numbers, Gary Urton (1997, 2003) points out how repeated sequences of numbers are referents to filial relations and embody in their own "succession" a sense of physical and material reproduction. In similar terms, the act of counting money among traders is perceived as a repetitive and auspicious act. The iconic statements of abundance and repetition produced in the Gran Poder parade through the performance of replicated sequences of dancers, costumes, and goods induce attraction and instantiate reproduction.

Such aesthetic patterns of abundance are not limited to ritual and religious practice. In fact, the market represents another domain where the provision of abundance constitutes a crucial aesthetic practice driving economic exchange and relations and whose similarity with the aesthetic patterns of dance parades is striking. If we look at the commercial area of Gran Poder, the first impression we gather is that of a repeated sequence of

Repeated sequences of *morenos* in the Gran Poder parade. Photo courtesy of Juan Yupanqui Rodríguez.

small shops trading in the same commodities. One finds not only consecutive and identical shops selling exactly the same goods, but also an overflow of commodities from their small premises onto the pavement.

If, on the one hand, the practice of concentrating such a large number of shops in the same commercial area heightens competition unnecessarily, on the other hand it creates a crucial aesthetic effect. Apart from generating a sense of repeated abundance, the small and consecutive shops are meant to *agarrar* (catch) the customers. Successful traders would not invest their profits in buying a bigger shop, as the logic of the liberal economy would require, but would rather buy another small shop. They would thus eventually find themselves owning two small shops, selling similar goods and perhaps next door to each other, a situation intended to maximize the possibility of attracting customers. This unusual practice is also explained as a consequence of the idiosyncrasy of the Bolivian buyer, who, instead of preferring a large shop with a variety of products, is convinced and "caught" by, and eventually gives in to, the repeated abundance of consecutive shops and their goods.

Through specific aesthetic patterns of repetition and abundance, the market itself can become an aesthetic performance, watched by and

Market stalls: repeated sequences of the same goods (red chili, tea, soap, etc.).

exerting its attraction on not only the layman but also cosmological forces. Catherine Allen (1988) has suggested that patterns of decoration placed on objects and animals may enhance the growth and "procreation" of such beings, not only because their "bodies" were physically affected but also because decoration and specific aesthetic patterns—abundance being one of them—attracted, stirred, and stimulated the activity of spirits. In this sense, it would be an error to understand the modern market as merely the space of competing individuals and playing a purely economic role.

"Planted Capital" and "Revolving Capital": Attachment and Circulation in Aymara Business Management

In the previous sections, I have tried to outline the tension between the concepts of circulation and abundance, anchoring and movement. I will now delve into how they operate concomitantly—in both antagonistic and complementary ways—in the logic of Aymara trade in the midst of global economic flows. In so doing, I seek to highlight how these Andean concepts are used and expanded in Aymara traders' practices of business management.

As we have seen, Rigoberto Ali owns two shoe shops in the *feria* 16 de Julio in El Alto, which he manages together with his brother, Máicol. As explained elsewhere (Tassi et al. 2013: 153), according to Rigoberto, two types of capital are involved in the management of the business. He talks of "planted (or grounded) capital" and "revolving capital."

> The planted capital is like an octopus holding onto (*agarrado*) a piece of ground or place with its tentacles and bit-by-bit it drips (*gotea*) onto the other capital—the revolving capital (*capital rotatorio*). The planted capital is the shop with all the goods stored inside. The revolving capital is what we use to replace the commodities sold and to buy more goods, to eat and party, to invest and consume (Rigoberto Ali, paraphrased interview, November 15, 2012).

In Rigoberto's description, the planted capital clings to the ground, highlighting the connection between this kind of capital and the specific *Pachamama* of the ground where the shop stands.[7] The animal quality attributed to this capital is not necessarily a coincidence or a metaphor because the *Pachamama* is endowed with a reproductive capacity or a tendency to "drip" (*gotear*)—a term often employed in the Andes to describe a repeated and sequential transmutation of substance, energy, and force from one recipient to another.[8] The interconnection and coupling between the capital and the *Pachamama* onto which it is grounded may be instrumental in the reproduction and growth of both the shop and the commodities stored in it.

In the Andes, objects, animals, and commodities are often thought to develop forms of grounded attachment to people (cf. Crain 1991; Allen 1988). As well as being one of the main means for many rural families to access cash, the bull is also considered the family "banker" and is thought to manage the household and guarantee its growth. In this sense, the bull maintains a specific attachment to the family and the local territory and is often the object of simulated wedding rituals with the children or included in reproductive ceremonies related to the fertility of the land and family[9] (Tassi 2012a). As we have seen, the identification and attachment among commodities, ground, and owner become expressly visible at Carnival when traders bless (*ch'allan*) their goods and the ground of the shop by decorating them with shiny confetti, flower petals, and colorful streamers and by drinking and eating with them. The blessing is intended as a propitiatory and regenerative act through which a process of reciprocal and communal growth is instantiated.

However, the tendency to generate grounded forms of growth and attachment is constantly complemented by forms of circulation and movement—as implied by the idea of revolving capital—included in wider circulatory processes. It is commonplace for traders to state that if you invest or simply spend money "with faith," it will be returned to you in a multiplied quantity. It is indeed common to emphasize the positive fluidity of economic "movement" as opposed to a static concentration of money in one's hands. Rather than only being conceived as the accumulation of resources and as saving, money is characterized as a means of facilitating movement and creating a sense of connectedness among different groups and cosmological forces. Both in the fiesta and in the market, debt, as well as expenditure (*gasto*), can be morally and socially highly valued because it implies a sacrificial spending for the communal well-being and presupposes relatedness and movement—a return of the money that has been invested in the economic/social reproduction of the community (see also Harris 1989).

If we go back to the bull, which I described as attached to local fertility, we can see how the sale of livestock on the market is equally followed by a propitiatory practice called *t'inkha*. Market sales are accompanied and complemented by a social and ritual act of drinking between seller and buyer as a propitiatory practice intended to seal the auspicious quality of the transaction. In fact, livestock markets may often take the semblances of festive events where producers and traders (*mañazos*) sit together drinking and eating in abundance. Economic transactions are always imbued with a social quality and with *suerte* (luck). *T'inkha* is a form of libation to spiritual forces in which the diverging interests of the buyer and the seller are suddenly joined together (cf. Platt 1992; Graeber 2011). In other words, competing interests and forms of grounded attachment between humans and animals give space to fluidity and movement and allow for trade to operate. In the case of the producer, the *t'inkha* is a welcoming ritual of "return" of the money invested, whereas for the trader the sum paid is the new beginning of the process of circulation.[10] These dynamics contradict a too-simplistic interpretation that has often identified the commercialization of livestock in the Andes as a stressful rupture or transformation from use value to exchange value (Crain 1991).

The sale of animals has often been associated with the tension between the impersonality of the market and the affective personal relation of the owner with his or her livestock, between the insubstantiality of exchange and the anchorage of family bonds. I would argue that such interpretation is the projection of Euro-American categories onto an indigenous Andean reality. As we have seen, the separation between the affection of family bonds and the impersonality of exchange, between use value and exchange value, is the foundation of the morality of Euro-American capitalist societies (Carrier 1995; Parry 1986). In the Andes, however, exchange is embedded with ideas of the reproduction of life and the health of the household. My butcher friend Nicanor used to say that his newly built house in a remote neighborhood of El Alto "ate" (*se comió*) twenty-four head of cattle, showing surprise at its unsuspected "hunger"—and at the costs of building materials. Although Nicanor had to sell most of his livestock to cover the costs of the building, he did not associate such a transaction with a process of loss but rather with a metabolic and reproductive transformation from one state to another. In other words, the emotional family bond with livestock is constantly paired with a sense of natural transformation of animals, objects and humans from one state to another. Domestic animals are invested with a supposed mobility and a constant tendency to "circulate" in space, time and substance. A precondition for that affective relation is the pre-emptive knowledge that the animal is only there temporarily almost as a guest; s/he will move on in its constant drive to circulate and transform.

Aymara traders repeatedly resort to local *yatiris* to pay offerings enabling their business to grow or for their investments to generate "multiplications." When talking to Don Daniel, I was often intrigued by the combination of forms of grounded attachment and circulation in the practices of ritual offerings of traders. When starting a business, an entrepreneur would generally pay four different offerings, or *mesas*, to multiple spirits or cosmological forces (Tassi et al. 2013). The first offering is paid to the specific *Pachamama* of the shop, namely, the spirit of the ground—or the building or the market—where the trader's business stands. The second *mesa* is dedicated to the *Pachatata* who is in charge of accompanying the offer along the path, thus linking the worshipper and the spirit, generating movement and activating the articulation. The third *mesa* is directed to the *Tío* with the intention to "stop the money" (*parar el dinero*), in the sense of slowing down the pace of circulation and consequently heightening the possibility for the trader to generate forms of accumulation. The last *mesa* is aimed at "attracting customers like flies," therefore increasing circulation and generating repeated sequences of buyers going through the shop.

I have previously explained (Tassi et al. 2013: 155) how among Aymara traders the idea of wealth and the basic economic dynamics appear to be defined by the constant search for an equilibrium between two opposed conditions: one of circulation (the revolving) and one of attachment (the planted or grounded), between movement and the interruption of movement. The excess of circulation and the excess of attachment are both envisioned as potentially dangerous conditions leading to social and economic disequilibria. If a trader becomes too attached to his property, commodities, or money, sudden economic damage such as the death of livestock, a robbery of goods, or a financial swindle may generate an illness that is referred to as *phustiga* (Velasco 2009), identified with the rejection of food and the loss of concern for personal care. In the Andes, a common and well-known illness is the so-called *amartelo*, a form of depression related to an acute nostalgia for a beloved person or place, which often degenerates into a physical and psychological illness with potentially deadly consequences. In general, as we have seen, forms of identification between, for instance, a godfather and a godson may be promoted. However, an excess of identification can be perceived as dangerous and it is usually reduced by making the two individuals eat from the same plate and ceremonially breaking the plate once the meal is over.

A different form of excessive attachment can be produced by a trading family that is gaining increasing power and spatial control in a market and either refusing to engage in forms of trade and exchange with local vendors or refusing to participate in the festive activities by accepting the role of steward. Similarly, it may happen that one of the religious fraternities in charge of the fiesta of Gran Poder acquires an excess of power and control of the fiesta, imposing rules and tasks on the others, monopolizing resources, and impeding the equitable circulation and distribution of means and benefits. In these circumstances, a series of forces both internal and external to the fraternity (or the family) begin operating in the attempt to fragment its monopolistic power (often this means breaking the fraternity in two), avoid an excessive centralization of power (cf. Platt 1987), and reestablish a more fluid equilibrium and circulation.

At the other end of the spectrum, the circulation of money and resources may need to be reduced or, as we have seen, stopped, to feed forms of accumulation. In fact, an excess of circulation and movement can also be identified with a similarly dangerous illness associated with the inability to retain money and resources or to activate processes of sedimentation. Such an illness is referred to with the name of *limpu* or *soplo* (blow) for its tendency to blow away all one's money and property as well as one's reproductive capacity (see Tassi et al. 2013: 155). In the previous paragraphs, we observed how individual forms of attachment and accumulation curtailing wider relational and circulatory processes can be deemed as dysfunctional and dangerous. Here we see how relational and circulatory processes are thought and meant to produce localized and individualized forms of accumulation and reproduction. The functioning of economic activities often depends on the equilibrium between attachment and circulation. Stopping the circulation of money and attaching it to a specific piece of ground or person is a legitimate and even necessary activity to foment forms of capital accumulation and successive reinvestment. However, money or commodities that have been held still for too long can actually "fall asleep" and become a nuisance for the trader. Rigoberto kept mentioning "nail-commodities" (*clavos*), which, after being stored in the shop for a long time, become "nailed" to the shop/ground, hampering the mobility of the trader and limiting his capacity to move to other markets.

The Andean cosmology is often characterized by a sense of complementarity of opposite and antagonistic terms. From the tension between the individual dimension and the community (Carter and Mamani 1982; Albó 1975; see also Chapter 5) to emotional features that alternate forms of acute sweetness and affection (*mojjsa*) with volcanic, irascible, and belligerent expressions (*ch'ajjwa*; see Platt 1987 and Cereceda 1987), these juxtapositions of opposed terms are conceived of as constantly producing a structuring and creative tension with no sense of anxiety or desire for synthesis (Rivera 1993, 2010a). The tension between forms of attachment and circulation I have described are inscribed in these same relational modalities between opposed terms that do not presuppose either integration of the one into the other or the generation of a new term that overcomes them.

In Chapters 1 and 2 of the book, I discussed a peculiar tension between territorial control of local markets and extended and flexible networks, highlighting a combination of localized strategies to control and defend the commercial space with heightened forms of mobility and plural and fluid connections with peoples and territories. In a similar way, Aymara traders' practices of business management are characterized by a comparable tension between planted capital and revolving capital, between attachment and circulation. This apparent contradiction seems to outline an idea of wealth simultaneously conceived as a process of physiological sedimentation, of growth tied to a piece of ground and a person, and a phenomenon of spatial and cosmological extension transcending the localized space and individual and articulating with other domains and subjects. Not only is the concept of wealth articulated with cosmological and social domains, but also it remains imbued with relational connotations both intersubjective and geographical. The constant search for an equilibrium between attachment and circulation is a constitutive pillar of the economic strategies of Aymara traders that defines their rhythm and modalities of investment in a global economy.

Popular Forms of Economic Operation

Such cosmological ideas and concepts of business management materialize into actual logics of investment, economic practices, and patterns. This does not preclude the possibility that global economic dynamics may in turn influence their rhythms of operation and their typology of investment. On the one hand, global economic forces and processes may be able to produce and foster locally specific forms and organizations (Goodale and Postero 2013). On the other hand, we have observed the capacity of Andean traders to appropriate foreign and external elements to consolidate and expand a local horizon.

Generally, the first type of investment or trade operation for Aymara traders is of a social rather than an economic kind, in the sense that it is often associated with the trader's insertion into the commercial flows, chains, and networks. Ramiro used to refer to these modalities of reinvestment and commercial operation as "making money without money" in the sense of resorting to a series of structures ranging from family networks to knowledges of markets, from commercial guilds to relations of trust to generate accumulation.

As we have seen, in the management of popular trade the so-called "social capital" becomes a key element pervading the whole economic structure and defining investments as well as making it possible to reduce costs and to make the functioning of this type of trade more dynamic. But the "religious capital" is another crucial recipient of investment because the lavish religious celebrations of Aymara traders are means both to activate and magnify the pathways and bonds with cosmological forces and to consolidate kin and networks. In fact, kinship bonds and networks often define how and in which direction this type of economy expands, as well as its scope and limits (see Chapter 5). Naturally, they become a recipient of both reinvestment and redistribution. One of the characteristics of the expansion of the Aymaras's trade is the simultaneous reinvestment in both their locally circumscribed institutions and their networks spread across vast territories. This generates a type of economic expansion and reinvestment "bit by bit," which, on the one hand, hints at a gradual consolidation of their socioeconomic system and, on the other, leaves space for possibilities of flexibility.

As much as the reinvestment in social and religious capital, among Aymara traders' practices of investment appear to be driven by the abovementioned tension between attachment and circulation. This means that investment in fixed assets requires a constant pairing with parallel investments in the revolving capital and vice versa so as to avoid the equally pathological conditions of stalemate and excessive circulation.

The house is an example of this specific tension. Among traders it is common to conceive of the dwelling as an investment or a space that must produce (*tiene que generar*). Made of bricks or adobes, the house is a natural extension of the *Pachamama* and therefore understood as an enveloping womb protecting and stimulating growth and production. This incentivizes a tendency among traders to combine commercial and dwelling spaces, building shops and stores on the ground floor, an events hall on the first floor, and lodgings and apartments on the upper floors. In the recently built Asodimin market you can find buildings hosting apartments, shops, warehouses, and dance halls simultaneously. Rather than a static residence, the dwelling becomes an element that notably contributes to the reduction of fixed costs by combining familial and business logics and serves as a multifunctional space where social and economic domains overlap. In a context of heightened velocity in the replacement of capital and high frequency of reinvestment, the investment in the dwelling where a large chunk of capital stands still or asleep for a relatively long time is revitalized or "woken up" by the multiple commercial and social functions that the house acquires.

As fixed assets, shops also present similar patterns of reinvestment and similar levels of multifunctionality as the dwelling. Traders prefer not to reinvest in expanding the size of their shop. They would rather buy another shop right next to the old one or to diversify by renting a space or stall in a different market or neighborhood. Mercedes Limachi, a successful Aymara entrepreneur running a spinning mill in Santa Cruz, started off the comercialization of her own textiles in the central and popular Los Pozos market of Santa Cruz. She later acquired two stalls in the Mercado Mutualista, which was at the time located in the northern outskirts of the city, and recently she has bought two stands in the wholesale *feria* of Barrio Lindo and a shop a few blocks away from the main square. These small and multiple investments in different urban locations and markets enabled her to diversify her practices of commercialization—that is, by combining retailing and wholesaling—but also to access a variety of social sectors in the stratified urban space. Such strategies of reinvestment are a consequence both of the modalities of attraction of customers we mentioned previously and of the often rigid structuring of local markets by trade unions that operate to avoid the concentration of property in a few hands. All these dynamics feed forms of small and "repeated" reinvestments in different shops, markets, and product categories, outlining a scenario of repeated sequences of small shops and markets that are highly diversified in terms of commodities.

In recent years when the country's economy is enjoying an unusual epoch of bonanza, the multiplication of possibilities, connections, and articulations with regional markets has led to some reshuffling of the modalities of investment in fixed capital by popular enterprises. The constant fluctuations of the global economy, the tendency of certain markets to quickly saturate, and the emergence of new markets in economically depressed areas of the country not only was paralleled by the traditional capacity of local traders to move around but also induced the replacement of various shops in local markets with weekly or seasonal trips to multiple markets, increasing the level of spatial mobility and expanding the economic radius of operation. This tendency not only reduced traders' fixed costs but also increased their investment in social and translocal networks as a result of the tendency to operate in multiple markets and because they required the logistical support of local actors during their commercial trips.

In the markets of both La Paz and El Alto, the dimensions of shops are exiguous. Ramiro was running his wholesaling activity and imports from China from a room measuring fifty square feet in the Huyustus market where he had managed to squeeze both an office and a showroom for his products. He shared this space with his wife, his goddaughter—in charge of dealing with customers—and her two baby daughters. In the shop there was no running water or toilet and Ramiro's investment in display cabinets, hangers, and shelves had totaled about $50. Several traders had negotiated with large brands such as Sony, LG, and Samsung for neon signs to be installed. Such costs were covered by these companies, which in some cases even paid yearly quotas to the shop owners. Usually the costs of rent, furniture, and electricity were not even taken into account in defining the price of goods. In addition, the location of most popular markets in marginal urban areas that in recent years have undergone a process of appreciation in value has enabled traders to minimize expenses and fixed capital costs (Antonio Rodríguez-Carmona, personal communication).

Shops themselves often take on the role of multifunctional spaces transcending their mere economic meaning or a coherent economic function. On Saturdays and Sundays bible-reading groups gather in different shops or stalls in the market, producing an interesting intersection of litanies and commercial negotiations. Sitting on cardboard boxes or sacks full of flour and rice, bible readers wait until they have finished the passage before answering questions about prices and demands for discounts from customers. Shops also play a fundamentally social role, both as spaces where people meet for amusement and entertainment and as spaces where confessions and advice are exchanged. In this sense, shops replace taverns and bars but also provide fundamental spaces where social and family problems are addressed, discussed, and potentially solved. As we have seen in the case of Ramiro's, several shops and stalls functioned as daycare centers where babies, toddlers, and children of the guild members would gather to play and rest.

The tendency to reduce fixed costs and the heightened forms of mobility is paired with forms of continuous and repeated reinvestment in acquiring new commodities to enlarge and diversify the stock—something that according to Rigoberto's definition should be included in the planted capital category. This leads to the emergence of a series of shops/stores exhibiting an abundant variety of products and where, as we have seen, the large number of goods tends to overflow from the small shops onto the sidewalk. The capacity of the market to elicit attraction is produced by the repeated sequences of abundance that encourage us to think of the market as a communal endeavor of concatenated merchants that parallels the competitive and individualist anchoring of each trader to his own space/shop.

This is magnified and reproduced through a system of internal circuits of supply and distribution within markets such the Eloy Salmón and

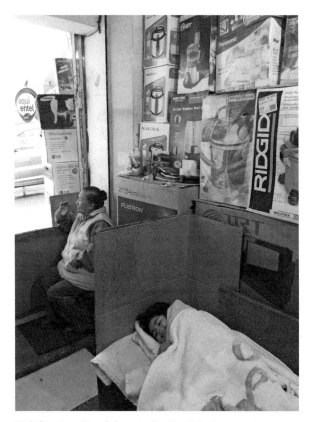

Multifunctionality of shops in the Eloy Salmón market.

Huyustus. Traders operating in the Huyustus market redistribute commodities in large quantities at a discounted price to local retailers and even wholesalers. It is not infrequent among traders in the same market to place orders for commodities of different brands from each other to diversify their stock. For instance, my friend Alex from the Eloy Salmón market retails two-thirds of his imported goods and wholesales one-third to friends and guild members in the same Eloy Salmón market. The profit margin on this kind of wholesale transactions can be as low as 3%. However, these practices activate and maximize the movement of money and the number of transactions. As suggested by the most basic economic theory, the influx of a large quantity of money or the increase of money in circulation will raise prices. However, when the increase of money in circulation is accompanied by a proportional increase in the number of transactions, inflation does not tend to grow.[11]

Even among long-distance importers we observe a tendency to rapidly reinvest in commodities once the earnings are sufficient to place a new order, quickly reconverting the revolving capital into planted. In several cases, the reinvestment in and expansion of stock coincided with the expansion of the radius of operation of the traders, who moved into—and invested in—new markets with purchasing potential either on the border or in economically emerging areas of the country such as mining towns or intermediate cities. This centrifugal movement of expansion toward new markets not only counteracted forms of economic concentration but also heightened the possibilities for the business to expand geographically and diversify.

The unusual combination of forms of flexible relationality with forms of localized attachment fosters practices of control of territories but also of commercial routes. In addition, it incentivizes repeated although not huge forms of social and economic investment in multiple markets, providing Aymara traders with the possibility to venture into new economic spaces without the degree of dependence and deference traditionally associated with these subordinate economic actors. In practical terms, the mobility and agility of Aymara trade was translated into an economic modality characterized by a form of commerce across large distances, generating a relatively modest movement of commodities in comparison to multinational companies (Tassi et al. 2013).

Conclusions

A series of Aymara forms and practices that remain rooted in local cosmological principles play an important role in structuring Aymara traders' involvement in the global economy. This encourages us to think beyond the perception of the global economy and market as all-powerful entities engendering awe among subaltern groups and hierarchically defining them for what they are not (proper, formal, or modern). In the first three chapters I discussed the social structures and institutions granting Aymara traders a degree of control over economic activities in a global economy. In this chapter I have shown how Aymara cosmology and its tension and complementarity between abundance and circulation, attachment and movement constitute tools not only for appropriating and resignifying capitalism and global commodities but also for defining specific microeconomic practices, logics, and strategies of business administration. Although with limitations,

Aymara traders have been able to reconfigure rhythms and modalities of operation in their economic management based on their cosmoeconomic principles. In Escobar's words, this places them as "economy makers" in the sense that "the economy is something they do rather than something that is imposed on them" (Escobar 2008: 100). In the next chapter, I will explore another of the tensions that characterize the Andean cosmology—namely, that between the individual and the community—to further understand the role of cosmological concepts and ideas as tools to structure and define forms of participation in the global economy.

CHAPTER 5

"Individual Capital" and Collective Relations in Business Administration[1]

The specific tensions we have observed between a solid and locally rooted institutionality and flexible and extended networks and between practices and forms of attachment and circulation also extend to another crucial "dichotomy" of Andean sociology, namely, the individual versus the collective (Albó 1975; Carter and Mamani 1982).

Today, at a time when indigenous sectors are at the core of social and economic transformations menacing traditional hierarchies, we are witnessing attempts among urban elites and intellectuals to reframe the dichotomy between the individual and the collective as the benchmark defining or measuring who and how indigenous a group might be (Crabtree and Chaplin 2013). Such a tendency appears to reflect a more or less explicit intention to exclude from the "indigenous" category those highland groups—particularly the Aymaras—who have been entertaining long-lasting relations with urban markets (cf. Harris et al. 1987) and therefore have been "contaminated" by individualist economic forces. With some notable exceptions (Canessa 2007; Rivera 2010a), a predisposition to operate in the market is often seen as a symptom of a liberal individualism and a lack of indigenous character, whereas communal ownership of land, disregard for economic convenience, and respect for nature rather than its exploitation embody the crucial principles of indigeneity.

In the following sections, we will explore a series of counterintuitive forms of articulation between the individual and the collective at the heart of Aymara traders' business management practices. I argue that specific Aymara modalities of conceptualizing and delimiting individual and collective domains become instrumental in the division and administration of business. I outline how specific forms and possibilities of autonomy, individuality, and transformation are granted within collective spaces. I also sketch the multiple levels of decision making and labor practices in Aymara enterprises. In so doing, I suggest that the tendency to dichotomize the individual and the collective runs the risk of interpreting local cultures and indigeneity through an analytical framework based on the morality of modern capitalism, which, as we have seen, tends to create a sense of incommensurability between the domains of individualist market relations and the reciprocity of community bonds.

Economic Collective Strategies of Aymara Entrepreneurs

In Chapter 1 we dealt in depth with the framework of social organizations that guaranteed the operation of Aymara trade in a context of exclusion from the formal economy and conventional institutions. In particular, we emphasized the role of such organizations in producing forms of social control and regulating access to local markets. In this section, we explore how local collectivities and a particular typology of social relations may generate specific forms and practices of business management and economic functioning.

Family-run Aymara enterprises generate strategic collective alliances to share the cost of international transport, access discounts for large orders, and generate economies of scale. Among Huyustus and Eloy Salmón electrical goods traders, it is common to get together to place large orders for televisions from *casero* suppliers in the Iquique duty-free zone. For orders of more than $100,000 (usually two full truck loads), *caseros* provide a discount of 5%, a practice that allows televisions to be sold in Bolivia at a cheaper price than in Chile.[2] The possibility offered by China to fill up a container with a variety of different commodities has enabled local traders to share the costs of transport and in some cases to access commodities that they would not have been able to import individually.[3]

In the case of large wholesalers traveling cross-country with a truck to distribute their commodities, they often stop in improvised wholesale spots within the urban perimeter of the major cities because of the lack of infrastructure to host these kinds of activities. To avoid the nuisance of local authorities asking for bribes or issuing fines, groups of traveling merchants generate strategic collective alliances coordinating their simultaneous arrival at the same wholesale spot in a specific city. In these circumstances local authorities feel much less comfortable in confronting a whole group of combative traders. This often implies developing alliances and extended networks among traders from different regions of the country converging in the same cities to wholesale their products.

As we have seen in the previous chapter, this inflow of a large quantity and variety of commodities generates a circular movement of redistribution and wholesale of goods to the other traders operating in the market. These continuous and reciprocal practices of wholesaling among traders and importers participating in the same markets determine an interesting overlap in the dynamics of competition and cooperation (Colloredo-Mansfeld and Antrosio 2009). Competition—even among members of the same union, family, or fraternity—is usually connoted in positive terms because it magnifies innovations and creativity and improves the performance of the fraternity or community. In the fiesta, the competition between the different *bloques* that compose a fraternity, each displaying innovative dance steps and outfits, is unavoidably connected to practices of cooperation and the joining of efforts and resources aimed at amplifying circulation and abundance and conducive to the fortune and success of the whole fraternity. This tension can be observed even in the market and specifically in the exchanges of goods among traders that take place at almost cost price. For instance, a television bought by a trader in Iquique for $80 and usually sold on the market for $105 can be sold for $90 to another trader in a different location who wants to increase the variety or quantity of his or her goods. In the same way as the fraternity can be imagined as a communal, solid guild composed of competing *bloques* aimed at delivering a sequential and repeated display of plenty, the market can be envisioned as a system of competing shops engendering a communal and repeated attraction of customers. Rudy Colloredo-Mansfeld and Jason Antrosio describe communal conceptions of markets among handicrafts producers in the Ecuadorean Andes in a similar way:

> First, competitors (who in fact may not cooperate in systematic ways) combine imitation and innovation to cogenerate a shared economic value; second, commercial goods and places produced through competition can become culturally marked and defended as community patrimony. (Colloredo-Mansfeld and Antrosio 2009: 135)

In other words, the conception of the market as a space where single and individual entrepreneurs compete is constantly complemented by the idea of multiple and repeated commercial transactions and connections among market vendors. Not only is the market a space that is gradually being constructed in a communal fashion, but also its capacity to attract customers is produced by forms of communal—although competing—performance and participation. In the grocery market of *Villa Dolores* in El Alto, the local union of producers has been trying to draw indigenous communities from different ecological areas into the market to heighten the attraction of the market through the variety of products on offer and also reinforcing the conception of the market as a space of convergence of different groups and localities (see Chapter 4).

The Family-Run Market Research Culture

When it comes to the management of popular enterprises, the extended family is a structure playing a crucial role. For instance, in a context of socioeconomic invisibility and chronic neglect by conventional institutions, the family networks both foment a series of skills to understand the market and its variations and encourage the consolidation of specific practices and knowledges to read local markets.

One of the most striking features of popular traders is their visual memory in relation to multiple products as well as the capacity to memorize their retail and wholesale prices. In particular, secondhand clothing retailers such as Rigoberto would be able to recall the price of hundreds of different products without any use of price tags. Large importers and distributors of electric goods with their shop in the Huyustus and operating in multiple markets of the country were able to memorize not only the retail and wholesale price of several dozen products but also the price discrepancies among different markets, such as Santa Cruz or Cochabamba, where they regularly distributed their products. In fact, this impressive mnemonic knowledge of prices often applied not only to a variety of different products but also to different markets in the country or region operating under different economic conditions, currencies, and regulations.

It is interesting to observe here the resonance with the capacity of Andean cultures with an established tradition of mnemonic skills linked to products and territories. Andean agriculture involved the simultaneous care of hundreds of plots of different products spread across a vast and climatically highly differentiated territory. Under such conditions, the peasant family turned into a pool both of mnemonic knowledge about the different plots, products, and territories and of division of tasks to organize the multiple agricultural activities in the different ecological niches and epochs of the year (Rivière 1994).

Today, the family network works as a crucial space for discussion and comparison of prices and economic possibilities, economic variations and discrepancies between a rural *feria*, an intermediate town, or a border market. This transforms the family network into an important database of constantly updated experiential, oral, and practical economic knowledges feeding a culture of economic comparison and analysis. While dining after a day of work, I was often impressed by how the family was able to quickly identify on the base of the retailing prices of fellow guild members whether they were reselling or whether the commodities were imported in large quantities or smuggled. The capacity to retrieve, compare, and combine these multiple pieces of information about territories, prices, and commercial strategies conjured into a mental map identifying multiple markets, niches, and possibilities across the country or region for the specific product category and commercial strategies adopted by the trader. Rigoberto, for instance, knows the exact day of the month when the miners from different mining towns on the high plateau are paid their salaries— knowledge that is considered crucial given the reputation miners have for spending their wages all at once.

At a time of widespread access to information technology, it is impressive to observe how this oral and empirical knowledge is quickly updated to cope with market fluctuations and price volatility. Carlos Mamani, an Alteño optician and a distributor of Chinese-produced sunglasses in the southern border towns with Argentina, was recalling how, with the fall of the Argentinian peso in 2013, the activity of the Aymara traders and truck drivers in the region came quickly to a halt and they suddenly relocated toward the Amazonian towns on the border with Brazil.

Such sophisticated, family-managed, and complexly articulated skills are valuable in conducting market studies in increasingly complex marketplaces characterized by a vertiginous inflow of new commodities. Mercedes Limachi, before beginning the production of new pieces of garments in her mill in Santa Cruz, would send drawings and pictures of the model to her family in El Alto, *caseros* in Cochabamba, and retailers/*compadres* in the border towns with Brazil and Argentina to explore the potential sales price and profits. This would quickly mobilize a network of interconnected actors to find out the prices of a similar commodity in a series of local markets, who would inquire with local competitors, wholesalers, *caseros*, and guild members. In just two or three days, Mercedes would get a detailed "report" on this family-run market study, on the basis of which she would decide whether an investment of several thousands of dollars was worthwhile.

Popular traders appear to have developed great skills in reading the market, its variability, and its fluctuations, not so much by means of expensive, complex, and conventional market studies but through family networks maintaining historically rooted mnemonic skills and a vast knowledge of market/territorial discrepancies. Such a family-managed (*casero*) database of market knowledge provides Aymara traders with a comparative commercial advantage in relation to foreign and state enterprises who are often unaware of these differences and information and whose professional study of highly segmented local markets would be too costly and unsustainable.

Social Accountancy

Accounting is another domain where social structures such as the family tend to perform an important economic role, often feeding a series of practices challenging conventional ideas on the subject. In the case of Rigoberto, for instance, his semilegal business induced him to reduce its visibility by cutting to a minimum the written records of economic and financial information and resorting to local mnemonic skills about prices and sales of the nearly 1,000 pairs of shoes exhibited in his shop. During the research, I was often struck by the scarcity of accounting records registering purchases and sales employed in the administration of local enterprises. In fact, most of the family members resorted uninhibitedly to the cash flow of the shop for their domestic expenses, lunches, or grocery shopping. Instead of paying salaries to family members, everybody simply used the cash box to cover family-related expenses. This implied that in the vast majority of these popular establishments there was no calculation of monthly and yearly earnings, much less of a break-even point. Even in the case of large importers who had stores of commodities scattered about in relatives' homes across the city, they would not keep a delivery note or any kind of written record of the commodities stored in or taken out of these *casero* warehouses. These commercial establishments with yearly turnovers of tens or sometimes hundreds of thousands of dollars and a precise knowledge of the profit margins of each product would not bother about accounting records.

In several cases I realized that conventional accounting practices were replaced by a series of family-run social control mechanisms aimed at reducing the risk of swindles and robberies. In some cases, the importer's godsons and daughters or brothers and sisters would live rent free in the apartment above the warehouse. They are often in charge of safeguarding the commodities and maintaining a constant mental record of the goods stored and products that needed to be ordered. Something similar can be seen in the shops where, despite the overwhelmingly large number of commodities often squeezed into the tiny space, each family member keeps a detailed visual record of the products, to the point where even the smallest changes in the display are noticed and shared by the family.[4] The proximity of the shops also generates a concatenation of different control agents, ranging from relatives to guild members who are also often able to identify suspicious behavior.

The story of the foodstuff trader Nelson Rodríguez is emblematic of this link between accounting and social control as well as of the role of one's social entourage in detecting possible sources of economic threat. Nelson started off as a small trader buying a small quantity of products on credit from large food brands to the point that he could barely fill in the shop he was renting in the Huyustus. However, after a few years of success, the value of his business grew considerably. He shifted to wholesaling and moved to *Villa Dolores* in El Alto, where the wider and less crowded spaces facilitated the logistics of wholesaling. In the past decade, Nelson's imports and wholesale activities grew considerably thanks to the connections that he and his family managed to establish with *casero* retailers in the expanding markets of the Amazon region. So steep was the growth of his business that Nelson had to resort to renting new warehouses as well as hiring two employees to take charge of the frequent loading and unloading of products, something new for an enterprise that had been traditionally family run. A few months later, a local retailer who was one of Nelson's customers pointed out to him that his two employees appeared to lead a lifestyle above their means. Because of the lack of an actual accounting system, Nelson began monitoring the activities of the employees and realized that, on arrival, some of the imported commodities were being diverted to the warehouse of another trader.

This was a recurring problem that I observed in several commercial establishments. Whenever the volume of the commercial activities exceeded the family's social control capacity, the enterprise was faced with two possible options to avoid the problems encountered by Nelson: one, to shift to forms of institutionalized and more formal accounting with bookkeeping and accounting records, employees, and administrators; or two, to reduce drastically the volume of the commercial activity for the family to recover its full social control. Generally, as in the case of Nelson, this last option was preferred because the cost increase resulting from the abrupt transition to accounting records was considerable and also because there was a tendency among traders to favor forms of direct and independent management. Successful traders expanding their radius of operation to other cities would be faced with the dilemma of whether their extended family network was solid and reliable enough to cope with this transformation. In the case of small families or of traders not involved in the festive cycle of the Aymara urban community, they preferred to disregard appealing opportunities for business expansion toward other cities and markets because of the lack of trustworthy relatives who could manage the business in another location and follow up on, control, and account for the transport of commodities. Extended but reliable circuits of relatives, goddaughters, and *compadres* not only guaranteed the necessary forms of control of the business and its accounts but also defined the possibility and directions of business expansion.

Individual Capital and Family Business Management

A series of social structures such as the family or the guild are certainly key collectives in the construction of economic knowledge and strategies specific to this form of popular trade. However, rather than rushing to define these economic forms and practices as "communitarian trade" (Héctor Parra, personal communication), it is worth understanding and specifying the idea of "collectivity" of these actors more precisely. On several occasions, Silvia Rivera (1993, 2010a) has emphasized the paradoxical tendency among Aymara indigenous groups particularly to fight for forms of equality while simultaneously defending specific differences. According to Rivera, the expression of ideas of commonality does not preclude the possibility of recognizing differences and individualities. She uses the Aymara term *ch'ejje* or *ch'ixi* to refer to such a juxtaposition of opposing terms and possibilities, suggesting a coexistence of heterogeneous or opposed elements without aspiring either to their fusion or to the development of a new term encompassing and overcoming the tension. As in the case of attachment and circulation, such a view of things expresses a creative tension where opposed or different terms simultaneously antagonize and complement each other.

One of the elements that most struck my curiosity in business management by the extended family was the coexistence of heightened practices of cooperation and mutual help with a series of "individual" strategies, forms of management, and capital. In the case of Rigoberto and his brother Máicol, they jointly manage two shoe shops in El Alto with the help of the extended family but they maintain independent and complementary economic strategies. Rigoberto buys goods from large wholesalers and importers in the city of Oruro, where some of the largest suppliers operate and where secret warehouses of secondhand clothes have been installed. He buys directly from the patio of two *casero* suppliers with whom he enjoys a high degree of trust, to the point where he is allowed to choose the products that best fit his line and the demands of his customers. Rigoberto often brings presents to his suppliers, particularly food items such as *marraqueta* bread or lake fish readily available in El Alto but not always in Oruro. He also helps them out with a series of bureaucratic and administrative tasks such as the release of the container from the companies who only operate in La Paz. However, Rigoberto finds himself exposed to a high degree of risk, particularly during the nighttime transportation of these illicit commodities by bus from Oruro to his shop in El Alto.

Máicol's commercial strategies and networks are completely different from Rigoberto's. He buys from resellers in El Alto by sealed bale at a lower price than Rigoberto but without really knowing what he is buying. There-fore, the relationship he maintains with his suppliers is much more flexible and less strict. Although they run a family business, they developed differ-ent and independent business strategies and networks and manage indi-vidual capital and profits. Whereas Máicol specializes in kids' footwear, Rigoberto's favorite niche is young adults. Although they run the shops together, Máicol collects the income from the sales of kids' footwear inde-pendently and autonomously defines his own business strategies and forms of reinvestment.

In most of the commercial establishments I have worked with, the different members of the family managed their own capital independently, linking strategically with each other and even lending each other money with interest. The Kataris, for instance, run a well-furnished electrical goods shop in the Huyustus market. Despite the general appearance of uniformity of the shop, I slowly realized that the refrigerators belong to the father, the washing machines to the mother, and the blenders and mi-crowaves to the son. This generated a system of three separate cash "regis-ters." each belonging to a different member of the family, as well as different forms and strategies of reinvestment of the income. Rather than administering the capital collectively or defining a clear division of labor or specialization of functions among family members, each one is in charge of his or her own management and sales, taking full responsibility for the entire commercialization process, strategies of specialization, and diversification. What this structure appears to guarantee is the possibility for each family member to develop his or her own space and path (*camino*), thus granting spaces of autonomous decision making and reducing the

Multiple cash boxes for each member of the family in an appliances shop in the Eloy Salmón.

possible interference of vertical forms of authority as well as dependence on parental guardianship. Instead of a vertical structure patriarchally led by the head of family in charge of the management and economic tactics, the family-run enterprise often takes the semblance of a more horizontal system of articulated activities and strategies within which each member enjoys a certain degree of autonomy.

"Luck" is another crucial element in defining offspring's role and specialization in the family-run enterprise. Hilarión has named the importing company he runs together with his three brothers "Kayla" after his twelve-year-old daughter because she is apparently lucky (*suertuda*), and that luck might drip now onto the whole company. Every box or product imported from China has the name Kayla stamped in large letters. But the luck of a son or daughter can also be identified with a particular disposition toward a specific product category or activity. Rosalía, an auto part importer and retailer in the *feria* 16 de Julio, often mentioned to me that her son Leonel was lucky with vehicles and that he could drive repeatedly and across large distances on the uneven Yunga roads without any mechanical inconvenience. She therefore envisioned Leonel to get on and develop the family enterprise in the branch of transport. At the time of this writing she was still struggling to decipher which kind of transport—commodities, fruit, people—would be Leonel's lucky choice.

Among Aymara traders traveling collectively to China to share the costs of the containers and generate economies of scale by placing collective orders, it was not infrequent for them to engage in individual negotiations with the suppliers and owners of the Chinese family-run consortia. In fact, they even established preemptive verbal agreements to avoid competition on certain products thought to be a prerogative of specific traders. What these dynamics appeared to guarantee was the shielding of autonomous forms and practices of business operation in a context highly controlled by collective structures and organizations. If we look at land tenure alone, the Aymaras combine forms of ancestral and communal ownership of land (*aynuqas*) with spaces under individual ownership where families build the house and cultivate cash crops (*sayañas*). Whereas the *sayañas* belong to individual families and constitute a form of tenure predating the colonial period and the formation of markets (Carter and Mamani 1982: 23), the communal *aynuqas* are divided into plots rotationally assigned to each family in the community, who then independently decide on the crop to plant and productive strategies.

In the current political debate over "who is (really) indigenous," which has reemerged with vehemence in Bolivia in the past few years, the indigenous status of highland communities is often demeaned since despite the existence of communal lands, members of the community commercialize their products in an "individual" fashion (Crabtree and Chaplin 2013). In other words, not only is the Aymaras's complex articulation of collectivity with forms of personal and familial autonomy distorted, but also "indigeneity" is measured through idealized, 19th-century European ideas of the noble savage.

Offspring as Tools of Business Diversification

Intergenerational relations are the ideal space to look at both the reproduction and consistency of the popular institutionality of Aymara traders and the peculiar articulation of enhanced autonomy with strict and capillary forms of social control and collective structures. As we have seen in the case of my godson, who at the age of ten was elected fiesta steward for the year 2025, youngsters are often caught up from an early age into the mechanisms of the sophisticated and multiform structures of Aymara institutionality. Simultaneously, however, sons and daughters are guaranteed important spaces of autonomy in decisions about their studies and professional life. In fact, from an early age children are exposed to meticulous observation of their tastes and preferences that are recognized as unique features although they may be influenced or dripped onto (*gotear*) by relatives and godmothers. Interfering with such features and preferences or with children's decisions is associated with the production of dangerous forms of resentment and disequilibrium.[5]

In his work on El Alto, the anthropologist Xavier Albó has pointed out the flexibility of Aymara social organizations. Albó describes the celebratory tradition of the urban Aymaras as a key moment in urban social life that enables the social and cultural insertion of young people into the social fabric and simultaneously promotes innovation through new forms and practices.

> In an energetic environment such as El Alto it is possible to develop a young, syncretic and dynamic version of the urban Aymara culture. The existence and expansion of a powerful urban festive tradition facilitates the social and cultural insertion of youngsters through the local community, the school or the numerous groups they themselves create by providing a wide range of options (. . .) They create and develop their own spaces and styles, sometimes including techno and rap music, to which they sometimes add the adjective "Aymara." (Albó 2006: 341, my translation)

In other words, the celebratory structure of urban Aymara sectors provides local youngsters with a framework within which they can—and are encouraged to—express diversity and produce innovation. Aymara celebratory practices outline a sustainable way to link different generations, producing a sense of continuity within transformation (Robbins and Wardlow 2005). A son or daughter's wedding is another crucial social event that in the Aymara tradition implies a sociopolitical transformation.[6] With the wedding, the couple is tied to multiple godmothers and godfathers, sealing bonds of "reciprocity" that become constitutive of the social life of the couple. This means that the newlyweds become connected simultaneously to multiple lines of fictive kinship as well as to varied and diverse socioeconomic environments. It is this multiplicity, diversification, and variability of options that constitute a key difference from the socio-economic dynamics of a more endogamous and fragmented local oligarchy whose offspring's social and economic options appeared to be more circumscribed.[7]

Intergenerational relations in the market operate in similar terms. In the main grocery market of La Paz, one can observe an increasing number of young female vendors, often holding university degrees in engineering or accountancy, working on the stalls they inherited from their mothers (cf. Scarborough 2013). In some cases, this was a consequence of the difficulty for these younger generations belonging to the urban popular sector to land a "professional" job. However, it was common for these educated youngsters to work as grocery sellers on the stall in the morning, while in the afternoon and evening they worked as receptionists or accountants for private firms. Such a strategy enabled them not to lose a sure source of income (the stall) while diversifying and multiplying their revenue options. Although this modus operandi reflected the peculiar flexibility and diversification strategies of the Andean economic organization, it also revealed the local distrust toward the idea of a single, formal, and permanent job providing social security and constituting the economic foundation of the family. Whereas the white urban middle-class bought into the modernist narrative of a progressive and linear transition from trade to NGO consultancy and office work, paradoxically nowadays experiencing unexpected forms of economic decline, popular traders diversified their businesses but also reinvested in their original product categories and commercial enterprises.

In the Andes, local agriculture's high exposure to climate risks had traditionally encouraged heightened forms of diversification, in terms of both crops with varying degrees of resistance to frost and plots in different ecological niches. In this context, the family worked as a pool of different resources, distributing its workforce according to the demands of the various activities in the attempt to maximize access to multiple products and possibilities. These Andean practices of diversification were further expanded with the participation of family members in forms of seasonal waged labor connected to national or regional agroindustrial (Dandler and Medeiros 1988) or mining enclaves (Platt et al. 2006).

In this sense, the rural kin viewed a son working in the sugar cane harvest in Argentina as a necessary local strategy of economic diversification to cope with the uncertainty and variability of local economic trends. Whereas modernist theories forecast the disintegration and subordination of local structures when they link with global capitalism (Platt 1982b;

Sánchez 1982; Calderón and Rivera 1984), from an Aymara point of view this was perceived as an expansion and stretching of historically rooted indigenous structures and strategies of diversification (Dandler and Medeiros 1988).

In such circumstances, rather than offspring being invested with the task of reproducing and improving the parents' business, they become recipients of the expectation to diversify the parents' enterprise and develop it in unexpected directions. For sons and daughters of established traders, this often implied the identification of an independent commercial niche that nonetheless maintained a degree of articulation with the parental business. As we have seen in the case of Ramiro, he imports video games from Guangzhou. A few years ago he installed a workshop in the basement of his house for assembling memory boards with imported Chinese technology and he wholesales these to business partners in the Paraguayan duty-free zone of Ciudad del Este (cf. Rabossi 2012). Once his daughter, María, got a degree in medicine from La Paz University, they began the paperwork to obtain a license to import and distribute Chinese medical equipment and drugs. Ramiro used to explain the business partnership with his daughter both in terms of access to a variety of products before local markets become saturated through increasing competition and in terms of a beneficial form of economic diversification. In the words of Ramiro,

> if instead of a single cow producing five liters of milk per day, you have three cows—videogames, memory boards and medical equipment—you save on forage, meaning transport, foreign business networks and export paperwork, and you now have enough milk that you can even start producing cheese. (Ramiro Yupanqui, paraphrased interview November 14, 2012)

Particularly among long-distance traders such as Ramiro, such an economic diversification promoted and produced by the participation of offspring in the family business is viewed not only as a reduction of risks but also as a possibility to generate economies of scale. This also meant that despite the forms of collaboration with parental authority, María was also granted an important degree of autonomy in the management of her business, both in financial terms and with regard to decision making. If, on the one hand, this once again proposed the idea of the family business as a concatenation of multiple activities, on the other hand, it suggested that personal independence was a precondition for engaging in familial and collective endeavors.

In the context of highly mobile families scattered across large distances, the emphasis on filial and individual dispositions was constantly counteracted by the necessity to avoid the "splitting" (*partirse*) of the family. When a son or a daughter living on his or her own in a remote border town or a faraway regional market faced problems or lingered on the brink of amoral or asocial behavior, the network of local *padrinos* would firmly intervene in often intimate matters, giving advice but also tightening the system of social control by mobilizing a number of local actors. It was common for an entire family to use the pretext of a social gathering to get together, recalling offspring and *padrinos* living in other cities for a whole week, disregarding business, working hours, and any kind of economic activities to "talk over" any social or economic dysfunction in the family.

Independent Workers in a Social Contract

The characteristics of local social structures and intergenerational relations as well as the economic history of this specific social sector all seem to incentivize high levels of employment diversification and even multiple, fragmented, and overlapping forms of labor. This resonated with neoliberal policies and practices that promote diversification and flexibilization. Once again, Aymara economic actors not only perceive such labor dynamics as dominant imperatives forced upon them but also and simultaneously metabolize them as tools for reproducing their local power structure and economic system.

These counterintuitive dynamics roundly contradict the analyses of local leftist economists who aspire to promote stable and formal employment, solid wage labor, state-run pension schemes, and a social security system. Even at a time when local popular sectors find themselves massively and successfully participating in economic networks of commerce and consumption, they still maintain a high degree of skepticism regarding the capacity of both formal institutions and the economy to provide stable forms of employment, consistent wage increases, and job promotions or a social security system able to guarantee a comfortable and healthy old age. In contrast to the local white-*mestizo* middle class that had traditionally benefited from the employment and ad hoc policies provided by the state or aspired to work as local representatives of foreign multinationals, Aymara traders maintained a strong sense of independence both in terms of external social security systems and regarding employment.

In El Alto, I often came across schoolteachers, priests, and policemen "diversifying" and complementing their income by locally reselling goods provided to them by Aymara wholesalers and importers. Although interpretations of the informal economy have tended to depict it as hierarchically dependent on the investments made by formal waged workers, particularly bureaucrats and civil servants (Hart 1973), Aymara traders appear to be able to coopt representatives of official institutions such as the church and the state into their networks and systems. Recent research conducted on employment in El Alto has begun to show that supposedly appealing formal waged employment—nursing, teaching, police work—were being rejected by locals either because of the limited possibilities for social mobility they were able to guarantee or because they hampered the performance of complementary economic activities (Pascale Absi, personal communication). The historic, chronic defectiveness of local capital reproduction and popular sectors' distrust of stable jobs and social security systems provided by conventional institutions, as well as their heightened sense of autonomy, fostered ideas and practices of labor that exposed the inadequacy of preconceived categories of "formal employment" and "wage labor" in any attempt to grasp the economic transformations enacted by Aymara traders.

The "Voice" Contract and the Interstices of Wage Labor

Within popular enterprises, labor relations were sanctioned through so-called "voice contracts" (*contratos a voz*). Despite their "informal" and unwritten quality, such verbal agreements imply, as we shall see, a series of both formal and customary rights and obligations. As well as being recognized as a thorough and effective bond socially enforced by local institutions, from the side of the employee the voice contract appeared to be valued for its open-endedness: in other words, for guaranteeing tolerated spaces of ambiguity that allowed the employee either to devote time to other economic activities or to earn extra (*aparte*) and independent profits—in addition to her salary—based on her entrepreneurial initiative.

On her own initiative, my friend Lourdes, who worked for a popular enterprise in the Huyustus market, would take advantage of the hours of the afternoon when sales slowed down to go and "offer" (*ir a ofrecer* or *ir a acomodar*) goods at the wholesale price to other popular retailers and traders willing to diversify their stock. She agreed with the owner beforehand on the wholesale price of each commodity and she then charged an extra (*aparte*) fee to the buyer, as remuneration for her own initiative, entrepreneurship, and negotiation skills. Although the owner would not be informed about the extra fee, these practices were sustained by a generalized and implicit social tolerance. Lourdes's success and skillfulness in the offering activities enabled her to produce 30% of the enterprise's profits and also double her salary. After a few years, Lourdes began retailing directly—with the help of her mother and from a smaller stall—some of the commodities that the enterprise's owner imported from the Iquique duty-free zone (Arbona et al. 2015: 98). In a way, Lourdes tried to conceal her own business from the owner and she even changed the name on the receipts so as not to arouse suspicions. However, every night the owner granted her time to go and collect payments from the customers of her stall.

The voice contract does not presuppose a strictly dependent form of waged labor since it creates ambiguous spaces where employees operate their own entrepreneurial initiative with a limited degree of risk, because the owner is still in charge of the products. As we have observed in the case of Lourdes, the other advantage that this type of working relationship guarantees for the employee is access to the economic networks of popular markets and their chains of distribution and supply, to the point where the employee is able to build actual partnerships with other local actors and entrepreneurs.

Vladimir, a middle-age employee of a local importer in the Eloy Salmón market, has specialized in negotiations with El Alto officials in charge of clearing customs, as well as dealing with highway patrols and taking care of relations with truck drivers. In addition to his network of key contacts and negotiation skills, his empirical knowledge of import procedures often surpasses the knowledge of the importers themselves. His services are so highly rated that he is "hired" by other importers, supposedly behind the back of his employer, who openly tolerates the nonexclusivity of the verbal employment contract. Whereas Vladimir receives a monthly salary of barely $300, it is in the negotiations with customs officials, policemen, and truck drivers that he gets most of his income. Sometimes, in his role of acting as a broker between different guilds or networks, Vladimir receives compensation from both sides.

Although the local commercial guilds often function as structures allocating jobs for local youngsters and loyal employees, in the past few years the benefits or, more accurately, the possibilities offered by the popular economy's voice contracts have been attracting several employees or accountants shifting from formal to informal employment. To join the Huyustus, Lourdes quit her sales position at Burger King, which in Bolivia is considered a formal establishment for urban middle-class customers and that has been recently at the center of a press scandal for the supposed impediments the company was posing to the unionization of its workers.[8] Usually these decisions are framed in terms of better opportunities for personal development or a wider set of socioeconomic options and possibilities.

Large brands such as Burger King often implement strategies of disciplining the workforce according to supposedly natural and often exploitative rules aimed at transforming the worker in a wage laborer. Undertaken as a civilizing project, capitalism's disciplining of the workforce, aspiring to instill respect for routinized working hours and days that sometimes clash with local religious and social events and so foregrounding labor as a priority in relation to kinship and tradition, has a long history of failure in Bolivia (Rodríguez Ostria 2014). Popular employers appeared to hold a clearer understanding of the local unsuitability and dislike of labor rules adopted by mainstream companies. They showed an unexpected degree of tolerance toward employees being absent from work for the three-day patron saint festival in their community of birth, for a cousin's marriage, or for a simple family gathering. Popular employers seemed to understand the local codes, aspirations, and priorities of their employees while challenging supposedly universal rules that regulate labor in a capitalist society: you can be a paid worker while maintaining a degree of autonomy in relation to your employer and from the label of "wage laborer" and uphold your social priorities and personal aspirations instead of being reduced to a modern proletarian uprooted from traditional forms of belonging, ideas, and practices.

Probably the most interesting feature of the local forms of labor and the voice contract was the series of benefits and rights that it entailed. In other words, the employees were included in the institutional structures and provision of services that the Aymara traders had generated in the interstices of official institutions. The first set of benefits was referred to as "constitutional rights." Although the voice contract was informal and not legally registered, it entailed a series of "informal obligations" on the part of the employer, such as paying the end-of-the-year bonus (*aguinaldo*, consisting of an additional month's salary) to employees and providing them with "health insurance," namely, a refund for health expenses such as those incurred because of accidents at work and, in some cases, childbirth. In 2013, the Morales government issued a decree that forced public institutions and private companies to pay a double end-of-year bonus to their employees because of the country's exceptional economic performance. Although some of the "companies" were not formally registered and their employees only had a voice contract, in the Eloy Salmón the employers regularly paid the double bonuses to their employees. Once again, the practices and rules of the formal and official world are masterfully appropriated by the popular economy to further legitimize their own social and economic system.

Exploitation and Deferred Solidarity

If, on the one hand, the ambiguity of voice contracts seems to stir up forms of subaltern resourcefulness among local employees, on the other hand, it also seems to promote certain forms of exploitation. In markets such as the Huyustus, Eloy Salmón, or 16 de Julio, a common figure is that of the orphan "adopted" by a family of traders and working as an employee or a helper in the family business. Another emblematic figure is the market porter (*aparapita* or *cargador*) turned into a workhand or, in some cases, even a technician in an electrical goods shop. Both the orphan and the market porter are quintessential figures associated with loneliness and displacement in melancholic Andean songs. The marginality of the orphan and the porter is conventionally associated with being severed from a place and from community bonds and thus being identified as "foreigners" (*forasteros*). It is this sense of displacement, dispossession, and severance that supposedly fosters heightened forms of loyalty once a trader's family takes them under its wing. In fact, the hiring of a porter in the family shop engenders an overlap of social and economic meanings as the formal salary paid for his work becomes intertwined with a sense of gratitude for rescuing him from the street. It is this overlap or confusion between social and economic domains[9] that makes the porter more available to work longer shifts and to perform duties not included in his voice contract—for instance, taking the employer's children to school.

In the popular markets of La Paz and El Alto, Aymara employees working for local Aymara entrepreneurs are not unionized, although they often participate in the meetings of the local traders' guilds, and, above all, they play an active role in the social and religious activities of traders' fraternities. In other words, employees of the Huyustus or the Eloy Salmón are not organized in a labor union connoted by a divergence of social and economic interests with their employers who run the local shops. On the contrary, they are careful to constantly and publicly convey their belonging to the wider community of traders. This is not because employee unionization is vetoed by local entrepreneurs, but because the conceptualization of labor differs from taken-for-granted definitions. The idea of the independent individual worker "freely" selling her labor (as alienable property) on the market is replaced by an understanding of labor as a social contract granting connections to a wider socioeconomic system. Not only is labor allocated, regulated, and linked to the networks and forms of kinship of the popular sectors, but also, from the point of view of the employees, it guarantees forms of participation in both traders' guilds and fraternities (or, as we have seen, even in forms of entrepreneurship and chains of supply and distribution). Employees mobilize popular and Aymara codes and forms of reciprocity to constantly reassert their participation and membership in a wider sociocultural community and thus force the employer to rebalance vertical forms of authority that are seen as detrimental to local alliances and even socially sanctioned.

In the Huyustus and Eloy Salmón markets, employees participate actively both in the urban battles against the raids of customs aimed at confiscating "unregistered" commodities and in the protests against the constitutionally shaky laws clamping down on the popular economy. In the late 2000s, Bolivian employees of the Bolivian sweatshops in Buenos Aires amazed local authorities when, after an intense media campaign against "slave labor" in the immigrant Bolivian sweatshops, they took to the street together with their employers to protest against the violence of the raids led by the police. Not only were employees openly protesting against the label of slave labor in the sweatshops, but also they were challenging the well-intentioned local media, defiantly accusing them of considering Bolivian workers stupid to the point of not understanding when they were being exploited (Forment 2014).

In the case of sweatshop workers in Buenos Aires, some manage to establish their own independent business even after six months of wage labor. During this short time, they are able to get acquainted with the networks of providers and distributors, identify strategic *caseros* to wholesale their products to, and eventually consolidate their participation in the activities of the guild and the fraternity. The Bolivian sociologist Silvia Rivera has been the most outspoken in facing the accusations against slave labor in Aymara shops and workshops and in proposing the necessity of different categories and ideas with which to think of Aymara wage labor. The frequent matrimonial alliances between family of traders and employees, the nonexistent record of labor claims against Aymara traders in the Ministry of Labor, and the frequent switches or even complementarity between dependent and nondependent labor give cause for greater caution when addressing the supposed slave quality of labor in trader's enterprises. Rivera suggests that Aymara workers undergo forms of "self-exploitation" and "payment of dues" (*derecho de piso*) as they conceive of their economic and social ascendance not so much as a straight line, but as a process going through hierarchical step-stages (*gradas*) where what you pay in one stage will be reciprocated or "paid back" to you in the following ones. Rivera uses the Aymara notion of "deferred solidarity" to refer to the idea that dues paid in one stage will benefit your future stages or generations in a logic of Aymara reciprocity that often involves not only employer and employee, but also cosmological forces and future generations not yet born.

These dynamics have impeded the materialization of a mere simplistic classist structure of local society where, supposedly, with the emergence of forms of social stratification within an ethnic group, the emerging sectors would join the interests and demeanors of the oppressors acting against their own people (Long and Roberts 1984; Poole 1988). On the one hand, traders keep functioning according to indigenous demeanors and codes and, within those same codes, employees have also been able to develop modalities of social pressure and forms of subaltern resourcefulness. On the other hand, an indigenous society that was often perceived as static, feudal (Lora, cited in Wanderley 2003), and based on fixed customs (Geertz 1979), as well as prone to decomposing because of internal diversification, has demonstrated an important capacity to accommodate local and translocal, vertical and horizontal (Guaygua and Castillo 2008) instances. The overlap among employees of wage labor and independent entrepreneurial initiative, their manipulation of Aymara codes and logics in order to access wider socioeconomic spaces, knowledge and even chains of supply and distribution make us understand the employees' outflow from an exclusive formal economy to the "informal" one. Beside, it blurs both the circumscribed identity of the "wage laborer" and the narrative of a linear proletarianization, severance and alienation of labor which, in fact, remains embedded in local organizational structures and cosmological concepts consolidated and expanded by the affirmation of Aymara trade.

As we shall see, these practices did not indicate a "parallel" socioeconomic system that was antistate or against public morality, but rather outlined a complex organizational structure that attempted to affirm legitimacy and "citizenship" on their own terms. The articulation between dependent and autonomous forms of labor, its conceptualization as a social and participatory tool instead of an individually owned resource, and its links with forms and ideas of the formal official world displace conventional and Manichean economic categories and interpretations that become unsatisfying hermeneutic tools unable to make sense of the ferment and quality of this type of economy.

Conclusions

The peculiar articulation between public and private, individual and collective domains and the capacity to guarantee and tolerate spaces of autonomous decision making in a context of strict social control are key features of the Aymara traders' economy. This produces a simultaneous reliance on the often-complex framework of local organizations and practices of mutual help and a heightened sense of autonomy of the single enterprise or entrepreneur. A single enterprise may present a high degree of internal diversification and multiple layers of decision making. This generates less hierarchical and patriarchal forms of internal organization (cf. Putnam et al. 1994), which appears simultaneously to promote newness—in terms of both strategies and ideas—and to facilitate the reproduction of the material and cultural stock on which the enterprise is based.

Offspring may be bearers of specific preferences for or luck (*suerte*) in certain types of business and/or regional markets. This generates both a process of flexibilization of the family-run enterprise and the extension of its radius or modalities of operation. In fact, such enterprises are often reluctant to plans of permanent expansion, either through new machinery and infrastructure or by taking on additional workers. In some cases this might be a result of the preference for coopting ill-paid members of the family not covered by social security (Long and Roberts 1984: 157). However, several enterprises of Aymara traders tended to amplify their radius of operation and networks rather than consolidating permanent and concentrated enterprises. The resulting modality of enterprise is a family-run "circuit-enterprise" (cf. Landolt et al. 1999) with multiple and articulated nodes of decision-making operating in different social networks and geographical locations. As we have seen, this type of circuit-enterprise appears to reconcile the benefits of large firms for its capacity to generate economies of scale with the heightened flexibility of small enterprises able to easily readapt and reconvert its structure in moments of market transformation (see Chapter 7).

Marx (1990 [1867]) argued that forms of primary accumulation in the absence of a free labor market might involve coercive practices, which, in the case of Aymara traders, would take the form of paternalistic ties and non-wage incentives. However, unlike conventional enterprises, Aymara traders were the advocates of forms of labor that reflected local ideas and aspirations. Instead of pushing for a proletarianization of workers and employees through an ideology of permanent but subordinate job specialization, their idea of labor reconciled forms of waged labor with autonomous initiative, work and pleasure, exploitation of family members, and inclusion in the guild of traders and entrepreneurs. As we have seen, employment does not necessarily respond to the demand-and-supply logic, nor is it an individualized service, since it remains tied to future generations and to the membership of kinship networks that, through specific redistributive forms, assures remuneration and social benefits. Although this does not imply the absence of forms of "exploitation," the collective dimension and relational dynamics in which labor is inserted hinders its conceptualization as alienable individual property.

CHAPTER 6

Economic Strategies in the Aymara World-System

In the prior two chapters we focused on the cosmological dimension of Aymara traders and its tendency to structure a series of economic practices and conceptions of the market, to carve out autonomous spaces at the heart of the global economy, and to define the rhythm of reinvestment in and withdrawal from the market. In their manifesto of "cosmoeconomics," da Col and Rio (2013) emphasized how the economy and cosmology are tied together by a "double bind" where material and financial conditions constantly influence cosmological practices and meanings while simultaneously being acted on by them. In the case of Aymara traders, the intersection of the flows of the global economy with a local socioeconomic structure, whose reproduction capacity was founded on its ability to appropriate and resignify external elements (see Chapter 3), revived and expanded a series of skills, knowledges, and strategies to both connect and disconnect global markets and local worlds. Although these strategies have deep historical roots, today they tend to acquire a series of global connotations while often not conforming to the expectations of conventional economic concepts and narratives.

Plurimarkets and Arbitrage

Drawing on the culturally specific ability to mobilize, memorize, and update information about a variety of market discrepancies and segments scattered across vast territories, Aymara traders have shown a well-developed capacity to operate between and exploit the different urban niches and social/ethnic frontiers, adopting diversified commercial modalities in their relations with different social sectors. Among white-*mestizo* middle-class traders, the idea and the practices of commerce are bound up with supposedly universal categories, preferences, and marketing strategies. In contrast, the Aymaras's capillary knowledge of the local territory and markets as well as of urban ethnic boundaries and economic discrepancies make them prone to operate in a variety of sociocultural spaces, embracing multiple strategies and practices fitting different economic logics and idiosyncrasies.

Migrants from the plateau town of Sica Sica have specialized in the trade of tools and construction equipment, mostly produced in China. Their retailing base is located in the central neighborhood of *La Ceja* in El Alto and in the *Isaac Tamayo* street of La Paz, only two blocks from the Eloy Salmón. Because the urban middle classes are often unwilling to venture in the crowded popular streets of the slope, in the past decade Sica Siqueños opened branches in the wealthy neighborhood of *San Miguel* in the *Zona Sur* retailing at 5–10% higher prices than in El Alto and thereby exploiting local social discrepancies.

Several importers alternate retail with wholesale in different urban locations. As we have seen, Ramiro runs his millionaire business from a fifty-or-so square-foot room in the Huyustus market where he exhibits video game samples for traders who come to visit him from the 16 de Julio and the Eloy Salmón but also from Peru, Amazonian towns on the border with Brazil, and other Bolivian cities in the south. More than ten years ago, with the help of a *compadre*, Ramiro rented a sales space in the Eloy Salmón market to retail video games. Despite being located only a few blocks down the slope from the Huyustus, the Eloy Salmón market has become an attractive place for the shopping sprees of the white-*mestizo* urban middle class in search of cheap appliances and electronics. In contrast to popular consumers, this kind of client is often not knowledgeable about the prices and technical features of electronic products, and higher profit margins are therefore possible in a context where prices are never fixed or exhibited and brand counterfeiting is likely.[1]

This logic of exploiting different social layers within a city is commonly complemented by a tendency to operate simultaneously or seasonally in a variety of markets across the country or the region (Tassi 2012a), exploiting social and commercial discrepancies. As we have seen, at the end of each month when salaries are paid, Rigoberto travels across the country to mining towns to sell shoes. Also, at the end of the year Rigoberto travels to the south of Bolivia and the border with Argentina to sell the large-size leftovers for which there is no market among the "short" residents of La Paz and El Alto (see Tassi et al. 2013: 189).

The regional understanding of commerce among popular traders is a relatively new phenomenon for economies that supposedly used to take no notice of regional partners. With the arrival of cheap leatherlike materials from China, leather jacket producers in La Paz and El Alto have begun finding new commercial niches in more sophisticated markets such as Lima and Buenos Aires, where their products are highly competitive in relation to mainstream brands. Simultaneously, they were increasingly searching for and finding new niches in Bolivia's quickly expanding intermediate cities with increasingly complex local markets where producers could retail their goods directly.

In the *feria* 16 de Julio in El Alto, the majority of traders operate in this vast market two days a week. The rest of the week they travel to other cities and towns across the country, carrying their commodities with them. This recreates a system of interconnected *ferias* stretching for hundreds of miles across a diverse territory and economy, with a rotation and concatenation of traders and services. For instance, Alteño garment producers who run stands on Thursdays and Sundays in the *feria* 16 de Julio send their spouse or offspring to Santa Cruz to retail and wholesale their products in the *feria* of Barrio Lindo on Saturdays but also to buy raw materials such as Brazilian thread. Barrio Lindo is a strategic wholesaling spot from which Bolivian garments are distributed to neighboring countries such as Brazil, Argentina, and Paraguay but also to the several intermediate cities around Santa Cruz enjoying an agribusiness boom.

The Andean concept of "discontinuous" community scattered across a variety of territories and ecological niches stimulates a set of social and economic skills enabling locals to operate simultaneously in multiple spaces and markets. As we have seen, this remains interwoven with a cosmological principle that identifies the flows of products across different ecological zones as a fecund and reproductive movement articulating different localities and territories, peoples and spirits (Harris 1989; Sallnow 1989; Platt 1992).

The Prestige of Mobility

Instead of specializing in one specific territory or investing in one single market, Aymara traders are increasingly operating in multiple commercial spaces across the region. For local traders, this has meant maximizing their geographical mobility while simultaneously building multiple bonds to generate forms of access to a variety of markets and concurrently reducing travel and accommodation costs. Such modalities of operation, often based on fictive kinship, resulted in the recomposition and expansion of a system articulating multiple territories and actors spread across large distances, as well as a practice of multiple domicile (cf. Harris 1989) that in the past guaranteed Andean peoples the capacity to control and administer extensive territories. Instead of renting a shop in Caranavi or on the border with Peru or Brazil, Aymara traders rely increasingly on existing local structures for the control of the market and traveling. At a time of economic bonanza, with the emergence of new "rural" markets and the increasing sophistication of existing urban segments, traders opt to maintain a degree of flexibility and openness to these multiple options.

Such increasing mobility is also stimulated by the recent improvement of macroeconomic indicators in Bolivia and the consequent enhancement of the purchasing power of rural sectors and remote regions—such as the Andean plateau—which had traditionally been seen as economically unviable (cf. Bebbington 2000). These economic improvements have been paralleled by the expansion and upgrade of the road infrastructure, followed by an exponential growth in the number of transportation companies as well as the forms of transportation (Medeiros et al. 2013), generating a much more fluid economic connection between urban and rural areas. Interestingly, it was mostly the indigenous and popular sectors that took advantage of these heightened possibilities of moving around. Just as one can find schoolteachers reselling clothes in the 16 de Julio on weekends, one can also find highly mobile rural families that combine farming, herding, or small-scale mining in the countryside with selling electronic products acquired from relatives on the Chilean side of the border.

My friend and fraternity brother (*fraterno*) Nicanor worked in El Alto as a butcher running two retailing kiosks in *Villa Dolores* and *Santiago II* and selling imported secondhand cars and auto parts in the *feria* 16 de Julio. Five years ago, Nicanór reinvested in his high-plateau community, where he decided to convert his family plot into a cattle farm, given the land's suitability for growing alfalfa forage. He converted a secondhand truck he had imported from Iquique into a livestock transporter to bring the cattle to the slaughterhouse in El Alto and decided to divide his working week between his community and the city.

My *compadre* Egidio is a small contractor in El Alto and he is now involved in building the headquarters of the construction workers' union. Originally from a high-plateau community by the lake, together with the other families from his community Egidio decided to form a cooperative to mine rocks from a local ravine and convert them into gravel for the construction industry in El Alto. A community-run truck cooperative transports the rocks to El Alto, where they are ground into gravel. This year Egidio has been chosen as secretary general of the community, so he can be seen in El Alto alternating construction overalls with ponchos and whip (*chicote*), the symbols par excellence of indigenous authority. These dynamics incentivize bidirectional reinvestments in the city and the countryside and consolidate their connections, turning El Alto into the hinge around which these ongoing transitions revolve.

Until the 1980s, the conception of the development of El Alto was tied to severing its connections with the backward rural regions through a "green belt" along the perimeter of the city, which should have sped up its modernization (Juan Manuel Arbona, personal communication). Nowadays, the Aymara logic of constantly generating economic and cosmological synergies between different territories appears to prevail, becoming a structuring mechanism of the city's economic expansion that remains inextricably entrenched in its connection with the rural regions.

Social and economic analyses in Bolivia are often faced with this novel tension. The deep-rooted stereotype of El Alto being nothing more than a hotbed of unemployment, a slum (Davis 2006), and a nonproductive "dormitory town" whose inhabitants daily invade the streets of La Paz is today reversed by the gradual transition of La Paz's popular economic activities and popular sectors toward El Alto, which is now nicknamed "the merchant city." In fact, we have recently witnessed a process of transition by popular entrepreneurs from La Paz's slope to the neighborhoods of El Alto that not only have become more convenient for business but also provide strategic locations for the social positioning of ascending traders and for their cultural reproduction. In the past few years, El Alto has also become the leading city in the transportation of both goods and passengers. Besides, 30% of Bolivia's registered incoming goods clear customs in El Alto.[2]

The boom in El Alto appears to be founded on its capacity to maintain and develop links with multiple economic spaces. Its growth is paralleled by processes of apparent decentralization such as the emergence of a new customs facility in the middle of the high plateau—Patacamaya—that, in certain product categories such as heavy machinery, takes an important percentage of the total trade. In the plantation and mining towns of the Yungas valleys and the piedmont, the expansion of transportation service seems to lead to the development of new and important communication networks tangential to the traditional central axis crossing the country from west to southeast. For instance, El Alto has become a stocking center for plateau vegetables, meat, and tubers destined for the markets of the Amazon region on the border with Brazil, such as Cobija, Guayaramerín, and Riberalta. Similarly, tropical products such as papaya, plantain, and cassava produced in the Yungas are redistributed through Alteño families to a number of highland cities including Potosí, Sucre, and Cochabamba. In other words, the economic boom in El Alto lies in its capacity to articulate and develop commercial alliances with a variety of other spaces and places, generating both virtuous synergies and an unexpected level of mobility.

Both ethnographic (Geertz 1963, 1979) and historical accounts of early forms of trade (Le Goff 1982; Braudel 1981; cf. Curtin 1984; cf. Polanyi et al. 1957) have suggested how these entrepreneurial ventures were organized through centralized and hierarchical structures (i.e., the *compagnia* or the *comenda*). Florentine traders' families in Italy such as the Medici, Peruzzi, and Bardi would hire services from middlemen and local traders in a variety of towns and *ferias* spread across Europe (Le Goff 1982). In other words, it was through their headquarters in Florence that the Medici ran their trade and hired people to handle business locally. Something similar happened in the bazaar economy of Sefrou studied by Clifford Geertz (1979). The bazaar economy appeared to be structured along the lines of a hierarchical system where civilized "sitting" merchants would dispatch their goods across long distances through the work of impoverished, unlearned, and "riding" peddlers (Geertz 1979: 134). Such a system stimulated a linear understanding of the development of trade and a progressive tendency toward sedentarization as small, itinerant, and successful merchants would gradually become urbanized and set up their emporium.

Particularly in the case of El Alto, the development of popular trade has taken on different connotations from both the bazaar economy and the Florentine families. Rather than concentrating on managing trade across long distances from a comfortable office and hiring peddlers to handle business in local markets, the family—through a system of networks and *compadrazgo* bonds—takes charge of the entire trade cycle, from the clearing of customs in El Alto (or even the purchasing in China) to the distribution of products in remote rural areas and border towns. First, this system guarantees the family forms of direct access (cf. Salomon 1985) to multiple markets; second, it allows forms of direct control over chains of supply and distribution, thus limiting the incursion of foreign competitors into those routes; and third, it is rooted in forms of heightened mobility, the capacity to travel regularly, and multiple forms of domicile across the territory. Despite traveling repeatedly to mining and border towns, Rigoberto blamed his supposedly weak capacity for geographical mobility on the fact that he was a bachelor (*yokalla* in Aymara). Because he was not married, he had not developed an extended network of kin and trusted *compadres* with whom to share his workload and expand his business properly at a national and regional level.

As we observed in Chapter 5, this system is based on the counterintuitive combination of a strong sense of independence of popular trading enterprises with constant and multiple articulations and bonds with other actors and businesses. Geertz's subaltern riding peddlers are here replaced by autonomous and highly mobile traders who prefer to take on risks, responsibilities, and profits directly. Particularly in the *feria* 16 de Julio, commercial mobility was considered a social imperative. Retailers who only traded in the *feria* were often the object of scorn because that implied either a small family network or a limited commercial capacity and an inability to expand their economic activity geographically. In other words, rather than social pressure to move toward a supposedly more civilized sedentary trade, what we observe particularly in El Alto is a simultaneous emphasis on the social and economic benefits of mobility that can be seen as a sign of prestige and well-being.

These dynamics outlined an unusual politicoeconomic scenario. In fact, this system of interspersed and overlapping networks posed a political and economic challenge to conventional institutions and local elites for the control of the national territory and the economy. Aymara traders worked as connectors of these different economic spaces linking the country with the city and the nation with the region, while generating economic axes crosswise to the conventional ones.

Rosalía Urquizo is a secondhand auto parts retailer who runs two stands in the *feria* 16 de Julio in El Alto on Thursdays and Sundays. On Mondays, Rosalía travels to Iquique to buy auto parts from her cousin, Pablo, who purchases beyond-repair Asian cars from Pakistani vendors and has them disassembled (*charqueados*) in his own workshop within the Iquique duty-free zone to retrieve usable spare parts. Rosalía's husband, Mario, owns two Volvo trucks and travels between El Alto and Yungas valleys to buy papaya, which he then resells in the highlands. Taking advantage of his knowledge of local networks, Mario sells and distributes auto parts to mechanic workshops in the Yungas intermediate cities of Caranavi and Palos Blancos before returning to the highlands with a truckload of papaya. On a weekly basis, Rosalía also supplies her sister Marina and her fellow guild members retailing secondhand auto parts and running mechanic workshops in the Alto San Pedro market in Santa Cruz.

The specialty of economic actors such as the Urquizos is once again the capacity to operate with a variety of actors and markets, large companies and retailers, small-town *ferias*, and international brokers. Together with thousands of other highly mobile families, the Urquizos have played a key role in redesigning the economic geography of the country.

Handling Multiple Economic Niches

The detailed knowledge of multiple local and regional markets and the capacity to exploit the economic and social discrepancies of different markets and segments are constantly paired with heightened forms of diversification by product and the ability to handle a variety of complex product categories simultaneously with astonishing sophistication. The uncommon sedentarization of traders and the lack of specialization by market is paralleled by the rarity of specialization by product as a source of competitiveness. Instead, traders maintain a network of overlapping product categories, allowing them to constantly reduce risks and the possibility to redirect trade at times of economic upheaval.

One common economic strategy is the seasonal or even daily diversification of product categories to reflect the cyclical changes in consumption trends. I have recounted elsewhere (Tassi et al. 2013: 191) the story of Nemesia Huanca, a vegetable wholesaler/retailer who buys her merchandise from rural relatives and *comadres* who come to the *Villa Dolores* market in El Alto on Thursday nights, carrying their products on shared trucks. Nemesia runs a garage/storehouse where she stockpiles newly acquired vegetables and where her rural relatives and suppliers spend the night resting after the tiring trip. Her wholesaling activities begin as early as 3:30 in the morning as she supplies products to vegetable retailers from other urban markets in both El Alto and La Paz. At 6:30 am, her retailing activities begin as Nemesia starts selling in smaller quantities to local clients, restaurant owners, and other customers coming to *Villa Dolores* for their weekly stock of staple food. Around midday, when retailing slows down, her daughter Lucy arrives in the market with a pushcart she picks up from home after leaving school. For a couple of hours, Nemesia and Lucy close the garage gate and start selling juices and homemade beverages from the pushcart to local traders, truck drivers, and the *yatiris* who have established their tents and practices (*consultorios*) next to the market.

In commercial neighborhoods such as Gran Poder in La Paz and Chacaltaya in El Alto, a new business phenomenon has begun to materialize in the past few years. With the boom in ritual and festive celebrations in popular neighborhoods, commercial establishments, market stalls, and grocery shops are converted in the evenings or on weekends into gift shops for guests attending christening or wedding celebrations at the nearby popular reception halls. Rambo runs a butcher's shop in front of a reception hall. On Saturday evenings, he slides the meat counter to a corner of the shop, covers up the meat hooks and rails with old bed sheets, and brings in hundreds of potential presents, from blankets to tea sets, textiles to silverware. In forty minutes, Rambo converts his butcher's shop into a gift shop. Generally, this flexibility is enabled by the small size of these enterprises and their informal character, which avoids the bureaucratic burden of having to change their business description or obtain a new license. This not only implies a reduction in costs and paperwork but also requires the dexterity to constantly read the transformations in the market, to rapidly observe when the demand for a product approaches its saturation point, and to identify new business opportunities (Tassi et al. 2013).

Interestingly, the ability to handle multiple product categories simultaneously and the high level of product diversification do not apply only to small and semiformal entrepreneurs such as Nemesia and Rambo. In some cases, the level of diversification has increased either with the expansion of the business or with the consolidation of the commercial bond with China, given the insuperable inventive capacity of the Asian giant and its ability to constantly dish out onto the market new products with a short lifecycle.

Aymara importers from the region of Sabaya established in the plateau city of Oruro take advantage of their proximity with the harbor of Iquique and their privileged connection to some of the main cities of Bolivia—La Paz–El Alto, Cochabamba, Potosí—to operate seasonal wholesaling activity of a number of product categories for short periods of time. For instance, Sabayeños sell school supplies wholesale until September; from October to November they shift to Christmas decorations and New Year fireworks; in December they shift again to Carnival supplies. Over the year, they are able to handle five or six different and complex categories of commodities that require specialist knowledge and know-how, as well as links with multiple and often-foreign suppliers. Their wholesaling activities are articulated to a number of small and seasonal retailers scattered across the country that seasonally travel to Oruro to purchase from the Sabayeños, making this dusty plateau city one of the most diverse in terms of buyers.

Today, Aymara traders not only use product diversification as a tool to reduce the risks of the sudden and uncontrollable fluctuations in the global economy, but also turn it into a strategy to expand their commercial reach based on a series of local skills and knowledges. As we have seen, the inflow of younger generations in the family-run enterprise is not framed in terms of modernization of the business structure or technological specialization. To use a botanical metaphor, sons and daughters are often entrusted with the duty to generate and develop new branches of the economic family tree, either by gaining commercial spaces in new markets or by expanding the business toward other product categories and activities. This modality of business expansion bears interesting resemblances to the Aztec long-distance traders (*pochtecas*) studied by Anne Chapman (1957). Organized as a guild with distinctive gods and rites, the business activities of *pochteca* traders were driven by the conception of trade as an expansive act of "conquest" of markets and territories. In this sense, trade preceded tribute, administration, and commerce in the process of conquering a province. Aymara trade operates in the political and economic interstices of the global economy but it deploys similar strategies and structures to reach out to or "conquer" spaces and domains that official institutions have been unable (or uninterested) to reach.

Trade as Seed Capital

In this logic of the family business conceived of as an expanding tree with repeated conquests of new spaces and domains, it becomes interesting to follow Aymara traders' overflow into other, complementary economic activities and particularly toward production (Tassi et al. 2013). In a country such as Bolivia, whose economy has been characterized by the export of raw materials and high levels of informal commercial activities (UNDP 2005), the traditional problem economic experts have been trying to address has been the gap between primary export activities and the tertiary sector, namely the scarcity or absence of a productive vocation in the country. With the popular trade boom in the country, a counterintuitive phenomenon has begun to materialize. Probably for the first time in history, part of the profits from trade is being reinvested in local productive activities, highlighting a series of unexpected synergies and articulations between trade and production and suggesting that trade is playing the role of generating start-up capital for other types of economic activities.

Born in the plateau town of Guaqui, Mercedes Limachi worked a few years in the family business distributing Chinese semimanufactured textiles to a number of workshops across the country. Building on her experience and network developed as a textile distributor, Mercedes first traveled to São Paulo to work in the garment business and then, eventually, as we have seen, settled in Santa Cruz, where she established her own spinning mill. Mercedes's scope of operation was simply impressive. She traveled monthly to the Gamarra shopping center in Lima to buy cotton and new models of tops, shirts, and jackets and she regularly received drawings of Brazilian-designed garments from her Bolivian colleagues who had settled on the industrial hubs on the Atlantic coast, items that she then had reproduced locally. Her brother José, based in Shanghai, acted as a sentinel, spotting new fabrics and threads on the market that were suitable for Mercedes's production activities.

After importing canned and bagged condiments and spices from Peru through the border town of Desaguadero for ten years, René had his packaging company installed in El Alto by Mercedes's cousin, Mariano. Mariano worked for a few decades in Brazil at a company repairing industrial machines. Once back in El Alto, he created his own company that semiartisanally produced industrial machines (*hechizos*) for local industry. In the meantime, René had established contact with spice producers from Sucre and the southern Andean valleys of Bolivia. After having the spices processed and packaged in El Alto, René began distributing his highly competitive spices to the whole country, particularly to the Northern Amazon regions traditionally culturally connected with Brazil and that had recently been showing an interest in the cheaper products of Bolivian cuisine (see Arbona et al. 2015).

In the case of René and Mercedes, commerce and distribution provided them with the seed capital (*capital semilla*) to invest in a proper, full-size factory. However, in most cases reinvestment by popular traders in productive activities has been directed toward forms of light industry. Silveria's nephew set up an assembly workshop for Chinese motorcycle parts with capital of less than $5,000. Ramiro's workshop assembling flash memory sticks in the garage of his own dwelling consisted of a tiny conveyor belt and a soldering iron. The Choque family, who had been importing pots and pans first from Brazil and then from China, established a workshop in El Alto to cut and laminate aluminum as well as their own brand of pots made in Bolivia. The Choques began importing aluminum from China, which they successively cut and laminated on site, but they also continued to import pots and pans from Asia to diversify their stock. From supplying small retailers in La Paz and El Alto, their distribution network expanded dramatically, both nationally and regionally. Once again, popular traders' reinvestment in productive activities is carefully considered so as not to hamper their mobility and flexibility. Workshops such as the one owned by the Choques are often characterized by minimum levels of investment so they can be quickly readapted to new functions and businesses in case of a sudden shift in the global economy or new emerging possibilities. Interestingly, despite having established their own brand, the Choques kept importing specifically designed pots and pans from China to heighten the diversification of their stock and activities, as well as to maintain their networks and connections with China.

For people such as Mercedes and the Choques, trade is a tool to get to know the markets, their fluctuations, and their discrepancies as well as to access information about the demands and tricks of how the economy operates in a context of infrastructural and institutional limitations. But trade is also a key instrument through which people consolidate and expand their social network. Once one has gained such connections, knowledge, and information, one might then be able to identify and control more solid economic niches that provide enough guarantees to venture into productive activities. In the case of the Choques, their expertise in import procedures, knowledge of foreign manufacturers and mechanical devices, and acquaintance with local producers and production systems led them to reinvest in a workshop producing pots to meet a specific local demand. In El Alto, most of the commercial establishments for the sale of processed food are run by street vendors who cook the food at home and then transport it to strategic locations such as the city center, schools, and churches. They therefore require types of pots of specific dimensions that can be carried on a minibus and are light enough to be easily handled and transported.

Particularly in El Alto, where the articulation between productive and commercial activities appears more immediate, the synergies between trade and production have begun shaping a type of economic know-how adjusted to the specificities of the country. In the case of fabric importers, they would design new fabric patterns more suited to the local demand and aesthetic (e.g., *matizado*, a combination of colors in the fabric generating the visual effect of a gradual transition from dark to brighter colors or viceversa) and they would negotiate with multiple clothes manufacturing workshops in Bolivia to reach a volume sufficient to place an order with a Chinese producer and make it cost-effective. In most cases, Aymara traders traveling to China would function as strategic intermediaries with the necessary knowledge to identify cheap Chinese fabrics that could be imported, manufactured locally by Bolivian producers and retailed at a price competitive with the Chinese end product.

As we have seen, Alteño mechanics' workshops would interact with fellow Aymara importers to negotiate improvements that would need to be implemented on imported Chinese tools and products according to the characteristics of the local market and the specificities of the local manufacturing process. This not only created a synergy between local traders and producers but also allowed foreign technology to be adapted to the requirements of a specific production system and to the local economic structures. The mechanics in El Alto needed tools resistant enough to cut the stainless-steel chassis of old trucks that they used to assemble new machines or wheel rims and nuts resistant to the repeated oscillations caused by a rough and mostly unpaved road system. Such improved products enabled them to assemble trucks both affordable to popular drivers and more resistant and suited to the local transportation and infrastructure network than imported products. The synergies between trade and production appeared to outline a type of knowledge strengthening, specializing, and consolidating a local production system and know-how (cf. Arbona et al. 2015).

Conclusions

El Alto has been stereotypically viewed as the home of microenterprises incapable of producing economies of scale or effective access to information (UNDP 2005). The supposedly conflictive, fragmented socioeconomic environment and scant access to formal education was said to have engendered an intrinsic inability to generate virtuous synergies among different enterprises and actors and required forms of structural adjustment to the canons and knowledge of mainstream entrepreneurs. What emerges from the strategies we have analyzed in this chapter is an impressive dynamicity of local entrepreneurs and the ability to access multiple types of economic knowledge, from territorial knowledge and market discrepancies to specialized technologies that they manage to readapt and connect to the local reality and know-how. Their web of social, productive, and commercial activities highlights effective flows of information and responses to local economic needs and an ability to constantly read and react to market transformations and possibilities, based on strategies rooted in their own social structures and cultural forms. As we shall see in the next chapter, instead of adjusting to the conventional recommendations of economic experts, the capacity of Aymara traders to build on their own strategies and structures has enabled them to defy local economic hierarchies and even to solidify their own pattern of socioeconomic affirmation.

CHAPTER 7

The Upsurge of Aymara Traders: An Indigenous Project of Social Affirmation

In Bolivia, it was not until recently[1] that the idea of a socioeconomic reconfiguration of the country led by the emergence of economic actors neglected by conventional analysts began to gain a foothold. However, the acceptance of such transformations was often accompanied in the local scholarship by an emphasis on the deterioration of the socioeconomic and political conditions of the country (Ayo et al. 2013; cf. Chatterjee 2004). First, the new emerging economic and political actors would not hold the skills or the democratic capacity to lead the country toward sustainable forms of development. Second, through tailored economic policies and benefits, the government would be fomenting from above illicit economic actors and the substitution of traditional elites with the emerging popular sectors.[2] Third, given their lack of education and moral rectitude, these emergent sectors turned into "new elites" would be even more exploitative, antination, and undemocratic than the traditional white oligarchy (cf. Ayo et al. 2013).

The socioeconomic reconfiguration in Bolivia was defined by three overlapping transformations. First, the urban middle class had entered a process of gradual decline, partially losing control of the political and administrative apparatus that was being occupied by new political sectors and social movements (Soruco et al. 2014). In some cases, middle-class sectors had supported the *proceso de cambio*, creating political islands within the government whose political project and concepts differed from the ideological stances and aspirations of indigenous and social movements. In economic terms, the middle class had suffered from the gradual withdrawal of international cooperation, a traditional provider for these social sectors, both because of the scarcity of funding at a time of economic crisis and because of Morales's attempt to recover decision-making power in internal matters (Rodríguez-Carmona 2009). In addition, the traditional economic role of the local middle class in providing services to foreign enterprises and opening franchises of foreign brands had been curtailed by the government's policy of subordinating foreign investment to internal economic interests in the attempt to grant equal access to resources to local popular sectors.

The second important element in the economic restructuring of Bolivia was the increasingly hands-on role of the state in defining and leading the economic orientation of the country. In his end-of-the-year speech (*El Universal*, December 27, 2013), Morales claimed that 35% of Bolivia's economy was in the hands of the state, compared to 16% in 2006. Although countries in the region such as Peru, Colombia, and Brazil had handed over the extraction of raw materials to transnational capital, the Bolivian government had opted for increased state control of natural resources and for channeling the revenues from the extractive industries toward social policies.[3] Not only had the state played a central role in a series of infrastructure projects aimed at improving transportation networks and the education system, but also it handed over to local municipalities an important percentage of the revenues from natural gas, thus increasing their availability of financial resources by more than 30%. This not only helped to generate economic ferment in a series of local municipalities (Spedding et al. 2013) but also ended up outlining a system of multiple economic hubs as opposed to the traditional concentration of the economy on the main urban centers. In a more conventional sense, the state also became the promoter of a series of state-run enterprises and economic clusters intended to function either as development stimulants in remote areas or as sources of state institutionality and control, particularly along the borders. Although the aim was to attract investment from private entrepreneurs in these state-run enterprises, such initiatives were—as expected—not always successful.

The third element in this process of economic restructuring of the country was the emergence of popular entrepreneurs. The consolidation of the state as a key economic player was counterintuitively paralleled by the upsurge of popular traders, a sector that—because of its informality and illicit practices—was thought to habitually circumvent the state. In fact, in a context of historically unparalleled economic bonanza, tighter regulation of foreign investment, and gradual decline of the traditional middle class, popular economic actors such as Aymara traders came to play a more active and central role in the administration of the economic surplus (Tassi et al. 2013). Their heightened sense of autonomy, their small, highly flexible enterprises adapted to the reality of the country, and their historically rooted control of territory aimed at keeping foreign companies at bay coincided with the intention of the "revolutionary" government to bring back the control of the economy in Bolivian hands. However, top-down, state-run, large economic projects that sometimes miscalculated local limitations and possibilities found Aymara traders doubting their real profitability and unwilling to invest in them.

Literature on the informal and interstitial economy has often depicted these actors as "entangled in a parallel pariah economy of international scale" or as feeding a "free-for-all" crime industry accompanying processes of "democratization" and "globalization" (Comaroff and Comaroff 2006: 7). It is interesting to observe how the upsurge of popular Aymara traders is taking place at a time of "interruption" of neoliberal policies and frenzy (Goodale and Postero 2013), generally adduced as leading to processes of either democratization and globalization or informalization and subalternization of local peoples to the interests of global capital. Counterintuitively, the emergence of these popular and interstitial economic forms and actors is happening at the time of an unprecedented economic boom in the country and increasing nationalization of the economy.

On the one hand, the redistribution of wealth produced by the revolutionary government and the increased influx of cash produced by the high gas revenues created new purchasing power in markets in remote parts of the country that Aymara traders were quick to detect. Although beyond the scope of this book, it would be interesting to reflect on the role played by Aymara traders and other popular entrepreneurs in reconverting the volatile royalties from the exploitation of raw materials into locally grounded economic ferment and dynamics, consolidating economic processes more engrained in the reality of the country. On the other hand, for Aymara traders the *proceso de cambio* provided key symbolic tools, strengthening the possibility to "be what we are" in the sense of being able to frame their emergence not in terms of an adaptation to the social canons and demeanors of the conventional middle class while concealing their indigenous provenance, but to experiment with forms of social mobility defined on their own terms. If for decades Aymara traders had been defined for what they were not—formal, licit, modern—the new political circumstances and the radical attempt at a redefinition of the social foundations of the nation produced the possibility for traders to reposition themselves more centrally in the new socioeconomic equilibrium.

The political transformation in Bolivia granted new legitimacy and visibility to popular economic modalities and socioeconomic structures predating neoliberal policies and the *proceso de cambio* itself. Their emergence is not constructed and expressed in antistate, antisocial, or illegal terms but through the affirmation of ways to "make the country" (*hacer país*) on their own terms. In fact, Aymara traders have preceded the current government in connecting the country's territories, in establishing their presence and control on traditionally shaky borders, and in installing forms of unofficial institutionality in remote regions that the "illusory state" (*estado aparente*, Zavaleta 2009) had traditionally disregarded, considering them at best impediments to social and economic development. If state institutions historically run by the family interests of white-*mestizo* sectors had been permeated and coopted by the power and fashions of modern/global/neoliberal ideologies, Aymara institutions demonstrated a high degree of resilience and a capacity both to protect themselves from and to appropriate those external forces. Throughout his literary and ethnographic writings, the Peruvian intellectual José María Arguedas (1975; 2001) has repeatedly attempted to address this contradiction. Often marginalized, excluded, and oppressed by highly racialized social hierarchies, Arguedas affirms that those indigenous sectors carried a natural and crystalline conviction to be the depositaries of the destiny of the country (cf. Condarco Morales 1982; Zavaleta 1986).

The Social Hegemony of the Subalterns

Despite mainstream media's numerous attempts to portray Aymara traders as smugglers circumventing their citizen's duty to pay taxes,[4] the self-perception of traders and their political leaders often emphasizes their "social" role as the "backbone of the country's economy." The national leader of a traders' federation, Erwin Collo, affirmed that in just one market with nearly 1,000 affiliates each vendor paid 400 bolivianos per year in license fees. This would make a total of 400,000 bolivianos ($57,000) per year, in contrast to one of the most popular supermarkets, which would only pay 4,000 ($570). Erwin affirmed that as the merchants and market traders are stereotypically identified as responsible for the unhealthiness and uncleanliness of the city, they are forced to pay higher tariffs to benefit from services such as water, garbage collection, and electricity. In the same market with 1,000 affiliates, each month they pay

5,000 bolivianos ($715) for each of the fifty electricity meters they have in the market (cf. Arbona et al. 2015: 128).

In Erwin's opinion, it was simply for racial reasons that traders are associated with uncleanliness, underdevelopment, and natural antagonism toward regulations and formal enterprises. Out of their own pockets traders had not only set up the commercial structures, built the markets, and provided the services without which the urban economy today would collapse, but also engineered the forms and channels of supply and distribution that local authorities had simply disregarded. Erwin's stance also counteracted the simplistic interpretation provided by large corporations feeling threatened by the disloyal competition of illegal actors overlooking regulations and adopting policies of price reduction through illicit mechanisms. In particular, leaders such as Erwin underlined the role of traders in regulating the investments of foreign enterprises and their access to local markets through practices of commercial control that enable business and labor opportunities to stay in the hands of Bolivians. Besides, in contrast to large enterprises that often require both large-scale financial services and a supply of electricity beyond the country's means, popular entrepreneurs operated strategically within the existing local possibilities, limitations, and resources, shaping an economy made to measure for the country.

On several occasions during fieldwork, Aymara traders asserted a moral hegemony over official institutions and white-*mestizo* sectors. Traders from the popular sectors insinuated that without their preponderant role in the economy and control of the national territories and borders, white-*mestizo* entrepreneurs would sell the country off to transnational companies and foreign investors. While they implied that the white-*mestizo* entrepreneurs yearned for quick and without-scruples money, they emphasized their own gradual and constant reinvestment in the social and economic infrastructure and local services, without which the country would be unable to operate in the increasingly complex times of globalization. Conscious of their capacity to displace formal institutions in the definition of practices of supply and distribution and even in the definition of the economic direction of the country, popular traders reverted the deep-rooted stereotype that they were the ones not abiding to the "shared rules" by questioning the economic and moral behavior of the "high class."

At a time when international agencies rated Bolivia as one of the worst places to do business in Latin America, together with Venezuela and Haiti (World Bank 2012), Aymara traders had begun to reinvest their surplus steadily in economic activities within the country. These sectors were able to produce an economic ferment that made the number of popular traders mushroom to nearly 2 million in a country with 10 million inhabitants (Radio FIDES, December 13, 2011). As the traders' leaders like to affirm, not only had their activities consolidated the stability and articulation of the country's economic islands, but also they connected Bolivia to other markets in the region and the world with nonsubordinate relations, thus transforming a landlocked country into a key player in regional distribution.

The discrepancies with the traditional white-*mestizo* business sector—connoted by a profound disregard for the country and its peoples (Montenegro 1982), a preference for reinvesting abroad[5] and for keeping their savings in banks in Miami, and a tendency to bow to the demands of foreign investors regarded as agents of development and modernity—were often raised by popular sectors battered by discrimination and disparagement. Flashy Aymara traders with their marked style, their lavish social celebrations, and their abundant Far Eastern goods overflowing onto the sidewalk provided a constant reminder to the popular sectors of the decaying role of white-*mestizos* as paternalistic educators, economic experts, and modernizers dragging the masses onto the right path of development. In the same way as an uneducated indigenous president sending into space the first Bolivian satellite named after the indigenous hero Tupac Katari was perceived as a symbolic victory of a fierce indigenous world over indecisive white-*mestizos* who had repeatedly brought the country to the brink of default,[6] the economic ferment of Aymara traders originating from humble rural families and nowadays importing technology from China delineated a possibility of a homemade and locally tailored modernity.

The powerfully symbolic role of Aymara traders among popular sectors translated into heightened levels of legitimacy. Despite the repeated attacks against popular trade by the press, popular sectors emphasized that unlike white-*mestizo* entrepreneurs, they had not been the beneficiaries of institutional favors, purposely tailored policies, and interest-free loans.[7] The ferment and growth of Aymara traders were viewed as autonomous achievements defying the established socioeconomic hierarchies. Such a firm posture among popular sectors was repeatedly used to delegitimize the attempts by the municipality and government institutions to interfere with the practices, functioning, and institutions of popular trade. As we have seen, the efforts of foreign brands to impose standards of production and commercialization were often met with equal aversion by traders. The question of employment was often portrayed in similar terms.

Consolidated in often-marginal urban areas, popular trade had been able to provide employment possibilities in a context that both formal institutions and foreign capital were unable to reach. The expansion of popular trade had repercussions not only on sectorial employment in terms of employed vendors and small retailers buying from importers but also on services such as transport (both international and intercity) and repair workshops and eventually local crafts such as embroiderers and maskmakers for festive celebrations.

Another element granting legitimacy to Aymara traders was their capacity to provide popular sectors with affordable technological products from whose consumption they had traditionally been excluded. In contrast to the European tradition, where traders and money lenders were often represented as "foreigners" and religious minorities external to the local community (Simmel 1990), Aymara traders show an intimate complicity with and understanding of the neglected aspirations, ideas, and logics of the popular sectors. Unlike foreign investors who preferred to limit their direct involvement with local actors and operate from afar, Aymara traders have become closely involved in those socioeconomic activities that require them to compete for and organize local resources. All this stands in stark contrast to the traditional Bolivian elites whose manners, demeanors, and ideas were highly indigestible to the popular and indigenous sectors and who, in turn, repeatedly marked their difference and distance from those elites (cf. Zavaleta 1986). If the old elites were incapable of developing a genuinely hegemonic project able to seduce and coopt the indigenous sectors, emerging Aymara traders not only share cultural codes and demeanors with popular sectors but also have been able to retrieve and valorize their aspirations, values, and ideas. This has granted Aymara traders a widespread popular legitimacy that transcends by far the repeated attempts by urban intellectuals to represent them as illegal and lawless.

Popular Enterprises Reconfiguring the Economy

Interstitial economies and small enterprises such as the ones we have been outlining are often characterized by a series of important limitations. The main limitation is the scant availability of capital and technology, laying the foundations for economic endeavors with low productivity and little income. In fact, it has often been suggested that such semiformal enterprises will be unable to reproduce the capital invested, leading to minimal capital accumulation and a subsistence income rather than profit for reinvestment (Long and Roberts 1984; Calderón and Rivera 1984). Unable to access credit and with limited possibilities for financial maneuvering, small and semiformal entrepreneurs would need to leave manufacturing and large-scale commercial activities requiring sound investments in the hands of larger, formal, and/or foreign enterprises.

The other characteristic narrative about enterprises in the popular economy is that they are functional and subaltern to the requirements of large companies using capital-intensive technology that decide to reduce their costs and wage bills by allocating chunks of their productive/commercial cycle to local and informal enterprises. Generally, this is thought to imply the transfer of the benefits of family labor, local knowledge, and networks directly to the outsourcing company. Robert Neuwirth (2011) describes how a well-known U.S. food multinational operating in Morocco resorted to local informal enterprises and distributors to reach thousands of stalls as well as private families retailing products through their living room window. Through this interweaving of formal and informal domains, multinational and local spaces, products of the famous brand were able to reach millions of people in remote villages and isolated areas on the outskirts of the desert, unloading the distribution risks and difficulties onto local operators.

Although the enterprises of Aymara traders are not always immune from these characteristics and limitations, they began to show counterintuitive features and dynamics. First, in Bolivia the problem of capital reproduction extended far beyond small and informal enterprises. Even large and medium-size companies were unable to generate forms of access to technology or pay fair wages. In fact, factory workers were often forced to resort to their relatives in the countryside to provide them with staple food or to take on weekend jobs to complement their meager salary (Carmen Medeiros, personal communication). It is the urban popular enterprises that, particularly in the past decade, have begun to show important levels of reinvestment in a variety of diversified activities.

In multiple circumstances the hierarchy between formal enterprises defining the rules and the forms of economic operation and the subaltern informal Aymara enterprise appeared increasingly blurred. In El Alto a series of formal establishments and private service companies have sprung up around the *feria* 16 de Julio, the largest open-air market in the country mobilizing 300,000 vendors every Thursday and Sunday (Yampara et al. 2007). Such formal companies adapt their opening hours and services to the rhythms of the *feria* and attempt to exploit the institutionality, structure, and economic ferment produced by these largely informal traders. Local scholars' analyses of the informal economy had often suggested the inability of barely educated popular entrepreneurs to access basic forms of know-how or connect to more sophisticated and wisely run enterprises that understood about exports and technologies (Doria Medina 1988; Casanova 1988). Particularly in El Alto, the reverse was true. In the neighborhood of *Santiago II*, Aymara mechanics of rural origin had been able to create a large cluster of interconnected workshops and shops that most truck drivers in El Alto resorted to. Their capacity to provide a variety of services, from the sale of secondhand spare parts to the reconstruction of stub axles, from the welding of the truck's container to the full assembly of trucks, had attracted a series of formal enterprises in the perimeter of the neighborhood selling foreign brands of trucks or specialized in bending stainless steel for truck containers (Arbona et al. 2015).

From the *feria* 16 de Julio to the mechanics' workshops of *Santiago II*, local Aymara entrepreneurs had been able to solidify such an economic ferment that formal enterprises resorted to providing services to the "informal economic actors." Local small workshops and retailers defined the rhythms and the rules of the economic game, reconfiguring a hierarchy of the economic space that challenged the tension between center and periphery. Although formal enterprises keep taking advantage of small, semiformal entrepreneurs and popular markets, it is now the latter that define the dynamics, forms, and economic ferment to which the former must adapt. In other words, rather than a gathering of subaltern informal traders subcontracted to provide services for the formal sector, such popular markets not only embody the economy of the country but also define the forms and dynamics of how the economy expands.

As we have seen, among the clients of large importers of the Huyustus market one might find priests, policemen, bankers, or families of a decaying urban middle class "begging" (*rogándose*) Aymara traders for advice on products and categories with the highest profit margins. Reversing a commonplace interpretation, not only do representatives of official institutions and members of the formal economy come to insert themselves into the logic of the exchange of favors and *casero* relations of Aymara trade, but also they clearly recognize who is the holder of economic knowledge and who defines the rules of the economic game.

It was mostly small and autonomous popular enterprises highly articulated and economically synergized with each other that—despite their limited size and reluctance to engage in permanent forms of expansion—operated in a variety of territories and across long distances, outlining practices of spatial extension rather than a straightforward concentration of activities and capital. The combination of collective strategies with forms of individual autonomy, attachment, and control of specific territories with networks and circulation produced specific modalities of enterprise management I referred to as circuit-enterprises (cf. Landolt et al. 1999). In fact, these dynamics outlined a system of concatenated actors and enterprises that, on the one hand, were able to access economies of scale while, on the other, maintained an important degree of flexibility and capacity to economically reconvert according to the sometimes sudden transformations of the market. In other words, circuit-enterprises delineated a system of concatenated enterprises scattered across multiple markets and regions capable of accessing the benefits of larger companies—that is, economies of scale, capital, control of the different phases of the productive chain—while maintaining the structural advantages of small enterprises able to flexibly reconvert.

Probably the most emblematic example of how Aymara traders have been able to reconfigure traditional economic hierarchies and narratives, as well as concretely readapt formal structures and institutions to their requirements and forms, is their relationship with financial institutions and their strategies of access to credit. When in need of credit, Aymara traders had traditionally resorted to a series of internal practices and institutions, either because they preferred to mobilize inner resources rather than opting for a not really trusted banking system[8] or because they could not access formal loans because of their supposedly precarious socioeconomic conditions as well as being indigenous. The internal rotating loan system (*pasanako*) enabled the guilds, monthly or occasionally, to bring together financial resources to be destined to one of their members or to a potential new member, generally providing an important means of investment in his or her economic activity. In the past few years, we have witnessed a booming number of often informal and unregistered credit cooperatives,[9] which appear to outline mechanisms and forms of financial self-management by the popular sectors independent of conventional banking institutions.

The recent social and economic expansion of Aymara trade has generated the emergence of financial institutions run with local or national capital, clearly differentiated from traditional banks and willing to operate almost exclusively with popular economic actors. Begun as microcredit experiments for peasants funded by NGOs, such organizations quickly evolved into actual financial institutions providing credit by the millions of dollars to popular economic actors. In 2011, a guild of popular grocery importers took out a joint loan of $40 million to build commercial facilities in a dilapidated neighborhood of El Alto.

This not only suggests the potential profitability of popular trade, but also highlights the capacity of such financial institutions to adapt to the specific modalities of operation and financial requirements of popular trade, as well as a willingness to overcome the formal barriers that had traditionally impeded the provision of credit services to entrepreneurs who were not formally structured. The *Banco Nacional*, one of the oldest and most respected financial institutions in Bolivia, resorted to changing its logo and name to open branches in El Alto and the slope specialized in the provision of banking services to popular entrepreneurs. Interestingly, the *Banco Nacional* was eager to downgrade its posh image and reputation to make its services more like the style and practices of popular entrepreneurs.

Such financial relations evolved into actual extrainstitutional bonds between the credit managers and traders (Tassi et al. 2013), with reciprocal exchanges of favors and shared participation in the urban Aymaras's social and religious events. In most cases, such bonds were solidified by *compadrazgo* connections, where most likely the credit manager had to act as godfather at the christening of the trader's daughter. The connection became so profound that I came across credit managers who held the credit cards and checkbooks of the trader's whole family and, when necessary, paid creditors and provided cash to the members.

The function of the credit manager was not uniquely social and economic, since it extended into other domains. Ana María, a credit manager in El Alto, explained that she was in high demand among popular economic actors because she was invested with luck. Clients would refuse to accept the cash from the financial institution's loan unless it was touched and handed over directly to them by Ana María. They mentioned relatives who had taken out loans from other credit managers and whose investment did not "turn out" (*no resultó*). In fact, Ana María's role as credit adviser constantly had the semblance of a spiritual consultant. Traders would visit her office with an investment idea or plan and they would ask Ana María to "look into it" (*miramelo*) (Tassi et al. 2013: 145). This is the common request addressed to a ritual specialist when we want her to look into or "read into" coca leaves to forecast the future. Ana María had become a specialist in forecasting investments.

In recent years, the government has been cracking down on forms of unguaranteed credit to popular economic actors. However, the bond consolidated between credit managers and popular entrepreneurs had generated possibilities of credit that escaped the control of the official institutions. Rigoberto and his guild friends regularly received loans from Simón, a fellow member of the *bloque* "Los Mandarinas" in one of the most renowned fraternities of the city and a credit manager at the state-run bank. Although Rigoberto was a secondhand clothes retailer and therefore an illicit merchant, Simón managed to provide him and his guild friends with loans by crippling the name of the loan recipient and forging the documents guaranteeing the loan. Interestingly, such dynamics delegitimized a state producing stricter but unenforceable regulations unsuited to the reality of the country's economy in the attempt to show its muscle and new strength while providing new options of legitimacy to popular institutions such as the fraternity.

Popular economic actors had been able to transform the traditional formal, limited, and distant contact at the counter between the bank and its client into a *casero* relationship between the credit manager and popular entrepreneurs, with reciprocal extrainstitutional exchanges and repeatedly overlapping with spiritual and social domains. The forms of control over creditors used by this kind of financial institutions are based on social networks and connections rather than on the enforcement of formal financial regulations. Those same social networks can be mobilized when a creditor does not fulfill financial agreements. At the same time, both materially and symbolically popular economic actors are able to extend their forms of control and institutionality over a financial sector that had been seen as the ultimate obstacle to their expansion because of their inability to gain access to credit. If these modalities of extension by Aymara traders conquered formal and official spaces and sectors, readapting them to their forms and practices, it becomes particularly interesting to describe their heterodox relationship with the state.

Aymara Logics of Political Affirmation

The exuberance of Aymara traders and their reconfiguration of economic rules and hierarchies on the one hand coincided with the current government's intention to promote endogenous economic forms and practices and, on the other hand, clashed with the idea of a stronger state able to control the economy and define its rhythms and directions. This produced a vacillating and hesitant attitude toward Aymara traders on the part of the government. Policies and attempts to crack down on popular economic practices such as contraband and informality were followed by constant backoffs, given the organizational and mobilization capacity of these sectors, the weight of their vote in elections, and their centrality in regulating and organizing the local economy and literally allowing the country to operate.

One of the most illustrative examples of the centrality of Aymara traders in the functioning of the country is the provision of generators for the national elections (Tassi 2012a: 15–18). In the 2009 elections, the Bolivian National Electoral Court (CNE) began a massive effort to register all voters electronically, including communities at nearly 15,000 feet on the Andean Cordillera as well as seminomadic indigenous groups in the Amazon basin. Only a few days before the registration process was meant to start, CNE officers realized that they needed a few hundred generators for those rural areas that had not yet been reached by the electrification program. In despair, the CNE officers visited the *feria* 16 de Julio and found an Aymara woman trader sitting in a stall who had two electric generators "in stock." In a few days, this unassuming Andean woman was able to deliver the hundreds of generators that the CNE needed.

Given the fact that those generators needed to be imported from Chile and probably from the duty-free port of Iquique, behind that little stall in the "slum" there was a sophisticated international network of kin and a highly developed commercial circuit involving relatives in the countryside, truck drivers, customs police, border smugglers, wholesale dealers, and retailers. As our anecdote indicates, these economic circuits sometimes appear to be more efficient than formal economic enterprises and more structured, extensive, and far-reaching than some private and public companies. That is why they are capable of making official institutions bend to their own logic and practices, in this case forcing the state bureaucracy to accept that hundreds of generators could be imported into the country duty free and without formal receipt of purchase.

Even state institutions and the CNE must resort to the extensive and kinship-based networks and supply chains of informal Aymara traders to carry out their most basic function: organizing elections. The same national state that has been issuing tough laws against informality is forced to use those supposedly "illicit," "backward," and "inefficient" traditional economic channels, in strident contrast to the intentions of centralized economic development programs.

Such anecdotes hint at the complexity of the contemporary political conjuncture in Bolivia and the double-bind relationship between popular traders and the state. Indigenous economic actors solidly organized in compact local guilds and extended commercial networks daily circumventing the authority of the state are in fact a crucial commercial sector that the revolutionary government must resort to for its basic functioning.

In the case of the government's "social projects" in rural areas such as the construction of artificial turf football fields or sport arenas, Aymara entrepreneurs were instrumental suppliers. Their control of economic spaces enabled them to position themselves as the most convenient suppliers of synthetic grass imported from China, sand and rubber produced locally, and parquet flooring, beams, and goals. In some cases it was through the contacts of Aymara entrepreneurs that local and state institutions managed to get the certification of football pitches by FIFA authorities.

These anecdotes reveal a complex and counterintuitive relationship with the state that forces us to reconsider common notions about the construction of citizenship and participation in society (Lazar 2008) by popular sectors such as Aymara traders. One of the agendas of Morales's government has been the promotion of forms of participation by indigenous sectors in political institutions and their access to resources from which they had traditionally been excluded or marginalized. This promotion of citizenship and participation took the form of poverty reduction policies and social security benefits, which once again outline state-run patterns of social inclusion. Aymara traders have begun expanding such an integrationist notion of citizenship by outlining modalities of control of different territories and commercial spaces, trade routes, and markets that exceed the state's capacity to control the territory and provide access to resources, commodities, and employment.

The framework of popular institutions (see Chapters 1 and 2) created to regulate Aymara trade becomes an instrumental tool granting the possibility to exercise economic rights and to affirm the role and participation of popular sectors in the overall society. This reverses the role of the state in providing citizenship to popular and indigenous sectors by means of purposely tailored social and civil rights aimed at including them in predefined structures and concepts of state and society. Therefore, Aymara traders are citizens not by concession but through the constant affirmation that their economic services and institutions have become a matter of state and national relevance.

In the route connecting the harbors of the North of Chile with El Alto, a network of multiple actors including truck drivers, bus companies, mechanic workshops, and agents of local transportation firms had managed to generate a hegemonic economic system operating under the radar of the law, defining its own norms and rules and capable of displacing both the competition of Chilean transportation companies and the regulations of official institutions. Unable to operate within the foggy regulations of Bolivian customs and incompatible with the informal practices of local mechanics, Chilean truck drivers are now pressuring the Chilean government to grant them the unique right to transport goods from the harbors to the Bolivian border—in violation of the 1904 treaty between Chile and Bolivia. The hegemonic role of this Bolivian Aymara network, its capacity to define practices and quantities of supply and distribution, and its strategic geopolitical function of controlling the route to the Pacific place this ensemble of actors in a privileged and legitimate position to negotiate with the state and sometimes even to replace the state in the definition of norms and policies.

To safeguard both their status as experts and their employment, in several cases NGO workers and civil servants paternalistically continue to represent popular sectors as needy recipients of policies, aid, and training (Ayo et al. 2013). However, the institutionality and effervescence of Aymara traders and popular economic actors has begun to challenge the authoritative role of ministers in managing and defining central government policies. In a context of heightened geographic mobility connected to highly dynamic economic flows, increasing articulation between urban centers and intermediate towns, and the emergence of a type of economy based on multiple hubs (see Chapter 6), ordered, linear, and centrally planned public policies seem sometimes unsuitable. In fact, these emerging economic dynamics appear to require a less concentrated administrative power, further highlighting the inelasticity of a vertical and centralized management of the economy.

By affirming forms of citizenship from below, independent of the policies and benefits granted by the state, Aymara traders have promoted autonomous economic ideas and practices antagonistic to the role of the state that aspires to define the rules of the economic game. Ultimately, for Aymara traders this contradiction comes down not so much to a rejection of the state and its role but to participation in a plural national project and the aspiration to an "autonomous citizenship," namely a reciprocal recognition from the state of their legitimate institutions and their economic weight. What seems to be at stake is not the project of an indigenous minority demanding autonomy in a circumscribed territory in a corner of the nation—as the multicultural project appears to imply—but an indigenous project that aspires to be central in the definition of the nation.

This produced repeated tensions where popular institutions and official bureaucracy constantly attempted to file and polish each other. In this contradictory situation, Evo Morales played the role of a hinge between two superimposed political/normative structures: on the one hand, the horizontally articulated and self-normed institutions of popular sectors whose logics and aspirations Morales understood much better than traditional politicians, meaning he could "informally" negotiate with them outside of the official political/legal framework; and on the other hand, the conventional, vertical state bureaucracy aspiring to expand its control over the country and its resources but unquestionably not knowledgeable about the country itself. These dynamics outlined an unconventional project of emergence of Aymara traders that remains differentiated from what the traditional ruling sectors and the white middle class had devised for the indigenous sectors.

The Project of Emergence of Aymara Traders

The complex socioeconomic institutionality of Aymara traders, with their specific and autonomous pattern of affirmation, resulted in a mode of emergence with some divergences from the expected pattern that has been forecasting the simple integration of these nouveau riches into the socioeconomic categories and models of the middle class. Among the urban middle class, economic affirmation and the expression of success were conceived and manifested through partnerships with foreign capital and by opening franchises in the country (Rivera, cited in Soruco 2012). However, state contracts for infrastructure construction projects were the real "jackpot" that offered well-connected middle-class entrepreneurs a real chance to accumulate wealth and boost their socioeconomic status (Diego Muñoz, personal communication).

The affirmation of Aymara traders did not imply either a replacement of traditional elite families in their occupation of the bureaucratic apparatus (cf. Ayo et al. 2013; Spedding et al. 2013) to get state contracts and concessions or access to conventional business associations highly interbred with ministries in the definition of official economic policies. On the one hand, Aymara traders maintained a safe distance from the state to delegitimize its attempts to intervene in their institutional system. On the other hand, they remained socially and racially excluded from participation in the conventional business associations still run by the decaying elites. At the economic level, we previously observed how popular informal economies characterized by low productivity and investment were not really absorbed into more efficient, modern, and conventional economic forms. Something similar happened with the social emergence of Aymara traders, who appeared to outline patterns of socioeconomic affirmation that did not imply their linear integration or assimilation into the spaces, practices, and demeanors of the conventional middle class.

If the socioeconomic emergence of Aymara traders was manifested through symbolic practices of social "distinction" from lower social sectors (Bourdieu 1984), they also continually marked their difference from the traditional white elites. For instance, instead of buying comfortable one-story houses with a garden as a symbol of their economic success, Aymara traders resorted to architectural styles more suited to their specific economic ascendance and social aspiration. Born in El Alto, the so-called "neo-Andean architecture" has quickly consolidated into the expression of the emergence of the Aymara popular sector. With a garage for a truck, stores and commercial activities on the ground floor, a large hall for social events on the first floor, and dwellings on the second floor and the terrace, all decorated with expensive mirror glass and precolonial indigenous motifs, such buildings have become a statement of a specific style, social provenance, and economic emergence from below.

Both in El Alto and in La Paz, popular neo-Andean architecture experts such as Freddy Mamani have been shaping a nonacademic architectural

Neo-Andean architecture in El Alto.

movement fitting the aesthetic preferences as well as the pragmatic logic of these ascending popular sectors. While experts and the middle class continue to emphasize the lack of any architectural virtue in such a style,[10] among emerging popular traders neo-Andean architecture has today become an expression of their specific sociocultural aspirations. Instead of adapting to elitist aesthetic canons, emerging Aymara traders have preferred to mark their social and aesthetic difference by highlighting—in a rather defiant way—their presence, permeation, and conquest of urban spaces from which they had traditionally been excluded through flamboyant architectural forms.

Particularly in La Paz, dance parades and religious fiestas that have mushroomed in the past few years within the urban perimeter have come to embody the role of symbolic territorial conquests by popular indigenous sectors over the white-*mestizo* middle class. Although such parades and religious events have long been considered emblems of the national folklore (Abercrombie 1992), in the past few years the firm control of the fiesta by popular sectors has made tensions reexplode with the white-*mestizo* middle class. Feeling invaded in their own urban territory (cf. Matos Mar 1984), the white-*mestizo* middle class has begun to use barbed wire on the street to prevent the "illegal" parades characterized by the excess of alcohol, crime, and uncleanliness from entering their neighborhoods.[11]

Despite the repeated attempts to "nationalize" these socioreligious events by transforming them into tamed and normalized expressions of the national folklore, the protracted exaggerations during the parade and the mushrooming of unconventional religious practices have reignited the tensions and the differences between the popular sectors and the white-*mestizo* middle class. Rejecting locally dominant bourgeois values such as modesty and thriftiness, Aymara traders express their emergence through practices of conspicuous consumption and ritual exaggerations that, as we have seen, embody key cosmological concepts.

Interestingly, both the neo-Andean architecture and the religious dance parades do not aspire to "communicate" with the white-*mestizo* sectors and do not expect their appreciation. The sophisticated engineering features of Aymara traders' building, the complex process of bending long window glasses, and the meticulous knitting of the chandeliers are practical and aesthetic processes whose richness is not grasped by—or even directed to—the urban white-*mestizos*. Similarly, the complex and although immanent symbolism of dance costumes, the quality of the fabrics, and the sophistication of the embroideries speak to the heart and history of popular sectors: Alteño mechanics and constructors, market sellers, and porters—and not the Paceño middle class—are the ones who daily grasp this popular art. Such expressions not only engender legitimacy among popular sectors but also eventually materialize and allow visualizing a wider popular knowledge that has its circles and depths, just as the predominately erudite lore has.

In 2012, the daughter of an established and respected popular trader from the Huyustus market married a high-ranking civil servant from one of the city's "good families." Before the engagement was officially sanctioned, for two weeks in a row the mother of the bride took the bridegroom to have lunch at one of the humblest food stalls in La Paz's main market with no tables or forks (*agachaditos*). She said she wanted to test the character of her soon-to-be son-in-law and see whether he could adapt—being a *jailón* (a snob youngster)—to the practices, norms, and demeanors of the popular sectors. Traditionally in Bolivia, successful foreign traders—Italians, Germans, Croatians—would marry into the families of the local oligarchy in the attempt to merge commercial capital and social prestige. Today, however, popular traders do not seem to perceive their own social affirmation as dependent on the blessing of the urban elites or integration with the circles, practices, and manners of the traditional dominant sectors.

Interestingly, after an early experimentation with sending their offspring to study abroad (Llanque and Villca 2011), Aymara entrepreneurs in La Paz and El Alto have widely opted for both public and private "national" schools. Whereas the urban middle classes aimed for private, expensive, and racially exclusive high schools where their children could receive an education in a foreign language (German, French, English) and eventually be trained for a professional life outside of Bolivia, most Aymara entrepreneurs chose national schools, supposedly providing a kind of training more anchored in the reality of the country while sending their sons and daughters to study Chinese in the evening.

In El Alto in particular, I was often struck by the fact that despite the economic achievements of some entrepreneurs, they would continue to educate their children as to the hardships of life, sometimes making them work two jobs through high school. At the age of twelve, Hilarión's son Walter attended school in the morning, worked as a shop assistant in the afternoon, and worked at night as a minibus attendant (*voceador*). In the neighborhood of *Santiago II*, several teenage sons of well-off truck drivers and mechanics had seasonal work experience in the gold mine run by a local cooperative. For most of these Aymara entrepreneurs without formal education it was clear that their comparative advantage in relation to foreign firms and local middle-class businessmen was the ability to operate in the global economy and its simultaneous fluency in the mechanisms and tricks of urban street life (*lo callejero*). It was therefore strategically important to pass on to their offspring this kind of unofficial know-how that could not be subordinated to formal schooling. This appeared in stark contrast with a certain local bourgeois attitude that constantly emphasized the fact that the benefits of their entrepreneurial hard work were directed to their sons and daughters that they should not suffer as their parents did.

Aymara traders appear to have gained the legitimacy and economic power to design their own pattern and rules of social affirmation that, instead of being based on imitation of the urban middle class, remained anchored in the affirmation and expansion of their own world, codes, and cosmos. Aymara traders not only defied the taboo of indigenous peoples' "fixed customs" and unsuitability or unpreparedness to produce social transformations (cf. Robbins 2010) but also the local narrative that implied renouncing their ethnic self-representation (Van den Berghe and Primov 1977) to access possibilities for social mobility and political participation.

The informal economy was conceived of as destined for gradual absorption by official and large firms capable of correcting, remodeling, and educating small enterprises as to the correct economic behavior. Social mobility has been often and equally understood as a linear and transformative process of imitation and realignment of ascending popular sectors to the mannerisms of the enlightened urban middle class as well as of abandonment of ancient and unsuitable habits. On the one hand, we have observed the capacity of the popular economy to expand beyond any expectation to the point of being able to "lay siege to the state" (*cercar al estado*), to define the local forms of operation of the economy, and to force large and official firms to adapt to their knowledge, aspirations, and rhythms. On the other hand, Aymara traders' social mobility appears to be founded on the capacity to reinvest, consolidate, and expand local institutions, social codes, knowledge, and manners, thereby foregrounding them as the constitutive structures of an emerging nation. These dynamics clashed not only with a series of modernist narratives but also with a conventional revolutionary project aspiring to generate new ideas and horizons of transformation of the local subjectivity to produce an improved "new man" freed from the false consciousness of traditional ideas and structures. In this sense, popular entrepreneurs may offer us a privileged starting point from which to begin pondering different modalities of both social and political transformation.

These dynamics break with the historical and normative precepts that have been defining the "modern citizen." Narratives of modernity, as well as elites' discourses, place the moderns apart from their predecessors by infiltrating a sense of moral redemption into the "new" processes, events, and practices. These evolutionist and liberating prospects tend to confer a sense of indignity on the backward nonmodern and produce a consequent desire to overcome it. Among Aymara traders, one often experiences a simultaneous sense of obstinate reluctance and a natural tendency to embrace modern artifacts, ideas, and manners. As we have seen in the case of the efficient marketing strategies of multinational brands, some of these modern elements may be discarded, deemed useless, or seen as hindrances to traders' tools of self-affirmation based on local forms of autonomy and independent decision making. Others may be appropriated as instruments to strengthen and expand their system and structure and/or resignify within existing cultural frameworks, as in the case of Chinese entrepreneurs forced to operate according to the terms of local markets. Once again, this mode of dealing with modernity suggests a framework of continuity within transformation (Robbins and Wardlow 2005) or of appropriation that defies the conventional modern idea of rupture with a traditional past, the middle-class anxiety to adjust to modern/foreign canons and trends, and the indigenist radical sense of continuity and resistance (Temple 1997; Yampara et al. 2007).

Conclusions

The economic and social achievements of Aymara traders are often counterintuitive. In a context of persisting exclusion and discrimination, Aymara traders have not opted for a withdrawal to their own marginal and circumscribed territory. Instead, starting from the control of local commercial spaces, they have aggressively worked to push foreign capital, brands, and banking practices to adjust to local forms and practices. They have benefited from the latest policies of Morales's government that have increased the purchasing power of popular sectors, but instead of solidifying a nepotistic relation with the revolutionary state, they have been keen to repeatedly reassert their independence and autonomy. Finally, in a context of persisting racism among the decaying white-*mestizo* middle class, Aymara traders have opted and searched for forms of legitimacy among the popular sectors and shaped their own patterns of social affirmation based on their own cosmological practices and forms. This seems to outline a native socioeconomic system gone global, opening possibilities for conceptualizing and practicing global processes from indigenous perspectives.

CONCLUSIONS

O ver the past few decades, an unprecedented economic and geopolitical reconfiguration has affected traditional forms of hegemony and shaped new alliances transversal to the conventional north–south, west–east, first world–third world axes through which globalization, development, and modernity had been vertically interpreted. The emergence of China as a world power has been flanked by a process of economic decentralization highlighting multipolar economies and by the consolidation of regional economic agreements in peripheral areas (Mercosur, ALBA, ASEAN). The logic of economic blocs with their annexed spheres of influence appears to have been superseded by a configuration of multiple alliances and economic networks with a higher degree of flexibility and dynamicity. This process is paralleled by a shift in the global economy from large and highly bureaucratized enterprises to small and more flexible subcontracting firms (Harvey 1989). The process of flexibilization has incentivized an increasing segmentation, globalization, and deprofessionalization of production processes, which has resulted in a global division of labor that appears ever more disassociated from specific places and populations (Ong and Nonini 1997).

In several Latin American countries, whereas on the one hand the "timespace compression" (Harvey 1989) brought about by global communication and transportation systems has facilitated a series of non-hegemonic global economic alliances, on the other hand, such a process has led to the crisis of economic models, social sectors, and traditional economic groups unable to cope with such transformations, feeding a shift of hegemony toward more dynamic and mobile social sectors (Arellano and Burgos 2010; Salman and Soruco 2011). This redefinition of economic relations and equilibriums has been accompanied by grass-roots political transformations and, in some cases, by radical governments tackling social and economic inequalities in a region traditionally characterized by some of the world's widest gaps between rich and poor (Thorp 1998; Hoffman and Centeno 2003).

The combination of these factors has stirred a series of political and economic "innovations" on the ground (Santos 2008; Escobar 2005) as well as the emergence of unconventional economic imaginaries and epistemologies (Santos 2009) that still need painstaking exploration. In fact, these global economic processes and dynamics called forth new kinds of social organization characterized by a high degree of mobility, a capacity to move around repeatedly, detachment from a neatly circumscribed territory, and the ability to communicate and operate interculturally. These transformations have often been mapped onto preexisting sociocultural arrangements and organizational patterns (cf. Ong and Nonini 1997) engendering processes of resistance, (re)appropriation, and hybridization (Escobar 2008).

The Aymara sociopolitical organization has been often depicted as a ramified and heterogenous confederation rather than a centralized state. Often founded on extended kinship networks and culturally specific practices of geographical mobility, Aymara groups have been defined by a tendency to "inhabit the territory by crossing it" (Platt 2009), which enabled them to outline forms of control of the territory exceeding conventional institutions. Broken up, redefined, or overshadowed by the administrative organization of the state (Barragán 1982; Mayer 2004), such forms of political organization have reemerged and intensified with surprising vehemence in recent decades, reactivating networks and producing forms of mobility today much more closely tied to the global economy. Social structures, networks, and cosmoeconomic patterns that had remained latent, or had been overshadowed for decades, reemerged as the arteries of a new politicoeconomic scenario and also as tools capable of economically displacing less mobile mainstream entrepreneurs more dependent on foreign capital. Today one may find sons of Aymara traders settled in Guangzhou for most of the year liaising with local entrepreneurs and producers, the parents in La Paz in charge of the assembly and distribution of Chinese electronics, and the daughters shuttling among a variety of border towns, intermediate cities, and regional markets. Not only has the scope and territory of operation of Aymara families widened dramatically, but also the scale of their economic action has multiplied, ranging from importing containers from China to informal retailing in rural towns.

The specificity and scope of these arrangements have remained largely invisible because they did not coincide with the expectations and narratives of development and modernization of subordinate indigenous sectors such as the Aymara. In fact, their distinctive strategies of accumulation, their business rhythms, and their modalities of expansion remained founded on "traditional" forms of organization and kinship networks, on culturally specific patterns of mobility and on indigenous concepts, beliefs, and forms of self-determination. Unlike the early Chinese overseas diaspora (Duara 1997) or the Dutch and British expat communities that responded to the expansionist aspirations of their respective nation states and their need for capital accumulation, Aymara mobility and involvement with global flows has become a tool for reasserting their autonomous indigenous project and its expression.

Aymara traders highlight a multifaceted relationship with global capitalism. There is no doubt that they are living "under" the conditions of flexibility, "timespace compression," and deterritorialization that represent the cornerstones of global modernity. They operate in a variety of marketplaces, exploiting their economic discrepancies in accordance with the principles of a flexible globalization. Yet these conditions, cornerstones, and principles are simultaneously reworked, defied, and complemented. This configures a modern Aymara trader riding on multiple timelines, immersed in new geopolitical dynamics and economic flows but also anchored to indigenous conceptions of trade, kinship, and value as well as reworking both traditional and recent colonial conditions of exclusion and marginalization. It is through this overlap of timelines that a restructuring of socioeconomic rules is taking place, positioning Aymara traders as key actors in a national and regional politicoeconomic reconfiguration.

If the conditions of global modernity have ended up affecting the socioeconomic arrangements of Aymara structures and organizations, through their very mobility and versatility, Aymaras have been able to elude, take tactical advantage of, appropriate, and resignify the forms of international capitalism, outlining spaces and modalities of participation in the global market on their own terms. Paradoxically, Aymara traders' interstitial participation in the global economy has been an instrument for consolidating, reproducing, and expanding forms of reterritorialization. Unlike liberal conceptions of transnationalism that identify global flows of goods and peoples as possibilities for redemption and liberation from the burden of an anchorage to place, territory, and nation, Aymara participation in the global economy is constantly paired by a consolidation of local institutions, control of marketplaces, and economic rules. But the opposite is also the case. It is the expanded anchorage in specific territories and markets that grants Aymara traders the capacity and possibility to flexibly and malleably link with multiple translocal spaces. Rather than happily participating in a liberating process of deterritorialization and displacement, Aymara traders invest in consolidating indigenous institutions and codes both to prevent the incursion of foreign conglomerates in local spaces and to outline forms of participation in the global economy rooted in specifically Aymara forms and logics.

Their interstitial participation in the global economy has led to multiple non-hegemonic alliances with translocal actors and spaces, outlining practices of globalization that transcend both the positivist rhetoric of the mainstream media and the universalist interpretations of global processes. Aymara traders' imbrication of traditional indigenous institutions, practices, and logics with modern global flows and technologies not only delineate a non-hegemonic global condition, as experienced by most of the world's people (Mathews and Alba 2012), but also calls into question the supposedly universal rules of the global economic game and exposes its legalistic apparatus that favors the interests of large conglomerates. Despite or because of their unequal participation in the global economy, Aymara traders have been able to impose banking practices and rules based on *casero* relations and reproduced through festive and religious events. They are shaping a system of transnational flows and global transactions under the radar of the law but highly regulated and legitimized by informal translocal alliances, institutions, and networks.

Such strategies enable Aymara traders to elude the rules and the recipes of conventional global institutions and development agencies and bypass the brokerage of formal investors and marketplaces (i.e., Miami or Singapore) to directly articulate with other non-hegemonic global actors. On the one hand, they problematize the idea of a supposedly formal global economic system in which only a small minority is entitled to participate. On the other hand, they expose the fallacies of a regulatory global apparatus unconcerned with regulating specific spaces, routes, and actors (Nordstrom 2007).

Probably the most significant transformations brought about by Aymara traders are connected to the series of challenges they have been able to confront in relation to established discipline regimes (Ong and Nonini 1997), colonial divisions of space (Arbona 2011), and hierarchies of knowledge on which the national and regional economic structure and its forms of exploitation have been founded (Rivera 1993). In the Andes, the market has repeatedly been envisioned by both progressive and conservative thinkers as a rationalizing agent that could curtail religious ceremonies and beliefs, install rational forms of property and organization, and normalize indigenous actors into disciplined "farmers" or "laborers" (Ávila Molero 2000) and also citizens subjected to an enlightened ruling class (Seligmann 2004). Aymara traders' interstitial participation in the global economy coincided with a mushrooming of their religious and ritual activities, a consolidation and expansion of their institutions and organizations, and an appropriation of urban spaces and domains traditionally a prerogative of the white-*mestizo* sectors.

Although conventional narratives forecast the unequal economic integration of indigenous groups into the national and global economy through the intervention of foreign experts and enlightened entrepreneurs, the emergence of Aymara traders outlines practices and knowledges rooted in indigenous forms of regulation and mobility that displaced white-*mestizo* entrepreneurs from their traditional role of defining the rules of the economic game. These dynamics suggests a series of patterns that subvert modernity's regimes of truth, where progress, development, and globalization are achieved by means of formal education, mimesis of the more advanced economic sectors, abandonment of feudal beliefs and forms of organization, and adjustment to "true" ideas and rules.

The affirmation of traders is generally associated with a secularization of society, calculation, and rationalization. The incursion of modernity and the global market in local spaces is often associated with a halt in the production of ideas, myths, and techniques by local cultures to adjust to the rules of the market and operate with the instruments and technologies modernity offers. Aymara traders' contact with modernity and the market economy has sometimes heightened their capacity to creatively produce economic concepts and narratives of their own, in contrast to the local elites' historic inability to generate local forms of internalization of surplus (Zavaleta 1986; Langer 2004; Rivera 1993) and lack of creativity in dealing with the interests of foreign capital. In fact, the tension between global and local forms, or between deterritorialization and reterritorialization, cannot be severed from the domains of cultural creativity and cosmological production. Aymara cosmoeconomic principles are turned into actual tools that operate at the heart of the global economy, defining the rhythms and practices of investment, the forms of interaction with foreign partners, the modalities of business expansion, and its limits.

Aymara traders have been defining the economic rhythms and logics of participation in the global economy according to their own cosmological principles, outlining ideas of wealth, property, labor, and investment that remained rooted in indigenous beliefs, practices, and concepts. Their different perspective on the ontological divide between the religious and the economic, between God's ethereal truth and mundane scarcity and finitude (Sahlins 2000), allows them to experiment with different modalities and possibilities in the world economy, where cosmological principles such as abundance, attachment, and circulation become the constitutive "religious premise" defining economic activity and drawing people into relations of exchange.

REFERENCES CITED

Abercrombie, Thomas. 1992. "La Fiesta del Carnaval Postcolonial en Oruro: Clase, Etnicidad y Nacionalismo en la Danza Folklórica." *Revista Andina* 10, 279–352.

Abercrombie, Thomas. 1998. *Pathways of Memory and Power: Ethnography and History among an Andean People.* Madison: University of Wisconsin Press.

Aguiar, José Carlos. 2012. "'They Come from China': Pirate CDs in Mexico in Transnational Perspective." In *Globalization from Below: The World's Other Economy,* edited by G. Mathews, G. Lins Ribeiro, and C. Alba Vega, 36–53. London: Routledge.

Albó, Xavier. 1975. *La Paradoja Aymara: Solidaridad y Faccionalismo.* La Paz: CIPCA Cuadernos de Investigación 8.

———. 1981. "Bases Étnicas y Sociales para la Participación Aymara." La Paz: Mimeo.

———. 2006. "El Alto, La Vorágine de Una Ciudad Única." *Journal of Latin American Anthropology* 11, no. 2, 329–350.

Albó, Xavier, Thomas Greaves, and Godofredo Sandoval. 1981. *Chukiyawu, la Cara Aymara de La Paz. El Paso a la Ciudad.* Vol. I. La Paz: CIPCA.

Albó, Xavier, and Matías Preiswerk. 1986. *Los Señores del Gran Poder.* La Paz: Centro de Teología Popular Taller de Observaciones Culturales.

Allen, Catherine. 1988. *The Hold Life Has: Coca and Cultural Identity in an Andean Community.* Washington, DC: Smithsonian Institute Press.

———. 1997. "When Pebbles Move Mountains: Iconicity and Symbolism in Quechua Ritual." In *Creating Context in Andean Cultures,* edited by R. Howard-Malverde, 73–84. Oxford: Oxford University Press.

Andolina Robert, Nina Laurie, and Sarah Radcliffe. 2009. *Indigenous Development in the Andes. Culture Power and Transformation.* Durham, NC: Duke University Press.

Angé, Olivia. 2011. "*Yapa*. Dons, Échanges et Complicités dans les Andes Méridionales." *Social Anthropology* 19, no. 3, 239–253.

Appadurai, Arjun. 1986. "Introduction: Commodities and the Politics of Value." In *The Social Life of Things: Commodities in Cultural Perspective*, edited by A. Appadurai, 3–63. Cambridge, UK: Cambridge University Press.

———. 1996. *Modernity at Large. The Cultural Dimensions of Globalization*. Minneapolis: University of Minnesota Press.

Applbaum, Kalman. 2005. "The Anthropology of Markets." In *A Handbook of Economic Anthropology*, edited by J. Carrier, 275–289. Cheltenham, UK: Elgar.

Aramayo, Lucia. 2014. *Comercio Popular en Vías Públicas: Formas de Vivir el Espacio entre Centralidades y Vía Pública*. La Paz: PIEB.

Arbona, Juan Manuel. 2011. "Dinámicas Históricas y Espaciales en la Construcción de un Barrio Alteño." *Colombia Internacional* 73, 91–120.

Arbona, Juan, María Elena Canedo, Carmen Medeiros, and Nico Tassi. 2015. "El Sistema Económico Popular: Consolidación y Expansión de la Economía Popular en Bolivia". In *La Economía Popular en Bolivia: Tres Miradas*, edited by N. Tassi, A. Hinojosa and R. Canaviri, 25–140. La Paz: CIS.

Archondo, Rafael. 1991. *Compadres al Microfono: La Resurrección Metropolitana del Ayllu*. La Paz: Hisbol.

Arellano, Rolando, and David Burgos. 2010. *Ciudad de los Reyes, de los Chávez, de los Quispe . . .* Lima: Planeta.

Arguedas, José María. 1975. *Formación de Una Cultura Nacional Indoamericana*. Mexico: Siglo XXI Editores.

———. 2001 [1964]. *Todas las sangres*. Lima: Peisa.

Aristotle. 1962. *The Politics*. London: Penguin Books.

Arnold, Denise. 2008. *Entre los Muertos, los Diablos y el Desarrollo*. La Paz: ISEAT.

Arnold, Denise, and Christine Hastorf. 2008. *Head of State. Icons, Power and Politics in the Ancient and Modern Andes*. Walnut Creek, CA: Left Coast Press.

Arnold, Denise, and Juan de Dios Yapita. 1998. *Río de Vellón, Río de Canto. Cantar a los Animales, una Poética Andina de la Creación*. La Paz: UMSA, Colección Academia 8, Hisbol/ILCA.

Asad, Talal. 2010. "Thinking about Terrorism and Just War." *Cambridge Review of International Affairs*, 23, no. 1, 3–34.

Aspilcueta, Marco. 2007. "Migración y Empresarialidad Urbana: Comerciantes Aymara en Lima." *Debates en Sociología* 32, 33–49.

Assadourian, Carlos Sempat. 1982. *El sistema de la Economía Colonial. Mercado Interno, Regiones y Espacio Económico*. Lima: IEP.

Ávila Molero, Javier. 2000. "Los Dilemas del Desarrollo: Antropología y Promoción en el Perú." In *No Hay País Más Diverso,* edited by C. I. Degregori, 413–442. Lima: PUCP, UP, IEP.

Ayo, Diego, Marcia Fernández Morales, Ana María Kudelka Zalles, and Carlos Moldiz. 2013. *Municipalismo de Base Estrecha: Empresarios No-locales,*

Empresarios Golondrina y Empresarios Políticos como Estandartes Privilegiados de la Descentralización Municipal. La Paz: PIEB.

Bach, Jonathan. 2010. "'They Come in Peasants and Leave Citizens.' Urban Villages and the Making of Shenzhen, China." *Cultural Anthropology*, 25, no. 3, 421–458.

Barragán, Rossana. 1982. *Etnicidad y Verticalidad Ecológica de Sicasica, Ayo-Ayo y Calamarca (Siglos XVI–XVII).* Working Paper. La Paz: MUSEF.

———. 1990. *Espacio Urbano y Dinámica Étnica: La Paz en el Siglo XIX.* La Paz: Hisbol.

———. 1997. "Entre Polleras, Ñañakas y Lliqllas. Los Mestizos y Cholas en la Conformación de la 'Tercera República.'" In *Tradición y Modernidad en los Andes*, edited by H. Urbano, 43–73. Cusco: Centro de Estudios Regionales Andinos Bartolomé de Las Casas.

———. 2006. "Más Allá de lo Mestizo, Más Allá de lo Aymara: Representaciones de Clase y Etnicidad en La Paz." *América Latina Hoy* 43, 107–130.

Barragán, Rossana, and Cleverth Cárdenas. 2009. *Gran Poder: La Morenada.* La Paz: IEB.

Bastien, Joseph. 1985. *Mountain of the Condor: Metaphor and Ritual in an Andean Ayllu.* Long Grove, IL: Waveland Press.

Bebbington, Anthony. 2000. "Reencountering Development. Livelihoods Transitions and Place Transformation in the Andes." *Annals of the Association of American Geographers*, 90, no. 3, 495–520.

Benencia, Roberto. 2012. "De migrantes a ciudadanos. Procesos de ciudadanización de bolivianos en Buenos Aires". Paper delivered at CLACSO, México City, November 9th, 2012.

Benjamin, Nancy, and Ahmadou Aly Mbaye. 2012. *The Informal Sector in Francophone Africa. Firm Size, Productivity and Institutions.* Washington, DC: World Bank.

Bird-David, Nurit. 1992. "Beyond the 'Original Affluent Society': A Culturalist Reformulation." *Current Anthropology* 33, 198–209.

Bohannan, Paul. 1959. "The Impact of Money on an African Subsistence Economy." *Journal of Economic History* 19, 491–503.

Boot, Max. 2002. *The Savage Wars of Peace: Small Wars and the Rise of American Power.* New York: Basic Books.

Bourdieu, Pierre. 1984. *Distinction: A Social Critique of the Judgement of Taste,* translated by R. Nice. London: Routledge Kegan Paul.

Braudel, Fernand. 1981. *Civilization and Capitalism, 15th–18th Century,* vol. 1. New York: Harper & Row.

Brooks, Andrew. 2013. "Stretching Global Production Networks: The International Second-Hand Clothing Trade." *Geoforum* 44, 10–22.

Calderón, Fernando, and Alberto Rivera. 1984. *La Cancha: Una Gran Feria Campesina en la Ciudad de Cochabamba.* Cochabamba: CERES.

Canessa, Andrew. (ed.). 2005. *Natives Making Nation: Gender, Indigeneity and the Nation-State in the Andes.* Tucson: University of Arizona Press.

Canessa, Andrew. 2007. "Who Is Indigenous? Self-identification, Indigeneity, and Claims to Justice in Contemporary Bolivia." *Urban Anthropology* 36, no. 3, 14–48.

Carlo, Carol, Cesar José Aguilar Jordán, Laurimar Ventura Ecuari, and Ignacio Arauz. 2013. *Cobija, Migración y Zona Franca. Prácticas Sociales y Económicas en el Comercio de Importaciones, 1998–2011*. La Paz: PIEB.

Carrier, James. 1995. *Gift and Commodities. Exchange and Western Capitalism since 1700*. London: Routledge.

Carter, William, and Mauricio Mamani. 1982. *Irpa Chico. Individuo y Comunidad en la Cultura Aymara*. La Paz: Juventud.

Casanova, Roberto. 1988. "El Sector Informal Urbano: Apuntes para un Diagnóstico." In *El Sector Informal Urbano en Bolivia*, edited by CEDLA and FLACSO, 143–169. La Paz: EDOBOL.

CEPAL. 2012. *Panorama Social de América Latina 2011*. Santiago de Chile: United Nations http://www.eclac.org/publicaciones/xml/1/45171/PSE2011-Panorama-Social-de-America-Latina.pdf/.

Cereceda, Verónica. 1987. "Aproximaciones a Una Estética Andina: De la Belleza al T'inku." In *Tres Reflexiones Sobre el Pensamiento Andino,* edited by O. Harris, T. Bouysse-Cassagne, T. Platt, and V. Cereceda, 180–316. La Paz: Hisbol.

Chapman, Anne C. 1957. "Port of Trade Enclaves in Aztec and Maya Civilizations". In *Trade and Market in the Early Empires. Economies in History and Theory*, edited by K. Polanyi, C. M. Arensberg, and H. W. Pearson, 114–153. Glencoe IL: The Free Press and The Falcon's Wing Press.

Chatterjee, Partha. 2004. *The Politics of the Governed: Reflections on Popular Politics in Most of the World*. New York: Columbia University Press.

Choque, Roberto. 1987. "Los Caciques Aymara y el Comercio en el Alto Perú." In *La Participación Indigena en los Mercados Surandinos. Estrategias y Reproducción Social—Siglos XVII a XX,* edited by O. Harris, B. Larson, and E. Tandeter, 357–378. Cochabamba: Ceres.

Chu, Julie. 2010. *Cosmologies of Credit: Transnational Mobility and the Politics of Destination in China*. Durham, NC: Duke University Press.

Classen, Constance. 1993. *Inca Cosmology and the Human Body*. Salt Lake City: University of Utah Press.

Codere, Helen. 1950. *Fighting with Property*. Washington, DC: American Anthropological Association.

Colloredo-Mansfeld, Rudy. 1999. *The Native Leisure Class. Consumption and Cultural Creativity in the Andes*. Chicago: University of Chicago Press.

Colloredo-Mansfeld, Rudy, and Jason Antrosio. 2009. "Economic Clusters or Cultural Commons? The Limits of Competition-Driven Development in the Ecuadorian Andes". *Latin American Research Review* 44, no. 1, 132–157.

Comaroff, Jean, and John L. Comaroff (eds.). 2006. *Law and Disorder in the Postcolony*. Chicago: University of Chicago Press.

———. 2009. *Ethnicity, Inc.* Chicago: University of Chicago Press.

Condarco Morales, Ramiro. 1970. *El Escenario Andino y el Hombre*. La Paz: Renovación.

———. 1982 [1966]. *Zárate: El "Temible" Willka*. La Paz: Renovación.

Crabtree, John, and Ann Chaplin. 2013. *Bolivia: The Processes of Change*. London: Zed Books.

Crain, Mary. 1991. Poetics and Politics in the Ecuadorean Andes: Women's Narratives of Death and Devil's Possession. *American Ethnologist* 18, no. 1, 67–89.

Curtin, Philippe. 1984. *Cross-Cultural Trade in World History*. Cambridge, UK: Cambridge University Press.

da Col, Giovanni, and Knut Rio. 2013. "Cosmoeconomics Manifesto." Paper presented at the Annual Meeting of the American Anthropological Association, Chicago, November 23.

Dandler, Jorge, and Carmen Medeiros. 1988. "Temporary Migration form Cochabamba, Bolivia to Argentina: Patterns and Impact in Sending Areas." In *When Borders Don't Divide: Labor Migration and Refugee Movements in the Americas*, edited by P. Pessar, 8–41. New York: Center for Migration Studies.

Davis, Mike. 2006. *Planet of Slums*. London: Verso.

De Boeck, Filip. 1999. "Domesticating Diamonds and Dollars: Identity, Expenditure and Sharing in Southwestern Zaïre." In *Globalization and Identity: Dialectics of Flow and Closure*, edited by B. Meyer and P. Geschiere, 177–210. Oxford: Blackwell.

Degregori, Carlos I. 2012. *How Difficult It Is to Be God: Shining Path's Politics of War in Peru, 1980–1999*. Madison: University of Wisconsin Press.

DeHart, Monica. 2010. *Ethnic Entrepreneurs. Identity and Development Politics in Latin America*. Stanford, CA: Stanford University Press.

De la Cadena, Marisol. 2000. *Indigenous Mestizos. The Politics of Race and Culture in Cuzco, Peru, 1919–1991*. Durham, NC: Duke University Press.

de Soto, Hernando. 1986. *El Otro Sendero: La Revolución Informal*. Lima: Instituto Libertad y Democracia.

de Soto, Hernando. 2002. *El Misterio del Capital: Por Qué el Capitalismo Triunfa en Occidente y Fracasa en el Resto del Mundo*. Buenos Aires: Sudamericana.

Devisch, René. 1993. *Weaving the Threads of Life: The Khita Gyn-Eco-Logical Healing Cult among the Yaka*. Chicago: University of Chicago Press.

Díaz Brito, José Andres. 2007. *Análisis Logístico de la Evolución del Comercio Exterior en Iquique*. MA Dissertation, Universidad de Chile, Santiago.

Dilley, Roy (ed.) 1992. *Contesting Markets*. Edinburgh: University of Edinburgh.

Doria Medina, Samuel 1988. "La Economía Informal en Bolivia: Una Visión Macroeconómica." In *El Sector Informal Urbano en Bolivia*, edited by CEDLA and FLACSO, 175–186. La Paz: EDOBOL.

Dover, Robert V. H. (ed.). 1993. *Andean Cosmologies through Time: Persistence and Emergence*. Bloomington: Indiana University Press.

Duara, Prasenjit. 1997. "Nationalists among Transnationals: Overseas Chinese and the Idea of China, 1900–1911." In *Ungrounded Empires. The Cultural Politics of Modern Chinese Transnationalism*, edited by A. Ong and D. Nonini, 39–60. New York: Routledge.

Dumont, Louis. 1977. *From Mandeville to Marx: The Genesis and Triumph of Economic Ideology*. Chicago: University of Chicago Press.

Elyachar, Julia. 2005. *Markets of Dispossession. NGOs, Economic Development and the State in Cairo*. Durham, NC: Duke University Press

Escobar, Arturo. 1995. *Encountering Development. The Making and Unmaking of the Third World*. Princeton, NJ: Princeton University Press.

———. 2001. "Culture Sits in Places: Reflections on Globalism and Subaltern Strategies of Localization." *Political Geography* 20, 139–174.

———. 2005. *Más Allá del Tercer Mundo. Globalización y diferencia*. Bogotá: ICANH.

———. 2008. *Territories of Difference. Place, Movements, Life,* Redes. Durham, NC: Duke University Press.

Escobari, Laura. 1985. *Producción y Comercio en el Espacio Surandino en el Siglo XVII, Cuzco–Potosí, 1650–1700*. La Paz: Colección Arzans y Vela.

Espirito Santo, Diana, and Nico Tassi. 2013. *Materiality and Transcendence in Contemporary Religion*. London: I.B. Tauris.

Ferguson, James. 1999. *Expectation of Modernity. Myths and Meaning of Urban Life on the Zambian Copperbelt*. Berkeley: University of California Press.

Fernandez, Marcelo. 2000. *La Ley del* Ayllu. *Prácticas de* Jach'a *Justicia y* Jisk'a *Justicia (Justicia Mayor y Justicia Menor) en Comunidades Aymara*. La Paz: PIEB.

Ferraro, Emilia. 2004. "Owing and Being in Debt: A Contribution from the Northern Andes of Ecuador." *Social Anthropology* 12, 77–94.

Forment, Carlos. 2014. "Plebeian Citizenship and the Ethico-Politcal Practices of the Ungoverned: Buenos Aires's La Salada and Emergent Forms of Democratic Life". Paper presented at CUNY, Committee on Globalization and Social Change. November 4, 2014.

Gago, Verónica. 2012. "La Salada: Un Caso de Globalización 'Desde Abajo.'" *Nueva Sociedad* 241, 63–78.

Gallagher, Kevin, Amos Irwin, and Katherine Koleski. 2012. *The New Banks in Town: Chinese Finance in Latin America*. Report for Inter American Dialogue.

Gallagher, Kevin, and Roberto Porsekansky. 2008. "China Matters. China's Economy Impact in Latin America." *Latin American Research Review* 43, no. 1, 185–200.

———. 2009. *China and the Latin America Commodities Boom: A Critical Assessment*. Working Papers Series 192, Political Economy Research Institute, University of Massachusetts, Amherst.

Gao, Chong. 2011. "The Economic Implications of Kinship: Small Entrepreneurs in Guangzhou Garment Industry." *International Journal of Business Anthropology* 2, no. 2, 91–101.

García Linera, Álvaro. 2008. *La Potencia Plebeya: Acción Colectiva e Identidades Indígenas, Obreras y Populares en Bolivia.* Bogota: CLACSO.

———. 2011. *Las Tensiones Creativas de la Revolución.* La Paz: Vicepresidencia del Estado Plurinacional de Bolivia.

Geertz, Clifford. 1963. *Peddlers and Princes. Social Development and Economic Change in Two Indonesian Towns.* Chicago: University of Chicago Press.

———. 1979. "Suq: The Bazaar Economy in Sefrou." In *Meaning and Order in a Moroccan Society. Three Essays in Cultural Analysis*, edited by C. Geertz, H. Geertz, and L. Rosen, 123–313. Cambridge, UK: Cambridge University Press.

Gibson-Graham, J. K. 1996. *The End of Capitalism (As We Knew It).* Oxford: Blackwell.

Gill, Lesley. 2000. *Teetering on the Rim: Global Destructuring, Daily Life, and the Armed Retreat of the Bolivian State.* New York: Columbia University Press.

Giorgis, Marta. 2004. *La Virgen Prestamista: La Fiesta de la Virgen de Urkupiña en el Boliviano Gran Córdoba.* Buenos Aires: Editorial Antropofagia.

Gisbert, Teresa. 2001. *El Paraíso de los Pájaros Parlantes. La Imagen del Otro en la Cultura Andina.* La Paz: Plural Editores.

Glave, Luís Miguel. 1989. *Trajinantes: Caminos Indígenas en la Sociedad Colonial, Siglos XVI–XVII.* Lima: Instituto de Apoyo Agrario.

Goodale, Mark, and Nancy Postero (eds.). 2013. *Neoliberalism Interrupted. Social Changes and Governance in Contemporary Latin America.* Stanford, CA: Stanford University Press.

Goody, Jack. 2010. *The Eurasian Miracle.* Cambridge, MA: Polity Press.

Gose, Peter. 1994. *Deathly Waters and Hungry Mountains: Agrarian Ritual and Class Formation in an Andean Town.* Toronto: University of Toronto Press.

———. 2008. *Invaders as Ancestors. On the Intercultural Making and Unmaking of Spanish Colonialism in the Andes.* Toronto: University of Toronto Press.

Graeber, David 2011. *Debt: the first 5000 years.* London and Brooklyn: Melville House.

Grégoire, Emmanuel. 1993. "La Trilogie des Réseaux Marchands Haoussas: Un Clientélisme Social, Religieux et Étatique." In *Grands Commerçants d'Afrique de l'Ouest,* edited by E. Grégoire and P. Labazée, 37–70. Paris: Karthala and Orstom.

Grégoire, Emmanuel, and Pascal Labazée. 1993. *Grands Commerçants d'Afrique de l'Ouest.* Paris: Karthala and Orstom.

Grotti, Vanessa. 2013. "The Wealth of the Body: Trade Relations, Objects, and Personhood in Northeastern Amazonia." *The Journal of Latin American and Caribbean Anthropology* 18, no. 1, 14–30.

Gruzinski, Serge. 2001. *Images at War: Mexico from Columbus to Blade Runner (1492–2019)*, translated by H. MacLean. Durham, NC: Duke University Press.

Gruzinski, Serge, and Nathan Wachtel. 1997. "Cultural Interbreeding: Constituting the Majority as a Minority." *Comparative Studies in Society and History* 39, 221–250.

Guaygua, Germán, and Beatriz Castillo. 2008. *Identidades y Religión. Fiesta Culto y Ritual en la Construcción de Redes Sociales en la Ciudad de El Alto.* La Paz: ISEAT.

Gudeman, Stephen. 2008. *Economy's Tension: The Dialecticts of Community and Market.* Oxford and New York: Berghahn.

——— (ed.). 2009. *Economic Persuasions.* Oxford and New York: Berghahan.

Gudynas, Eduardo. 2009. *El Nuevo Extractivismo del Siglo XXI: Diez Tesis Urgentes sobre el Extractivismo Bajo el Progresismo Sudamericano Actual.* Washington, DC: IRC, Programa Américas.

Guss, David. 2006. "The Gran Poder and the Reconquest of La Paz." *Journal of Latin American Anthropology* 11, no. 2, 294–328.

Guyer, Jane. 2004. *Marginal Gains. Monetary Transactions in Atlantic Africa.* Chicago: University of Chicago Press.

Habermas, Jurgen. 2013. "¿Democracia o Capitalismo?" *Nueva Sociedad* 246, 32–46.

Hale, Charles. 2005. "Neoliberal Multiculturalism: The Remaking of Cultural Rights and Racial Dominance in Central America." *PoLAR*, 28, no. 1, 10–28.

Hall, Stuart. 1997. *Representation. Cultural Representations and Signifying Practices.* London: Sage in association with the Open University.

Harris, Olivia. 1982. "Labour and Produce in Ethnic Economy, Northern Potosi, Bolivia." In *Ecology and Exchange in the Andes*, edited by D. Lehmann, 70–96. Cambridge, UK: Cambridge University Press.

———. 1989. "The Earth and the State: The Sources and Meanings of Money in Northern Potosí, Bolivia." In *Money and the Morality of Exchange*, edited by J. Parry and M. Bloch, 232–268. Cambridge, UK: Cambridge University Press.

Harris, Olivia, Brooke Larson, and Enrique Tandeter (eds.). 1987. *La Participación Indígena en los Mercados Surandinos. Estrategias y Reproducción Social–Siglos XVII a XX.* Cochabamba: Ceres.

Harriss-White, Barbara. 2003. *India Working. Essays on Society and Economy.* Cambridge, UK: Cambridge University Press.

Harriss-White, Barbara, and Anushree Sinha. 2007. *Trade Liberalization and India's Informal Economy.* Oxford: Oxford University Press.

Hart, Keith. 1973. "Informal Income Opportunities and Urban Employment in Ghana." *Journal of African Studies* 2, no. 1, 61–89.

———. 2007. "Bureaucratic Form and the Informal Economy." In *Linking the Formal and Informal Economy: Concepts and Policies*, edited by B. Guha-Khasnobis, R. Kanbur, and E. Ostrom, 21–35. Oxford: Oxford University Press.

Harvey, David. 1989. *The Condition of Postmodernity*. Oxford: Basil Blackwell.

Harvey, Penelope. 2002. "Elites on the Margins. Mestizo Traders in the Southern Peruvian Andes." In *Elite Cultures: Anthropological Perspectives*, C. Shore and S. Nugent, 74–90. London: Routledge.

Himpele, Jeff. 2002. "Arrival Scenes: Complicity and Media Ethnography in the Bolivian Public Sphere." In *Media Worlds: Anthropology on a New Terrain*, edited by F. Ginsburg, L. Abu-Lughod, and P. Larkin, 476–500. Berkeley: University of California Press.

———. 2003. "The Gran Poder Parade and the Social Movement of the Aymara Middle Class: A Video Essay." *Visual Anthropology* 16, 207–243.

Hinojosa, Alfonso, and Germán Guaygua. 2015. *Economías Populares Transnacionales. Espacios y Dinámicas Festivas Transnacionales en el Altiplano Paceño*. Working paper (draft). Centro de Investigación Social de la Vicepresidencia del Estado Plurinacional de Bolivia.

Hoffman, Kelly, and Miguel Angel Centeno. 2003. "The Lopsided Continent: Inequality in Latin America." *Annual Review of Sociology* 29, 363–390.

Holmberg, Allan. 1952. "Proyecto Perú-Cornel en las Ciencias Sociales Aplicadas." *Perú Indígena*, 5–6.

Hylton, Forrest, and Sinclair Thomson. 2007. *Revolutionary Horizons: Past and Present in Bolivian Politics*. London: Verso.

Inda, Jonathan, and Renato Rosaldo (eds.). 2007. *The Anthropology of Globalization: A Reader*. Oxford: Blackwell.

Irurozqui, Marta. 1994. *La Armonía de las Desigualdades. Elites y Conflictos de Poder en Bolivia 1880–1920*. Madrid: Consejo Superior de Investigaciones Científicas y Centro de Estudios Regionales Andinos "Bartolomé de Las Casas."

Jameson, Fredric. 1998. *The Cultural Turn*. London: Verso.

Joxe, Alain. 2002. *Empire of Disorder*. New York: Semiotexte.

Karaganis, Joe. 2011. *Media Piracy in Emerging Economies*. New York: SSRC.

Keane, Webb. 2007. *Christian Moderns: Freedom and Fetish in the Mission Encounter*. Berkeley: University of California Press.

Kipnis, Andrew B. 1996. "The Language of Gifts: Managing Guanxi in a North China Village." *Modern China* 22, no. 3, 285–314.

———. 1997. *Producing Guanxi: Sentiment, Self and Subculture in a North China village*. Durham, NC: Duke University Press.

Klein, Herbert. 1995. *Haciendas y Ayllus en Bolivia, Siglos XVII y XIX*. Lima: IEP.

Knoke, David. 2012. *Economic Networks*. Cambridge, MA: Polity Press.

Kohl, Benjamin, and Linda Farthing. 2006. *Impasse in Bolivia: Neoliberal Hegemony and Popular Resistance*. London: Zed Books.

Lagos, María L. 1994. *Autonomy and Power: The Dynamics of Class and Culture in Rural Bolivia*. Philadelphia: University of Pennsylvania Press.

Lambert, Agnés. 1993. "Les Commerçantes Maliennes du Chemin de Fer Dakar-Bamako." In *Grands Commerçants d'Afrique de l'Ouest*, edited by E. Grégoire and P. Labazée, 37–70. Paris: Karthala and Orstom.

Landolt, Patricia, Lilian Autler, and Sonia Baires. 1999. "From 'Hermano Lejano' to 'Hermano Mayor': The Dialectics of Salvadoran Transnationalism." *Ethnic and Racial Studies* 2, 290–315.

Langer, Erik. 2004. "Indian Trade and Ethnic Economies in the Andes 1780–1880." *Estudios Interdisciplinarios de Latin América y el Caribe* 15, no. 1, 9–33.

Larson, Brooke. 1998. *Cochabamba, 1550–1900: Colonialism and Agrarian Transformation in Bolivia.* Durham, NC: Duke University Press.

———. 2004. *Trials of Nation-Making. Liberalism, Race and Ethnicity in the Andes.* Cambridge, UK: Cambridge University Press.

———. 2008. "Indios Redimidos, Cholos Barbarizados: Imaginando la Modernidad Neo-colonial Boliviana (1900–1910)." In *Visiones de Fin de Siglo: Bolivia y América Latina en el Siglo XX*, edited by D. Cajías, M. Cajías, C. Johnson, and Iris Villegas, 27-48. La Paz: IFEA.

Larson, Brooke, and Rosario León. 1987. "Dos Visiones Históricas de las Influencias Mercantiles en Tapacarí." In *La Participación Indígena en los Mercados Surandinos. Estrategias y Reproducción Social–Siglos XVII a XX*, edited by O. Harris, B. Larson, and E. Tandeter, 313–353. Cochabamba: Ceres.

Laserna, Roberto. 2005. *La Democracia en el Ch'enko.* La Paz: Fundación Milenio.

Laville, Jean-Louis. 2009. "Definiciones e Instituciones de la Economía." In *¿Que es lo Económico? Materiales para un Debate Necesario Contra el Fatalismo*, edited by J. L. Coraggio, 47–71. Buenos Aires: Ciccus.

Lazar, Sian. 2008. *El Alto, Rebel City: Self and Citizenship in Andean Bolivia.* Durham, NC: Duke University Press.

Lazar, Sian. 2012. "A Desire to Formalize Work? Comparing Trade Union Strategies in Bolivia and Argentina." *Anthropology of Work Review* XXXIII, 1, 15–24.

Lazarte, Jorge. 1991. "Partidos, Democracia, Problemas de Representación e Informalización de la Política (el Caso de Bolivia)." *Revista de Estudios Políticos* 74, 579–614.

Lederman, Rena. 1991. "'Interests in Exchange.' Interests, Equivalence and the Limits of Big-Manship." In *Big Men and Great Men. Personifications of Power in Melanesia*, edited by M. Godelier and M. Strathern, 174–196. Cambridge, UK: Cambridge University Press.

Le Goff, Jacques. 1980. *Time, Work and Culture in the Middle Ages.* Chicago: Chicago University Press.

Le Goff, Jacques. 1982. *Mercaderes y Banqueros de la Edad Media.* Buenos Aires: EDUBA.

———. 2003. *La Borsa e la Vita. Dall'usuraio al Banchiere.* Bari: Laterza.

Lehmann, David (ed.). 1982. *Ecology and Exchange in the Andes.* Cambridge, UK: Cambridge University Press.

León-Manríquez, José Luis. 2010. "Asian Noodle Bowl: La Integración Económica en el Este Asiático y sus Implicaciones para América Latina." *Nueva Sociedad* 228, 28–47.

Li, Zhigang, Michael Lyons, and Alison Brown. 2007. "Ethnic Enclave of Transnational Migrants in Guangzhou: A Case Study of Xiaobei." http://www.hkbu.edu.hk/~curs/Abstracts%20and%20Fullpapers/05/07.doc/. Accessed February 2, 2013.

Lin, Yi-Chieh Jessica. 2011. *Fake Stuff: China and the Rise of Counterfeit Goods*. London: Routledge.

Llanque, Jorge, and Edgar Villca. 2011. *Qamiris Aymaras: Desplazamiento e Inclusión de Elites Andinas en la Ciudad de Oruro*. La Paz: PIEB.

Long, Norman, and Bryan Roberts (eds.). 1984. *Miners Peasants and Entrepreneurs. Regional Development in the Central Highlands of Peru*. Cambridge, UK: Cambridge University Press.

Luo, Youmin. 2012. "Making Sense of Good Life: Local Modernity from a Traditional Industrial–Commercial Region in Southern China." *International Journal of Business Anthropology* 3, no. 1, 85–101.

MacCormack, Sabine. 1991. *Religion in the Andes. Vision and Imagination in Early Colonial Peru*. Princeton, NJ: Princeton University Press.

MacGaffey, Janet, and Rémy Bazenguissa-Ganga. 2000. *Congo-Paris. Transnational Traders on the Margins of the Law*. Bloomington: Indiana University Press.

Mandel, Ernest. 1972. *Late Capitalism*. London: New Left Books.

Marx, Karl. 1990 [1867]. *Capital: A Critique of Political Economy*, vol. 1, translated by B. Fowkes. London: Penguin Books.

Masuda, Shozo, Izumi Shimada, and Craig Morris. 1985. *Andean Ecology and Civilization. An Inter-disciplinary Perspective on Andean Ecological Complementarity*. Tokyo: University of Tokyo Press.

Mathews, Gordon. 2011. *Ghetto at the Center of the World. Chungking Mansions Hong Kong*. Chicago: University of Chicago Press.

Mathews, Gordon, and Carlos Alba Vega. 2012. "What Is Globalization from Below?" In *Globalization from Below: The World's Other Economy*, edited by G. Mathews, G. Lins Ribeiro, and C. Alba Vega, 1–15. London: Routledge.

Mathews, Gordon, Gustavo Lins Ribeiro, and Carlos Alba Vega (eds.). 2012. *Globalization from Below: The World's Other Economy*. London: Routledge.

Mathews, Gordon, and Yang Yang. 2012. "How Africans Pursue Low-end Globalization in Hong-Kong and Mainland China." *Journal of Current Chines Affairs* 2, 95–120.

Matos Mar, José. *1984. Desborde Popular y Crisis del Estado: El Nuevo Rostro Del Perú en la Década de 1980*. Lima: IEP.

Maurer, Bill. 2005. *Mutual Life, Limited: Islamic Banking, Alternative Currencies, Lateral Reason*. Princeton, NJ: Princeton University Press.

Mauss, Marcel. 1990. *The Gift*. London: Routledge.

Mayer, Enrique. 2004. *Casa, Chacra y Dinero. Economías Domésticas y Ecología en los Andes*. Lima: IEP.

Meagher, Kate. 2010. *Identity Economics. Social Networks and the Informal Economy in Nigeria*. Suffolk: Boydell & Brewer.

Medeiros, Carmen. 1995. "Lineamientos para el Ajuste Étnico de la Metodología de Planificación Participativa." Research Report. La Paz: Dirección de Planificación, Subsecretaría de Desarrollo Rural, Secretaría Nacional de Participación Popular.

Medeiros, Carmen, Giovana Ferrufino, Antonio Rodríguez-Carmona, and Nico Tassi. 2013. "Ensanchando los Intersticios. Institucionalidades y Estrategias Económicas del Comercio Popular." *T'inkazos* 33, 27–46.

Medinaceli, Ximena. 2011. *Sariri: los Llameros y la Construcción de la Sociedad Colonial*. La Paz: IFEA, Plural, Asdi, IEB.

Meyer, Birgit, and Peter Geschiere (eds.). 1999. *Globalization and Identity: Dialectics of Flow and Closure*. Oxford: Blackwell.

Michelluti, Lucia. 2008. *The Vernacularisation of Democracy: Politics, Caste and Religion in India*. Delhi: Routledge.

Mignolo, Walter. 2000. *Local Histories/Global Designs*. Princeton, NJ: Princeton University Press.

Milgram, B. Lynne. 2012. "From Second Hand Clothing To Cosmetics: How Philippine-HK Entrepreneurs Fill the Gap in Cross-border Trade." In *Globalization from Below: The World's Other Economy,* edited by G. Mathews, G. Lins Ribeiro, and C. Alba Vega, 120–137. London : Routledge.

Miller, Daniel. 2009. *Stuff*. Cambridge, MA: Polity Press.

———. 2012. *Consumption and Its Consequences*. Cambridge, MA: Polity Press.

Mitchell, Timothy. 1990. "Everyday Metaphors of Power." *Theory and Society*, 19, no. 5, 545–577.

———. 2002. *Rule of Experts. Egypt, Technopolitics, Modernity*. Berkeley: University of California Press.

Molina, Fernando. 2013. *¿Por qué Bolivia es Subdesarrollada?* La Paz: Fundación Pazos Kanki.

Montenegro, Carlos. 1982. *Nacionalismo y Coloniaje*. La Paz: Juventud.

Montes Ruiz, Fernando. 1982. *La Mascara de Piedra: Simbolismo y Personalidad Aymaras en la Historia*. La Paz: Comisión Episcopal de Educación.

Munn, Nancy. 1986. *The Fame of Gawa*. Cambridge, UK: Cambridge University Press.

Murra, John. 1975 [1972]. "El Control Vertical de un Máximo de Pisos Ecológicos en la Economía de las Sociedades Andinas." In *Formaciones Económicas y Políticas del Mundo Andino,* edited by J. Murra, 59–116. Lima: IEP.

———. 2002. "¿Existieron el Tributo y los Mercados en los Andes antes de la Invasión Europea?" In *El Mundo Andino: Población, Medio Ambiente y Economía,* edited by J. Murra, 237–247. Lima: Instituto de Estudios Peruanos.

Naím, Moisés. 2005. *Illicit*. New York: Doubleday.

Narayan, Deepa. 1999. *Bonds and Bridges: Social capital and Poverty.* Washington, DC: World Bank, Policy Research Working Papers 2,167.

Nash, June. 1979. *We Eat the Mines and the Mines Eat Us: Dependency and Exploitation in Bolivian Tin Mines.* New York: Columbia University Press.

Neuwirth, Robert. 2011. *The Stealth of Nations: The Global Rise of the Informal Economy.* New York: Anchor Books.

Nordstrom, Carolyn. 2007. *Global Outlaws: Crime, Money, and Power in the Contemporary World.* Los Angeles: University of California Press.

Ong, Aihwa, and Donald Nonini (eds.). 1997. *Ungrounded Empires. The Cultural Politics of Modern Chinese Transnationalism.* New York: Routledge.

Orlove, Ben. 1977. *Alpacas, Sheep and Men: The Wool Export Economy and Regional Society in Southern Peru.* New York: Academic Press.

Orsi, Roberto. 2005. *Between Heaven and Earth. The Religious Worlds People Make and the Scholars Who Study Them.* Princeton, NJ: Princeton University Press.

Orta, Andrew. 2006. "Dusty Signs and Roots of Faith: The Limits of Christian Meaning in Highland Bolivia." In *The Limits of Meaning: Case Studies in the Anthropology of Christianity,* edited by M. Engelke and M. Tomlinson, 165–188. Oxford: Berghahn.

———. 2008. "Catechists at the Crossroads: Neo-Catholicism, Neoliberalism and the Shifting Sociopolitical Landscape of Aymara Life." *Politics and Religion,* 2, 99–120.

Parry, Jonathan. 1986. "The Gift and the Indian Gift." *Man* 21, 453–473.

Parry, John, and Maurice Bloch (eds.). 1989. *Money and the Morality of Exchange.* Cambridge, UK: Cambridge University Press.

Perry, Guillermo E., Luis Serven, William F. Moloney, J. Humberto Lopez, and Omar Arias. 2006. *Poverty Reduction and Growth. Virtuous and Vicious Circles.* Washington, DC: World Bank.

Pinheiro-Machado, Rosana. 2008. "China-Paraguai-Brasil: Uma Rota para Pensar a Economia Informal." *Revista Brasileira de Ciências Sociais* 23, no. 67, 117–133.

———. 2011. *Made in China.* São Paulo: Hucitec.

Platt, Tristan. 1982a. *Estado Boliviano y Ayllu Andino. Tierra y Tributo en el Norte de Potosi.* Lima: IEP.

———. 1982b. "The Role of the Andean Ayllu in the Reproduction of the Petty Commodity Régime in Northern Potosi (Bolivia)." In *Ecology and Exchange in the Andes,* edited by D. Lehmann, 27–69. Cambridge, UK: Cambridge University Press.

———. 1987. "Entre *Ch'axwa* y *Muxsa*: Para una Historia del Pensamiento Político Aymara." In *Tres Reflexiones sobre el Pensamiento Andino,* edited by O. Harris and T. Bouysse-Cassagne, 61–132. La Paz: Hisbol.

———. 1992. "Divine Protection and Liberal Damnation: Exchanging Metaphors in 19th century Potosí (Bolivia)." In *Contesting Markets,* edited by Roy Dilley, 131–158. Edinburgh: University of Edinburgh.

———. 1996. *Los Guerreros de Cristo*. La Paz: Plural Asur.

———. 2009. "From the Island's Point of View. Warfare and Transformation in an Andean Vertical Archipelago." *Journal de la Société des Américanistes* 95, no. 2, 33–70.

Platt, Tristan, Thérèse Bouysse-Cassagne, and Olivia Harris. 2006. *Qaraqara-Charka. Mallku, Inka y Rey en la Provincia de Charcas. Historia Antropológica de una Confederación Aymara*. La Paz: Institut Français d'Études Andines/Plural Editores/University of St Andrews/University of London/Fundación Cultural del Banco Central de Bolivia.

Plietz, Olivier. 2012. "Following the New Silk Road between Yiwu and Cairo." In *Globalization from Below: The World's Other Economy*, edited by G. Mathews, G. Lins Ribeiro, and C. Alba Vega, 19–35. London: Routledge.

Polanyi, Karl, Conrad M. Arensberg, and Harry W. Pearson (eds.). 1957. *Trade and Market in the Early Empires. Economies in History and Theory*. Glencoe IL: The Free Press and The Falcon's Wing Press.

Poole, Deborah. 1988. "Landscapes of Power in a Cattle-rustling Culture of Southern Andean Peru." *Dialectical Anthropology* 12, no. 3, 367–398.

Poole, Deborah. 1992. "Antropología e Historia Andinas en los EE.UU: Buscando un Reencuentro." *Revista Andina* 10, no. 1, 209–245.

Postero, Nancy. 2013. "Bolivia's Challenge to 'Colonial Neoliberalism.'" In *Neoliberalism Interrupted. Social Changes and Governance in Contemporary Latin America*, edited by M. Goodale and N. Postero, 25–52. Stanford, CA: Stanford University Press.

Poupeau Frank. 2010. "El Alto: Una Ficción Política." *Bulletin de l'Institut Français d'Études Andines* 39, no. 2, 427–449.

Putnam, Robert, Robert Leonardi, and Raffaella Nanetti. 1994. *Making Democracy Work: Civic Traditions in Modern Italy*. Princeton, NJ: Princeton University Press.

Quijano, Aníbal. 1998. *La Economía Popular y sus Caminos en América Latina*. Lima: Mosca Azul Editores.

Rabossi, Fernando. 2012. "Ciudad del Este and Brazilian Circuits of Commercial Distribution." In *Globalization from Below: The World's Other Economy*, edited by G. Mathews, G. Lins Ribeiro, and C. Alba Vega, 54–68. London: Routledge.

Ramírez, Susan E. 2008. "Negociando el Imperio: El Estado Inca como Culto." *Bulletin de l'Institut Français d'Études Andines* 37, no. 1, 5–18.

Randall, Robert. 1993. "Los Dos Vasos. Cosmovisión y Política de la Embriaguez desde el Inkanato hasta la Colonia." In *Borrachera y Memoria. La Experiencia de los Sagrado en los Andes*, edited by T. Saignes, 73–112. La Paz: Hisbol/IFEA.

Renard-Cassewitz, France M., Thierry Saignes, and Anne C. Taylor Descola. 1986. *L'Inca, l'Espagnol et les Sauvages*. Paris: Édition Recherches sur les Civilisations.

Ribeiro, Lins Gustavo. 2006. "Economic Globalization from Below." *Etnográfica* 10, no. 2, 233–249.

———. 2012. "Conclusion: Globalization from Below and the Non-hegemonic World-System." In *Globalization from Below: The World's Other Economy*, G. Mathews, G. Lins Ribeiro, and C. Alba Vega, 221–235. London: Routledge.

Rivera, Silvia. 1983. *'Oppressed but Not Defeated'. Peasant Struggles among Aymara and Qhechwa in Bolivia.* Geneva: UNRISD.

———. 1993. "La Raíz: Colonizadores y Colonizado." In *Violencias Encubiertas en Bolivia*, edited by X. Albo and R. Barrios, 27–138. La Paz: CIPCA–Aruwiyiri.

———. 1996. *Bircholas. Trabajo de Mujeres: Explotación Capitalista y Opresión Colonial entre los Migrantes Aymaras de La Paz y El Alto.* La Paz: Mamahuaco.

———. 2010a. *Ch'ixinakax Utxiwa: Una Reflexion sobre Prácticas y Discursos Colonizadores.* Buenos Aires: Tinta Limón.

———. 2010b. *Principio Potosí: Reverso.* Madrid: Museo Nacional Centro de Arte Reina Sofía (MNCARS).

———. 2010c. *Violencias (re)encubiertas en Bolivia.* La Paz: La Mirada Salvaje.

Rivière, Gilles. 1994. "El Sistema de Aynuqa: Memoria e Historia de la Comunidad (Comunidades Aymara del Altiplano Boliviano)." In *Dinámicas del Descanso de la Tierra en los Andes*, edited by D. Hervé, D. Genin, and G. Rivière, 89–105. La Paz: IBTA–ORSTOM.

Robbins, Joel. 2010. "Anthropology, Pentecostalism, and the New Paul: Conversion, Event, and Social Transformation." *South Atlantic Quarterly* 109, no. 4, 633–652.

Robbins, Joel, and Holly Wardlow (eds.). 2005. *The Making of Global and Local Modernities in Melanesia: Humiliation, Transformation and the Nature of Cultural Change.* London: Ashgate.

Rodríguez-Carmona, Antonio. 2009. *El Proyectorado. Bolivia tras 20 Años de Ayuda Externa.* La Paz: Plural.

Rodríguez-Carmona, Antonio, Miguel Castro, and Pablo Sánchez. 2013. *Imaginarios a Cielo Abierto: Una Mirada Alternativa a los Conflictos Mineros en Perú y Bolivia.* Madrid: ACSUR.

Rodríguez Ostria, Gustavo 2014. *Capitalismo, Modernización y Resistencia Popular, 1825–1952.* La Paz: CIS Vicepresidencia del Estado.

Rojas, José. 2009. "I'm in Hong Kong, I've Graduated." The Igbo Apprenticeship System and Hong Kong's Role in Informal Education. *Anual Meeting of the American Anthropological Association.*

Rojas Ortuste, Gonzalo. 2009. *Cultura Política de las Élites en Bolivia: 1982–2005.* La Paz: CIPCA and FES.

Sahlins, Marshall. 2000. "Cosmologies of Capitalism: The Trans-Pacific Sector of the 'World System.'" In *Culture in Practice: Selected Essays*, edited by M. Sahlins, 415–470. New York: Zone Books.

Saignes, Thierry. 1992. "De los Ayllus a las Parroquias de Indice: Chuquiago y la Paz." In *Ciudades de los Andes: Visión Histórica y Contemporánea*, edited by E. Kingman, 53–91. Lima: Institut Français d'Études Andines.

Sallnow, Michel. 1989. "Precious Metals in the Andean Moral Economy." In *Money and the Morality of Exchange*, edited by J. Parry and M. Bloch, 209–230. Cambridge, UK: Cambridge University Press.

Salman, Tom, and Ximena Soruco. 2011. "Anti-Elites as New Elites: Complexities of Elite Performance in Baffled Bolivia." *Comparative Sociology* 10, no. 4, 614–635.

Salomon, Frank. 1985. "The Dynamic Potential of the Complementarity Concept." In *Andean Ecology and Civilization. An Interdisciplinary Perspective on Andean Ecological Complementarity*, edited by S. Masuda, S. Izumi, and C. Morris, 511–531. Tokyo: University of Tokyo.

———. 1986. *The Native Lords of Quito in the Age of the Inca: The Political Economy of North Andean Chiefdoms*. Cambridge, UK: Cambridge University Press.

Samanamud, Jiovanny, Cleverth Cárdenas, and Patricia Prieto. 2007. *Jóvenes y Política en El Alto. La Subjetividad de los Otros*. La Paz: PIEB.

Sánchez, Rodrigo. 1982. "The Andean Economic System and Capitalism." In *Ecology and Exchange in the Andes*, edited by D. Lehmann, 157–190. Cambridge, UK: Cambridge University Press.

Santos, Boaventura de Sousa. 2008. *Conocer desde el Sur. Para una Cultura Política Emancipatoria*. Buenos Aires and La Paz: CLACSO, CIDES-UMSA, Plural.

———. 2009. *Epistemologías del sur*. México: Siglo XXI Editores.

Santos, Boaventura de Sousa and César Rodríguez-Garavito. 2005. *Law and Globalization from Below: Towards and Cosmopolitan Legality*. Cambridge, UK: Cambridge University Press.

Saravia, Joaquín, and Sandoval, Godofredo. 1991. *Jach'a Uru: ¿La Esperanza de un Pueblo?: Carlos Palenque, RTP y los Sectores Populares Urbanos en La Paz*. La Paz: CEP ILDIS.

Scarborough, Isabel. 2013. "Raising Awareness on the Importance of the Informal Market in Cochabamba, Bolivia." http://blog.wennergren.org/2013/11/engaged-anthropology-grant-isabel-scarborough-and-"raising-awareness-on-the-importance-of-the-informal-market-in-cochabamba-bolivia"/. Accessed December 29, 2013.

Schneider, Hartmut. 1999. "Participatory Governance for Poverty Reduction."*Journal of International Development* 11, no. 4, 521–534.

Schulte, Michael. 1999. *Llameros y Caseros. La Economía Regional Kallawaya*. La Paz: PIEB.

Seligmann, Linda. 2004. *Peruvian Street Lives. Culture, Power and Economy among Market Women of Cuzco*. Urbana: University of Illinois Press.

Simmel, Georg. 1990. *The Philosophy of Money*, translated by Tom Bottomore and David Frisby from a first draft by Kaethe Mengelberg. London: Routledge.

Simpfendorfer, Ben. 2011. *The New Silk Road: How a Rising Arab World Is Turning Away from the West and Rediscovering China*. London: Palgrave.

Siu, Helen. 2007. "Grounding Displacement: Uncivil Urban Spaces in Postreform South China." *American Ethnologist* 34, no. 2, 329–350.

Smart, Alan, and Josephine Smart. 2012. "Hong Kong Petty Capitalists Investing in China: Risk Tolerance, Uncertain Investment Environments, Success and Failure." In *Globalization from Below: The World's Other Economy*, edited by G. Mathews, G. Lins Ribeiro, and C. Alba Vega, 103–119. London: Routledge.

Soruco, Ximena. 2012. "Mestizaje y Ascenso Social en Bolivia." *T'inkazos* 31, 9–24.

Soruco, Ximena, Wilfredo Plata, and Gustavo Medeiros. 2008. *Los barones del oriente. El poder en Santa Cruz ayer y hoy*. La Paz: Fundación Tierra.

Soruco, Ximena, Daniela Franco, and Mariela Durán. 2014. *La Composición Social del Estado Plurinacional: Hacia la Descolonización de la Burocracia*. La Paz: CIS, Vicepresidencia del Estado Plurinacional.

Spedding, Alison. 2008. *Religión en Los Andes. Extirpación de Idolatrías y Modernidad de la Fe Andina*. La Paz: ISEAT.

———. 2009. "Esencialismo ¿Estratégico para Quiénes? Sobre el Ocaso del Discurso del Mestizaje." In *Memoria de la XXIII Reunión Anual de Etnología (RAE)*, edited by MUSEF, vol. 2, 503–523. La Paz: MUSEF.

Spedding, Alison, Gumercindo Flores Quispe, and Nelson Aguilar Lopez. 2013. *Chulumani Flor de Clavel. Transformaciones Urbanas y Rurales, 1998–2012*. La Paz: PIEB.

Stern, Steve (ed.). 1987a. *Resistance, Rebellion and Consciousness in the Andean Peasant World 18th to 20th Centuries*. Madison: University of Wisconsin Press.

———. 1987b. "La Variedad y Ambigüedad de la Intervención Indígena Andina en los Mercados Coloniales Europeos: Apuntes Metodológicos." In *La Participación Indígena en los Mercados Surandinos. Estrategias y Reproducción Social–Siglos XVII a XX*, edited by O. Harris, B. Larson, and E. Tandeter, 281–312. Cochabamba: Ceres.

Stobart, Henry. 2000. "Bodies of Sound and Landscapes of Music: A View from the Bolivian Andes." In *Musical Healing in Cultural* Contexts, edited by P. Gouk, 26–47. Aldershot: Ashgate.

Strathern, Marilyn. 1988. *The Gender of the Gift: Problems with Women and Problems with Society in Melanesia*. Berkeley: University of California Press.

———. 1990. "Artifacts of History: Events and the Interpretation of Images." In *Culture and History in the Pacific*, edited by J. Siikala, 25–44. Helsinki: Transactions of the Finnish Anthropological Society.

Sun, Zhenming. 2008. "The Role of Trading Cities in the Development of Chinese Business Cluster." *International Business Research* 1, no. 2, 69–81.

Tagliacozzo, Eric. 2011. "A Sino-Southeast Asian Circuit: Ethnohistories of the Marine Goods Trade." In *Chinese Circulations. Capital, Commodities, and*

Networks in Southeast Asia, E. Tagliacozzo and W. Chang, 432–454. Durham, NC: Duke University Press.

Tassi, Nico. 2010. *Cuando el Baile Mueve Montañas. Religión y Economía* Cholomestizas *en La Paz, Bolivia*. Praia: La Paz.

———. 2012a. *La Otra Cara del Mercado: Economías Populares en la Arena Global*. La Paz: ISEAT.

———. 2012b. "'Dancing the Image': Materiality and Transcendence in Andean Religious 'Images.'" *Journal of the Royal Anthropological Institute* 18, 285–310.

———. 2013. "Things We Grow With: Spirits, Matter and Bodies in La Paz, Bolivia." In *Making Spirits: Materiality and Transcendence in Contemporary Religions*, edited by D. Espirito Santo and N. Tassi, 179–204. London: I.B. Tauris.

Tassi, Nico, Juan Manuel Arbona, Giovana Ferrufino, and Antonio Rodríguez-Carmona. 2012. "El Desborde Económico Popular en Bolivia: Comerciantes Aymaras en el Mundo Global." *Nueva Sociedad* 241, 93–105.

Tassi, Nico, Carmen Medeiros, Antonio Rodríguez-Carmona, and Giovana Ferrufino. 2013. *"Hacer Plata sin Plata." El Desborde de los Comerciantes Populares en Bolivia*. La Paz: PIEB.

Taussig, Michael. 1980. *The Devil and Commodity Fetishism in South America*. Chapel Hill: University of North Carolina Press.

Telles, Vera da Silva. 2012. "Illegalisms and the City of São Paulo." In *Globalization from Below: The World's Other Economy*, edited by G. Mathews, G. Lins Ribeiro, and C. Alba Vega, 86–100. London: Routledge.

Temple, Dominique. 1997. *Las Estructuras Elementales de la Reciprocidad*. La Paz: Tari, Plural, UMSA.

Thompson, Sinclair. 2002. *We Alone Will Rule. Native Andean Politics in the Age of Insurgency*. Madison: University of Wisconsin Press.

Thorp, Rosemary. 1998. *Progress, Poverty and Exclusion: An Economic History of Latin America in the 20th Century*, Washington, DC: Inter-American Development Bank.

Toranzo, Carlos. 2007. "Burguesía Chola y Mestizaje." In *Democracia Boliviana: Un Modelo para Desarmar*, edited by D. Ayo, 470–484. La Paz: Oxfam y FES-ILDIS.

Trebat, Thomas. 1983. *Brazil's State-Owned Enterprises: A Case Study of the State as Entrepreneurs*. Cambridge, UK: Cambridge University Press.

Turner, Terence. 1995. "An Indigenous People's Struggle for Socially Equitable and Ecologically Sustainable Production." *Journal of Latin American Anthropology* 1, 98–121.

UNDP. 2005. *Informe Temático de Desarrollo Humano en Bolivia: La Economía Boliviana más Allá del Gas*. La Paz, Programa de Naciones Unidas para el Desarrollo.

UNDP. 2007. *Informe Nacional Sobre Desarrollo Humano: El Estado del Estado en Bolivia*. La Paz: Programa de Naciones Unidas para el Desarrollo.

Urton, Gary. 1997. *The Social Life of Numbers. A Quechua Ontology of Numbers and Philosophy of Arithmetics.* Austin: University of Texas Press
———. 2003. *Signs of the Inka Khipu: Binary Coding in the Andean Knotted-String Records.* Austin: University of Texas Press.
Van den Berghe, Peter, and George Primov. 1977. *Inequality in the Peruvian Andes: Class and Ethnicity in Cuzco.* Columbia: University of Missouri Press.
Vanhonacker, Wilfred. 2004. *The China Casebook.* Singapore: MacGraw–Hill.
Velasco, Oscar. 2009. "Aún nos Cuidamos con Nuestras Medicinas." Inventario Sistematizado de las Prácticas Sanitarias Tradicionales Existentes en las Poblaciones Originarias de los Países Andino. Consultancy report, Organismo Andino de Salud, Convenio Hipólito Unanue. http://www .orasconhu.org/documentos/SI%20Aun%20nos%20cuidamos%20con%20 nuestra%20medicina%20ORAS%20Oscar%20Velasco.pdf/. Accessed December 12, 2011.
Walley, Christine. 2004. *Rough Waters: Nature and Development in an East African Marine Park.* Princeton, NJ: Princeton University Press.
Wanderley, Fernanda. 2003. *Trabajo no Mercantil e Inserción Laboral—Una Mirada de Género desde los Hogares.* La Paz: CIDES-UMSA and Plural Editores.
Wang, Ya Ping, Yanglin Wang, and Jiansheng Wu. 2009. "Urbanization and Informal Development in China: Urban Villages in Shenzhen." *International Journal of Urban and Regional Research* 33, no. 4, 957–974.
Wank, David. 1996. "The Institutional Process of Market Clientelism: Guanxi and Private Business in a South China City." *The China Quarterly* 147, 820–838.
———. 2000. "Cigarettes and Domination in Chinese Business Networks." In *The Consumer Revolution in Urban China,* edited by D. Davis, 268–286. Los Angeles: University of California Press.
Weber, Max. 1978. *Economy and Society,* edited by Guenther Roth and Claus Wittich. Berkeley: University of California Press.
———. 1998. *La Ética Protestante y el Espíritu del Capitalismo.* Madrid: ISTMO.
Wolf, Erick. 1982. *Europe and the People without History.* Berkeley: University of California Press.
World Bank. 1997. *Expanding the Measure of Wealth: Indicators of Wealth: Indicators of Environmentally Sustainable Development.* Washington, DC: World Bank. Environmentally Sustainable Development Studies and Monographs Series, 17.
World Bank. 2000. *New Paths to Social Development: Communities and Global Networks in Action.* Washington, DC: Social Development Department.
World Bank. 2012. *Doing Business in a more transparent world. Economy Profile: Bolivia.* Washington: World Bank.
Xiang, Biao. 2005. *Transcending Boundaries. Zhejiangcun: The Story of a Migrant Village in Beijing.* Leiden: Brill.

Yampara, Simón, Saúl Mamani, and Norah Calancha. 2007. *La Cosmovisión y Lógica en la Dinámica Socioeconómica del Qhatu/Feria 16 de Julio.* La Paz: PIEB.

Yang Mayfair. 2000. "Putting Global Capitalism in Its Place: Economic Hybridity, Bataille and Ritual Expenditure." *Current Anthropology* 41, no. 4, 477–509.

Zavaleta, René. 1986. *Lo Nacional-Popular en Bolivia.* Mexico: Siglo XXI.

———. 1990. *La Formación de la Conciencia Nacional.* Cochabamba: Amigos del Libro.

———. 2009. *La autodeterminación de las masas.* Bogota: Siglo del Hombre Editores and Clacso.

Žižek, Slavoj. 1997. "Multiculturalism, or the Cultural Logic of Multinational Capitalism." *New Left Review* September–October, 28–51.

Zuidema, Tom. 1964. *The Ceque System of Cuzco: The Social Organization of the Capital of the Inca,* translated by Eva M. Hooykass. Leiden: Brill.

NOTES
....

Introduction

1. Throughout the text, names of people, companies, locations, and markets have been changed to protect the identity of the persons who have participated in this ethnographic study.

2. I employ the adjective "popular" in the Castilian Spanish sense of the term, namely with reference to the lower social sectors that, in Bolivia—and particularly among Aymara settlers of La Paz and El Alto—maintain sharp forms of differentiation from sophisticated white-*mestizos* whose cultural affiliation and referents are often nondomestic. Aymara traders such as Silveria have been generating multiple forms, strategies, and terms of self-identification. Silvia Rivera (1993; cf. De la Cadena 2000) has referred to this tendency as "*mestizaje ch'ixi*," alluding to the capacity of Aymara urban settlers to simultaneously look at reality from juxtaposed viewpoints as indigenous people of rural provenance and as *mestizos* who can fluently operate in the urban market and the global economy. Among Aymara traders, the adjective popular often embodies this tension with vindicatory, positive connotations referring to the energy, value, and force of "the ones from below," with an explicitly Aymara undertone.

3. According to the 2001 population census, in Bolivia 3.15 million adults (from a total of 5.07 million) declared themselves indigenous. Among them, 1.28 million self-identified as Aymara. The Aymara like to refer to themselves not as an ethnic group but rather as a nation given their numbers, the extensive territories they inhabit, and the social and economic heterogeneity of the population. It is worth clarifying from the beginning that when using

the word Aymara we are not referring to an undifferentiated and uniform population but to a dynamic group—or nation—sharing and acting in a specific territory and identified by common cultural traits.

4. In relation to Aymara traders, I employ the term "interstices" to identify spaces of historical exclusion from official institutions and the formal economy as well as a series of creative peripheral strategies. In peripheral areas and urban neighborhoods with scarce productive capacity and low purchasing power, both large companies and formal institutions were reluctant to provide basic socioeconomic services and invest resources. This placed local organizational forms in charge of regulating and reinvesting in the infrastructure of these areas as well as producing the emergence of a series of economic practices defined by the interactions of local codes and logics rather than conventional economic theory.

5. The mantra of "legal insecurity" or "uncertainty" in third world countries is often invoked by large conglomerates to obtain favorable conditions for their investments from national governments, to demand laws favorable to foreign enterprises, and to justify their unwillingness to distribute their products in small local markets and their need to subcontract regional firms, passing the risks on to them. As we shall see, family-run Chinese companies have been willing to engage in direct business relations with local traders (and vice versa), often generating alternative institutional frameworks to deal with legal uncertainty.

6. In the past few years a number of scholars (Milgram 2012; Nordstrom 2007; Rabossi 2012; Telles 2012) have taken pains to deconstruct the imaginary of illegality of small companies, popular, and informal actors to be blamed for circumventing "shared" economic rules. These scholars have been outlining the increasing participation of mainstream brands and formal enterprises in concealed or tolerated illegal practices of contraband, tax evasion, and money laundering.

7. The Andean case is certainly not an exception. In Braudel's analysis (1981) of the formation of capitalism in premodern Europe, the author himself is puzzled by the "infraeconomy"—referred to as *material civilization*—happening outside formal regulations and on which the market economy was built.

8. The word *feria* refers to markets held on a specific day(s) of the week. Traditionally, it referred to a system of interconnected and rotating markets.

9. A series of studies have emphasized the indigenous communities' links with the Chilean mining enclaves (Llanque and Villca 2011) or with the global wool trade (Orlove 1977). In particular, historical works have explained the early participation of Andean indigenous communities in the global market

(Harris et al. 1987). Such dynamics, however, have been overlooked by institutions, intellectuals, and ruling classes to reassert the discourse of indigenous unsuitability to modernity, progress, and the construction of sustainable nations. Tristan Platt (1992) argues that in Bolivia liberal governments purposely curtailed indigenous forms of mercantilism to weaken their socioeconomic organization and to avoid deviations from cosmopolitan ideas of liberal trade. With the agrarian reform of 1953, the unequal indigenous integration into the market economy came to be seen as a tool with which to transform and modernize their practices and institutions, thereby fostering their gradual conversion into peasants. When talking of the indigenous exclusion from the official economy, I refer to this tension and contradiction between indigenous participation in the market and officialdom's desire to oppress, ignore, and marginalize them.

10. In Bolivia since the Revolution of 1952, trade unionism became a legitimate and institutionally recognized political instance in the negotiations with the state but also funded and regulated by the state itself.

11. Silvia Rivera (1983) argues that this is different from the case of the Quechua from the interandean valleys of Cochabamba. Quechua settlers from the Cochabamba region have undergone repeated and intensive processes of interracial mixing with the white-*mestizo* sectors (see also Lagos 1994; Larson 1998), lowering their potential for ethnic differentiation and producing more harmonic forms of coexistence and *mestizaje,* although these were not necessarily less exploitative. Also, Aymaras' relations with external forms of social and political organization, from the trade union to the state, were often counteracted with a sense of primary allegiance to the idea of Aymara nation. Such idea of indigenous nation was anchored on specific cultural processes and long-term memories of colonial struggles (Rivera 1993). This translated in an enhanced effort to avoid that alien political ideas and actors interfered with their organizations, territory and decision-making (cf. Degregori 2012).

12. In the Andes, food offerings have traditionally been considered the central modality of interaction between worshippers and local cosmological forces (Bastien 1985; Gose 1994).

13. Salvation religions such as Islam or Christianity have often attempted to integrate the "heathens" and the popular sectors through the cult of marginal gods—such as the cult of saints or prophets—with the expectation to gradually adapt and transform them to the rational, ethical, and abstract forms and beliefs of salvation religion (Weber 1978). What we see in the case of the popular Aymara sectors is a heightened capacity to transform the

religious cycle and rationality of Salvationalism by reaffirming their popular religious forms and practices as structuring components of Christianity.

14. See *Página Siete*, February 9, 2013, "CANEB Dice que Debe Verse a China Más Como un Socio de Negocios" [CANEB encourages to look at China as business partner.]

15. The Bolivian Constitution recognizes four different economic forms: communitarian, private, state run, and social-cooperative.

16. The year 2009 is identified with the beginning of Morales's second term in office and with a deepening of the "process of change."

17. The word refers to members of the ruling party MAS (*Movimiento al Socialismo*).

18. In 2012 the government passed a law equating contraband with drug trafficking and attempting to expropriate the property of informal traders. In 2013 another law was approved incentivizing citizens to denounce smugglers in exchange for a percentage of the confiscated goods. More recently (2015), a Supreme Decree has abolished the validity of the legal status and documents of guilds unless personally signed by the president.

19. *Los Tiempos*, November 7, 2011: "73% de Carga que Pasa por Arica es Boliviana" [73% of Cargo Going through Arica Is Bolivian].

20. *La Razón*, January 19, 2014: "Choferes Bolivianos Bloquean Arica por Demora en el Servicio" [Bolivian Drivers Road-Block Arica due to Service Delays].

21. According to Gustavo Rivadeneira (President of El Alto Chamber of Transport), the transfer would be feasible without major costs to traders and truck drivers. May 22, 2012, interview with the author.

22. Eloy Salmón and Huyustus in La Paz; 16 de Julio, Asodimin, and Villa Dolores in El Alto.

Chapter 1

1. The word *reducción* refers to the colonial resettlement of the indigenous population implemented by Francisco de Toledo either to concentrate them in more stable and less scattered settlements for administrative purposes or to separate them from the Spanish population.

2. Indigenous administrative unit.

3. Juan Manuel Arbona and Giovana Ferrufino have provided me with important information about the Nueva Alianza-Asodimin market.

4. *Compadrazgo* is a form of fictive kinship established between two people who do not have blood ties. It is created through "sponsoring" Catholic rituals such as baptisms, weddings, and funerals or civic events such as graduations.

5. The word "founder" (*fundador*) is today used among traders to refer to the person, couple, or group of people who established the local fraternity. Such terminology is reminiscent of forms of addressing a common ancestor of the lineage (Ramírez 2008).

6. The *feria* of La Salada in Buenos Aires is thought to be one of the largest markets in the continent (Gago 2012; Benencia 2012), run mostly by associations of Bolivian traders and producers. The *feria* specializes in the wholesale of inexpensive clothes produced locally to retailers from the whole country. Because of their supposed involvement with counterfeiting, tax evasion, and exploitation of labor, in the past few years Saladas's traders and producers have been the recipients of repeated questionings from government and international trade organizations.

7. To better understand the syncretic articulation between Catholic religion and iconography with Andean animism and rituality, see MacCormack (1991), Classen (1993), and Gisbert (2001).

Chapter 2

1. Celebration performed to mark the end of mourning a year after the death of a relative.

2. This generates the paradoxical situation where Brazilian products are distinctly cheaper on the Bolivian side of the border than on the Brazilian side. This activates a flow of Brazilian buyers into Bolivia buying Brazilian products.

3. In 2011 the value of the manufactured goods that entered the Cobija duty-free zone legally amounted to $100 million (Carlo et al. 2013).

4. I thank Antonio Rodríguez-Carmona for the suggestions and ideas about this subject.

Chapter 3

1. The expression belongs to the Eloy Salmón trader Carlos Estrada in his attempt to describe the urban middle class when wandering in the unfamiliar territory of popular commercial areas, feeling both stressed about personal safety and insecure about the local social codes and modalities of interaction.

2. *La Razón*, January 6, 2014, "Villa Esperanza Tiene 'Pagodas' en Ocho de Sus Diez Callejones" [Villa Esperanza Hosts "Pagodas" in Eight of Its Ten Side-Streets].

3. The *matraca* is a religious-artifact-turned-musical-instrument that is today emblematic of the *morenada* dance.

4. In the local tradition, couples have multiple wedding *padrinos* (godparents) from both families' circles. Usually the *padrinos* cover specific wedding costs incurred by the newlyweds. For instance, different *padrinos* sponsor and cover the costs of the religious ceremony, the rings, the wedding cake, the dance hall, and the bands of musicians. There are even *padrinos de conteo de regalos* in charge of "counting presents," counting being an operation associated with luck and abundance but also a way to keep a record of who is giving what. In the case of an odd number of presents, the *padrinos de conteo de regalos* are supposed to make things even. Generally, being wedding *padrinos* constitutes a stamp of social recognition but also a possibility to expand one's social circles by linking up with the other *padrinos*.

5. Particularly among fraternity members, Aymara surnames such as "Mamani" or "Condori," traditionally stigmatized by exclusive official social and economic circles, have become powerful referents to their social and economic ascendance achieved without the support of official institutions. In the case of the Mamanis, a renowned family of embroiderers and founders of a religious fraternity, they have introduced as a rule the wearing of the *pollera* skirt among daughters and in-laws connected to the family, forcing them, in several cases, to change from the Western dress to the "local" outfit identified with the popular and indigenous sectors.

6. I thank Juan Manuel Arbona for suggesting that I look at the practices of appropriation in this way.

7. Some of the ideas and anecdotes described in this section have been reproduced from a book chapter published by the author. Tassi, Nico 2015. "Repensando el mundo desde las márgenes: la expansión cosmológica y económica de los comerciantes aymaras en Bolivia". In *Tecnología en Los Márgenes: Antropología, Mundos Materiales y Técnicas en América Latina*, edited by P. Di Giminiani, S. González Varela, M. Murray, and H. Risor. Mexico: Bonilla Artigas Editores.

8. In the Andes, the most important religious celebrations coincide with the moment of exchange following the harvest, when people travel to other ecological zones to exchange products. The Gran Poder fiesta in La Paz was originally celebrated by rural producers and traders from distant valleys and rural areas coming to sell their products in town. Several religious sanctuaries and festivals in the rural communities on the Bolivian high plateau are worshipped and celebrated not by local people but by groups from other regions coming to trade with the locals. In fact, the structure of the "community"—whose members were often scattered across multiple ecological zones—was reflected in multiple flows and pathways as well as

in a dispersed pattern of religious festivals celebrated in places that are sometimes located two or three days' walk from the community of origin.

9. In the case of Melanesians, Marilyn Strathern (1990) seems to suggest that instead of constantly interpreting new happenings and artifacts according to local categories of thought, the surprise generated by a new event may activate not only an impulse to control it but also a tendency to open it up to its possibilities, therefore constantly reshaping local hermeneutic categories. In the case of the Aymaras, I would argue that new events such as their involvement in global flows of commodities produce two simultaneous operations: one of appropriation of the external event or artifact and one of extension of local categories.

Chapter 4

1. Parts of this chapter are reproduced from an article and a book chapter published by the author, respectively: Tassi, Nico. 2010. "The 'postulate of abundance'. *Cholo* market and religion in La Paz, Bolivia". *Social Anthropology* 18, no. 2, 191–209; and Tassi, Nico. 2013. "Things We Grow With: Spirits, Matter and Bodies in La Paz, Bolivia." In *Making Spirits: Materiality and Transcendence in Contemporary Religions,* edited by D. Espirito Santo and N. Tassi, 179–204. London: I.B. Tauris.

2. In the early colonial period, the church's attempt to destroy local shrines and forms of worship resulted in both strategies to conceal the local ritual system and ruptures with it (MacCormack 1991); in the 17th century the scant success of forced conversion—or new strategies of integration instead of evangelization—encouraged the Catholic Church to promote forms of identification of local gods and cosmological forces with the Christian Holy Trinity and the saints (Gruzinski 2001). This was to change again with the Bourbon Reforms of the 18th century when the Spanish colonies were swept by a wave of rationalization of ritual expenditure and optimization of the exploitation of local raw materials. Thomas Abercrombie (1998) argues that at the time the appropriation of Catholic symbols and forms among local indigenous groups was so profound that Andean highlanders began promoting forms of resistance to "anti-Christian" reformists. The modernist wave that followed focused on amending the mistakes of a flawed colonial evangelization (see Orta 2006; Platt 1996), encouraging the transformation of Catholicism from an immature superstitious stage to a modern and rational morality; from the polytheistic cult of the saints to a Christ-centered faith (Orta 2008; cf. Orsi 2005: 9).

3. Loans with interest among family members are a practice that is both loathed by Western morality and a common habit within Aymara families.

In the case of Western morality, the domain of the family is connoted by reciprocal and selfless relations constantly threatened by economic interest. For Aymara traders, the form of monetary interest I have just described solidifies familial bonds and social relations and projects them across time.

4. The word *mesa* can be literally translated as "(dining) table." Alison Spedding (2008) suggests that both in Aymara and in Quechua, given the lack of a differentiation between the Spanish vowels "i" and "e" the word *mesa* is not phonetically different from *misa*—Mass. In fact, the Catholic Mass in the Andes is often reinterpreted as the performance of an offering to spiritual forces.

5. Note again the similarity between the minibuses all belonging to the same union and the fraternities of Gran Poder.

6. Depending on the shape of the vehicle, in the drivers' jargon different models and brands of minibuses are referred to with animal names: *lobito* (little wolf), *osito* (little bear), *búfalo* (buffalo).

7. Although the *Pachamama* is generally referred to in the singular, different pieces of ground and places are normally associated with different *Pachamamas*. For Don Daniel, it is not unusual during a *mesa* to spot various *Pachamamas* feeding jointly on the offering, an image often reflected in the communal meal (*apthapi*) laid out by and for the worshippers.

8. The godfather is thought to "drip" onto the godson and transfer to him his character, preferences, and morality. This process of dripping can also apply to the relationship between humans and cosmological forces. The Andean mountains' combination of a majestic and calm appearance with an irascible and "volcanic" nature is thought to be reflected in the human character.

9. After decorating the bull at Carnival, a tropical fruit associated with fertility (*lujjma*) is cut open and a coin of two bolivianos is introduced into the fruit, which is eventually buried under the stables. The body of the *Pachamama* where the fruit has been "sown" and the manure of the bull will make the money grow and reproduce. The coin of two bolivianos is no coincidence because reproduction requires the unity of two different parts.

10. The *t'inkha* does not solely apply to the sale of livestock. In fact, one can witness the same kind of ceremony in the *feria* 16 de Julio among car dealers.

11. I thank Tristan Platt for the suggestion to focus on these dynamics in the Aymara economy. The Bolivian economist Tomás Frías, quoting Ricardo probably without knowing it, had come to this same conclusion already in the mid-19th century (Platt 2008).

Chapter 5

1. Some of the ideas and examples of this chapter are drawn from this book: Tassi, Nico, Carmen Medeiros, Antonio Rodríguez-Carmona and Giovana Ferrufino. 2013. *Hacer Plata sin Plata: el Desborde de los Comerciantes Populares en Bolivia*, La Paz: PIEB.

2. Generally, this is also favored by forms of underinvoicing that are common among local traders and more seldom by skipping customs controls.

3. The cost of hiring large containers (Haiku) for the transportation of goods from the Chinese ports to Bolivia is roughly $5,000.

4. In her work in Sonqo in the Peruvian Andes, Catherine Allen (1988) noticed the tendency of local indigenous peasants to observe and record even the smallest natural transformations in the landscape.

5. Once again, we observe a tension between forms of extreme communization such as the communication between bodies and characters and a meticulous recognition of specific individual features, preferences, and tastes.

6. The wedding is considered not only a passage from youth (*imilla/yokalla*) to adulthood but also the crucial step to "personhood" (*jaqe*). Once married, both members of the couple are entitled to hold posts and responsibilities in the various structures and organizations of the community.

7. My friend Diego Muñoz used to refer to the self-enclosed white-*mestizo*, middle-class neighborhoods located in the southern part of La Paz as "the reservation," ironically countering it to the idea of the "indigenous reservation."

8. "Retiran a Dos Empleados de Burger King por Formar Sindicato" [Two Employees of Burger King Are Dismissed for Creating a Labor Union], *La Razón*, August 8, 2013.

9. Marxist scholarships have repeatedly warned about the tendency of dominant ideologies to disguise forms of exploitation for reciprocity and/or to naturalize them as intrinsic components of any economic process. Although we should not lose sight of such dominant mechanisms, what I have mostly focused on both here and in the previous chapters is how hegemonic ideologies may offer significant claims to those they are directed against (Mitchell 1990).

Chapter 6

1. In the case of the Eloy Salmón, importers who resell to middle-class buyers tend to import brandless electronic commodities from China to avoid confiscations at customs, although the products resemble the mainstream

large brands' models. Once they reach Bolivia, these commodities are retagged with labels of brands such as LG and Samsung and sold to mostly middle-class consumers with a relatively high profit margin.

2. The figure has been recovered from the statistics data of the *Aduana Nacional* of Bolivia (National Customs).

Chapter 7

1. In 2012 the *Programa de Investigación Estratégica en Bolivia* (PIEB) funded a number of studies on the economic reconfiguration of Bolivia and the emergence of new elites. A summary of such studies can be viewed in the journal *T'inkazos* (volume 33, 2013).

2. "Los Informales: Los Nuevos Reyes de la Economía" [Informal Entrepreneurs: The New Rulers of the Economy], *Santa Cruz Económico*, April 2013.

3. Although these countries in the region have shown explosive rates of economic growth and high levels of socioeconomic inequality, Bolivia's economy has achieved important goals in the reduction of poverty and inequality (CEPAL 2012). The still predominant extractive model, however, has been blamed for its high social and environmental costs and for reproducing a modernist idea of development (Gudynas 2009).

4. The discursive battle waged by the local middle classes against Aymara traders' tax evasion clashes with the inability of conventional institutions to provide suitable social security services for their citizens. However, particularly in the past decade such a discourse has been reinforced by the attitude of international development agencies facing an increasing failure of their investment, supposedly as a consequence of weak regulatory environments. The idea is that business corporations are undercut by informal economic actors who pay no taxes, evade costly regulations, and take advantage of often-illegal means to reduce prices. The irony here is that those same institutions and corporations, which in the past had promoted the deregulation and flexibility of informal arrangements for their own benefit, now wanted to deny it to those who would develop from behind (cf. Hart 2007).

5. "Comportamiento del Ahorro Interno y Mercado Financiero en Bolivia 1960–2001" [Behavior of Internal Savings and Financial Markets in Bolivia 1960–2001]. Superintendencia de Recursos Jerárquicos, La Paz, 2001.

6. On December 20, 2013, Bolivia launched into space its first satellite, named after the Aymara fighter Tupac Katari, from the Chinese Space Center in Xichang (Sichuan). Following the launch, the Bolivian president,

Evo Morales, addressed the crowd. After emphasizing how once again Tupac Katari would illuminate the path to liberation from oppression and imperialism, Morales pointed out that twenty-five years after neoliberal governments and economic experts had declared Bolivia economically moribund, the plurinational state was sending Tupac Katari into space and Bolivia had turned into a viable country as well as a regional referent for social battles and conquests. The symbolic impact of the satellite on urban popular sectors was profound. Coinciding with the beginning of ritual celebrations for the *Fiesta del Gran Poder*, over the following weeks the image of the satellite began appearing on invitations and posters announcing festive activities. A renowned *fraternidad* of traders in technology and appliances designed and produced a rattle (*matraca*) used by dancers in the Gran Poder celebrations in the shape of the satellite.

7. The process of establishing agribusinesses in the lowlands was financed by the dictatorship of the general Hugo Banzer through a system of state loans to local families, which in most cases were never repaid to the state (Soruco et al. 2008).

8. The issue of distrust in conventional institutions associated with the white-*mestizo* middle class such as the health or banking system is constantly raised and practiced even by the wealthiest Aymara traders I have been working with. In the case of the banking system, such distrust takes the form of an obstinate reluctance to let the bank manage their pensions or even to be the depository of their savings. This could be explained by the phenomenon of hyperinflation that hit Bolivia and the reputation of its banking system during the 1980s, together with its dependence on global fluctuations, and also by the corruption and untrustworthiness Aymara traders associate with bank administrators traditionally seen as stingy, unscrupulous profiteers "taking money abroad."

9. "Asfi Cerrará las Puertas de 311 Cooperativas de Ahorro y Crédito" [Asfi (the Financial Authority) Will Shut Down 311 Credit Unions], *La Razón*, October 2, 2012.

10. "Brillantes Oscuros" [Dark Diamonds], *La Razón*, December 1, 2013.

11. "En Chasquipampa Piden Controlar la Entrada Folklórica" [People Ask to Regulate the Dance Parade in Chasquipampa], *La Razón*, September 20, 2013.

INDEX

....